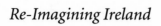

Re-Imagining Ireland

Re-Imagining Ireland

EDITED BY

Andrew Higgins Wyndham

University of Virginia Press

Charlottesville & London

University of Virginia Press
© 2006 by the Rector and Visitors of the University of Virginia
All rights reserved
Printed in the United States of America on acid-free paper
First published 2006

9   8   7   6   5   4   3   2   1

Library of Congress Cataloging-in-Publication Data

Re-imagining Ireland / edited by Andrew Higgins Wyndham.
    p.   cm.
  Includes bibliographical references and index.
  ISBN-13: 978-0-8139-2544-8 (acid-free paper)
  1. Ireland—Civilization—21st century. 2. Northern Ireland—
Civilization—21st century. 3. Ireland—Economic conditions—
21st century. 4. Northern Ireland—Economic conditions—21st
century. 5. Ireland—Social life and customs—21st century.
6. Northern Ireland—Social life and customs—21st century.
7. Ireland—Intellectual life—21st century. 8. Northern
Ireland—Intellectual life—21st century. I. Wyndham, Andrew
Higgins, 1949– .
DA966.2.R4 2006
941.50824—dc22

                                                    2006001345

Contents

Foreword

by Mary McAleese, President of Ireland

At the "Re-Imagining Ireland" conference in Charlottesville, Virginia, I recalled that a French nobleman once said that Thomas Jefferson had placed both his mind and his famous house "on an elevated situation from which he might contemplate the universe." The Virginia Foundation for the Humanities brought an impressive array of Irish scholarly and public talent, wit, and wisdom to engage our culture from the vantage point of Jefferson's reflective eminence. This book continues the wide-ranging conversations on Ireland which that extraordinary event initiated, deepening the discourse and enriching the contemplation begun there. I invite you to explore the dramatically changing Ireland that those at the conference conjured to re-imagine.

How Ireland has changed! A small and once impoverished island has come to symbolize the sort of economic success that everyone else wants to emulate. The country that up to the late 1960s offered the liberating key of education only to a very few has felt the surging energy of its greatest natural resource—the genius of its own people—empowered through widened access to second- and third-level education. The country that knew only emigration is now a place of net inward migration. The genius of Irish women, once corralled into narrowly prescribed spheres, is moving inexorably if slowly toward a flood tide yet to come. The politics of peace are transforming the landscape of possibilities within Northern Ireland, between North and South and between Ireland and Britain.

We cannot deny that there are casualties. Our widespread and heartening prosperity has proved liberating for many, but there are still those marooned on the beach, watching the uplifted boats sailing over the horizon. They too have to have a future to look forward to and champions to articulate and deliver it. Reassuringly we have shown ourselves capable of remarkable change, to be adaptable, to be willing to learn. And while there is still much to accomplish, there is a newfound confidence in our capacity to transcend and transform, to realize the imagined thing as reality.

Day in and day out I meet individuals who are making the crucial differences that are quietly building up to a better future. They are building up communities, breaking down sectarianism and racism, watching out for one another and especially the weaker members of Irish society. They are propelling us forward in the world of business, trade, tourism, and investment and—for all the untidy capriciousness of the marketplace—showing a resolve and creativity which still make us one of the most robust and stable economies in the world. Their work of human care also contributes enormously to underpinning our democracy and developing our ambition to be a society where all are included.

We are a connecting people, and this is our strength. Yet the very strength of our connectedness, the very ease of our intimacy can itself appear to be a powerful wall of exclusion for some of those who look at us with doubt and mistrust. There can be no hermetic seal on the Irish family and its circle of friends and neighbors, even its reluctant neighbors north of the border. Like strands of a rope, they all take their shape from each other, and they have an important voice too in the re-imagining of Ireland—for Ireland's future is also theirs.

This is a good time to be in Ireland and to participate in the changes in our society. We have too often before ransacked the past for arguments to deploy against the future. The road to that future lies in the imagination and in the courage it takes to take the first step to a world not known with certainty but longed for with passion. Twenty-first-century Ireland is at least in part living the Ireland imagined in past centuries. Now is a good time to sketch the imagined landscape of tomorrow's Ireland, and to inspire the champions who will take us to it. There is nowhere better to begin than in this collection of essays, the work of so many artists and bridge builders who—guiding us to that Ireland via Charlottesville—can help us see beyond where we are to where we could hope to be.

Preface

If you ask for directions in Ireland, or the West of Ireland anyway, the person you are addressing may begin by saying, "Well, first you go down to the cross," meaning not a Celtic cross but a crossroads, a place where people and traffic intersect. Not so long ago, I encountered just such a kindly representative of Old Ireland on the Dingle Peninsula near the village of Cloghane. She directed me to "the cross"—and a field there—to park my car, leaving it while I hiked an unnamed mountain on the Connor Pass, across the way from Mount Brandon.

From about age six to thirteen, I grew up in Ireland, mostly outside Dublin, near Stillorgan, then still a distinct village. We had a central "cross" too. My Polish father was a bit of an anomaly there, though an Italian opened up a fish-and-chip shop up the hill around that time also. We had come from England, to which my Dublin-born mother had emigrated to find adventure and work after finishing school. So when I arrived in Ireland, I had an English accent, not the most advantageous of assets among my schoolmates at the time, but mostly they let it go.

We had moved to Dublin at a kind of crossroads for the country, which was just beginning to scope out and implement plans to encourage foreign investment. Within a few years we were living at Shannon, with its then-nascent industrial park, where my father, who was an electronics engineer, got a job with a Rhodesian company and where most of my friends had foreign—meaning non-Irish—accents. Their fathers worked for American, South African, German, and Japanese businesses. But I went to school in Limerick, where I continued to learn a very curiously accented Irish, at least compared to the version given me by the priests at my Dublin school in preparation for the national Primary Exam.

My mother, Eileen Higgins, loved her country. But because she also relished the good things that the world had on offer, she spent her life mostly longing for Ireland at a distance, being impelled to seek abroad what the land of the Higginses could not then provide. It was she who encouraged my father to look across the Atlantic, where he found a new position with General Electric. Again she was up and leaving the land of her youth, and now mine. There was no Irish wake—we went down to the Shannon Shamrock Inn at Bunratty for a farewell dinner. And, having sold most all of our things, we headed off for the United States essentially empty-handed, save for our suitcases, taking not an emigrants' "coffin ship" but a gleaming vessel of the developing global transport system—a Pan American DC-8 jet. We arrived at the crossroads of New York but headed down south to Virginia, where I have lived, and from which I have frequently visited Ireland, since that time.

Ireland was at a crossroads then; it was a place of modest intersections, encounters, and change. Today it is at an "interchange" on a freeway, having taken a quantum leap, emerging as the most globalized society in the world. Now Stillorgan is subsumed by Dublin's urban sprawl, the original plan for Shannon has become the road map for the "siliconized" country, individuals with foreign accents and various skin colors are a commonplace, and people who speak different dialects of Irish are at home with each other on the Internet. Dublin airport is again expanding to accommodate the global traffic, and citizens like my mother are coming back to stay, permanently, because Ireland now offers most everything available in the world at large.

We kids used to go into the poorer areas of Dublin to buy illegal British fireworks that were, we were told, smuggled by rail from the distant and uninviting North and thrown off before the train pulled into Dublin—such was the myth. Today, those areas of Dublin are being renovated in concert with the long-time local residents; they are renewing and recovering community. Of greater moment, Northern Ireland and Ireland and the people within their respective polities have taken some giant steps to create genuinely democratic solutions to long-standing civil problems—and people of all allegiances are hopeful that gunrunning is permanently in the past. I knew nothing about such things then, just as I knew nothing about issues of civil rights and violence in the American South, where we were moving from Ireland. Today, the Enterprise Unlimited speeds back and forth about every two hours between Dublin and Belfast. The Belfast waterfront is booming, and people are getting used to a postwar environment, gradually building confidence.

The island of Ireland is in so many ways new to itself. It is also new—if, as Fintan O'Toole says, eerily familiar—to those who are returning. And it is often viewed as alien by those who have read Yeats and Synge and Joyce and who arrive on holiday, filled with visions handed down by literature, or their parents' and grandparents' stories, and recharged with longing by the latest glossy tourist brochures. In truth, there are still great treasures of heritage and landscape and tradition to be found in Ireland, but they can reasonably be seen as under threat. At the same time, while many Irish have assumed a palpable and justifiable sense of pride in the country's astonishing development, others are ambivalent and asking serious questions about the ultimate social and cultural costs and consequences of growth. The Irish, awash in change, globally connected, are asking who they are, what Ireland is, where their country or island is going, how to make sense of what it all means. They are, in short, at an intellectual and psychological—even a spiritual—crossroads.

This book of essays engages critical social and cultural issues raised by the groundbreaking "Re-Imagining Ireland" conference and festival, which itself proved a crossroads of a kind. President Mary McAleese set the keynote at the four-day event, held in Charlottesville, Virginia, during May 2003. The program involved some 130 speakers and performers, most of them from Ireland. On the agenda were thirty panel discussions, a series of concerts and musical presentations, poetry readings, a major exhibition of contemporary Irish visual art, a new Irish play, and other presentations, including short and feature film screenings. The event was organized and hosted by the Virginia Foundation for the Humanities (VFH), whose goal was to give a Virginia and U.S. audience an opportunity to experience Irish perspectives, from both North and South, on issues confronting their cultures. As VFH project director, I worked with a core group of Irish and American consultants (see the acknowledgments) to create a large and diverse cross-cultural conference, blending discussion and the arts. In a context of exchange, examining a wide range of issues anew, the program would allow Irish and American participants to explore what has been happening on the island. For the purposes of the conference, Charlottesville would become a crossroads for Ireland—out of Ireland—a place where influential Irish individuals drawn from throughout the culture, and who might never otherwise meet, could gather on neutral ground to explore matters of mutual concern, re-imagining some old pathways, discovering new directions.

From those intersections came this book. It is not a volume of proceedings but was largely written following the event and has its own integrity. Ten essays, composed by experts from different disciplines and fields, provide the superstructure of the collection. These are matched by complementary sections of "Voices"—selected, revised statements, about one-quarter of those originally delivered at the conference—which amplify, extend, and play off the emerging themes. The text addresses Ireland's history and contemporary dynamic, bringing together ways of talking about a society in transition, taking the country as a window on the world.

How do more to explain a book that is vastly diverse; intellectual, artistic, and visceral in its content; and that goes to the heart of the ways in which a nation is engaging and re-imagining its national identity? Certainly it is not easily done—in fact, to impose a facile and embracing logic would be to falsify the extraordinary view provided by this metaphorical "window" on the ferment that has characterized Ireland of late. Does that figure of a window itself suffice? Not really, because this book is no abstracted "take" on things—it is not just a looking-out on what is going on in Ireland today. Best to shift metaphors then and invite you on a "journey of discovery," especially if you are American.

Reading this volume, you can virtually breach the barrier, climb through that window, and, on the proposed trip, bridge differences and exchange views with a universe of personalities who come from all across Irish culture and beyond its geographical boundaries, and who are intimately engaged with its manifold meanings. You will be inspired, moved, stimulated, perhaps sometimes agitated by—and find much to enjoy in—their novel, diverse, and often challenging perspectives. From the standpoint of life experience as well as analysis, they will introduce you to an Ireland wrestling with its past and present, exploring how economics, race, religion, politics, language, and, above all, their new sense of being global players have changed and are changing what it means to be Irish. Why does this matter? Because it touches on the fortunes and futures of contemporary societies generally, on the universe of cultural change that nations and peoples are seeking to understand and negotiate worldwide in the twenty-first century.

If you don't quite believe all this, now is the time to turn to the table of contents and begin with what first strikes your fancy. Or you can move from beginning to end, following the natural, "national" logic of the text. This will take you from discussions of the significance of contemporary Irish experience, including Ireland's transforming economy and society, to views of Irish identity. You will plumb the meaning of being Irish in a global context, following those for whom America or Britain became alternatives to the homeland, and then questioning the nature of race, discrimination, and the colonial legacy. You will consider Ireland's core linguistic culture, how it is achieving new life, and how it links the island in an identity with Scotland. From here, you will focus on the challenges facing visual art in contemporary Ireland, as well as immersing yourself in discussions of Irish music, dance, and film. Cinema can provide an entry point to modern Dublin, but in the next section you will discover the city from a perspective unfamiliar to most viewers and visitors, considering how the built environment, though by some standards seen as impoverished, may sustain the riches of community. Through a final sequence of essays, you will engage in-depth analyses of Unionism and the many dimensions of the Northern Ireland Peace Process, as well as of revisionism and competing views of the historical fortunes and accomplishments of "Irish people" at home and abroad, and on the margins between.

The writers, the voices, the individuals are provocative, disarming, winning. They imaginatively introduce profoundly important reflections on economics and culture, world consciousness, the changing forms of expression through which individuals and nations gradually but inevitably negotiate their identity, and a movement from conflict to politics. These explorations are a journey well worth the taking.

Acknowledgments

Although the contents of this book are in most ways distinct from the record of the conference that preceded it, the book would not exist had the conference never taken place; one grew out of the other. There is thus a necessary overlap in the acknowledgments due those who contributed to these two phases of the "Re-Imagining Ireland" project, as well as to the television documentary that was made between them.

The Virginia Foundation for the Humanities is honored by and grateful to President Mary McAleese of Ireland for her endorsement of and commitment to the "Re-Imagining Ireland" project, from the conference to the publication of this book. That originating conference was planned in consultation with, and could not have happened without, an outstanding and dedicated board of ten Irish and American writers, scholars, and arts experts with whom I worked to shape the program. These consultants also made initial contacts with a multitude of extraordinary program guests, provided essential assistance in raising vital funds, spoke at the conference itself, and wrote the commissioned essays in this text. The group includes author and Irish studies scholar Angela Bourke; sociologist Mary Corcoran; poet, writer, and radio presenter Theo Dorgan; film scholar and cultural theorist Luke Gibbons; museum administrator, arts programmer, and academic director Declan McGonagle; journalist and author Susan McKay; film scholar Martin McLoone, who first suggested the topic of the program; emigration historian Kerby Miller; folklorist and performance artist Mick Moloney; and cultural commentator, journalist, and author Fintan O'Toole. I will always be grateful for the ideas, generous help, encouragement, and friendship of these individuals.

The project would never have blossomed and succeeded in the way it did without the hospitality, guidance, and logistical support of the Irish Embassy in Washington. The VFH extends a special thank-you to Ambassador of

Ireland Noel Fahey, and to former ambassador Sean O'Huiginn. I am personally grateful for the kind assistance and camaraderie of Tim Doyle, first secretary at the Embassy, and Owen Feeney, cultural attaché and third secretary, who partnered with us in planning for President McAleese's visit.

To make a project like "Re-Imagining Ireland" fly required substantial financial underwriting. Those who saw the potential at the earliest stages and came to the Foundation's aid with generous seed money include the Office of the President at the University of Virginia, the Anne Lee Ueltschi Foundation, and the National Endowment for the Humanities. VFH is particularly grateful to Anne Ueltschi for both planning and major implementation support, as well as kind counsel, helping to maintain our momentum from the beginning to the end of the project. We are greatly indebted, also, to UVA president John T. Casteen III for his ongoing interest and for providing essential targeted assistance throughout the planning and implementation phases. And it must be said that the conference and all that followed would never have happened without both a consultation and a major implementation grant from the National Endowment for the Humanities. VFH acknowledges and warmly thanks the Endowment's Division of Public Programs and its Special Projects team for their guidance and pivotal support—in particular, senior program officer Bonnie Gould and Division director Nancy Rogers.

Major funding and in-kind support were made available by many other "investors" without whom "Re-Imagining Ireland" would only have been a dream. These include Ireland's Cultural Relations Committee and Department of Arts, Tourism, and Sport, who provided extremely generous assistance for the conference. We especially thank Michael Grant, assistant secretary general of the Department, CRC director Christine Sisk, and former director Michael Fitzgerald for their gracious guidance in the application process. Also providing vital and very generous support for the project were Caroleen Feeney and the French-American Charitable Trust; the American Ireland Fund—with special thanks to director Kingsley Aikins and the kind assistance of Patrick Sweeney, founding president and CEO of ServerVault; and Delta Air Lines, which was the *Official Airline of Re-Imagining Ireland* and provided substantial and essential transatlantic travel support for our featured guests. We are especially grateful to David and Susan Goode for their counsel, encouragement, and vital assistance in communicating the potentials of the project to Delta and other underwriters. Particular thanks also are due to the Department of Culture, Arts, and Leisure (DCAL) in Belfast and to Maurna Crozier, special consultant to the minister, and Mark Mawhinney, head of the Arts and Creativity Branch at DCAL.

The VFH is grateful and extends special thanks to the City of Charlottesville, Virginia, for indispensable financial and transportation assistance, provided through City Manager Gary B. O'Connell's office, by way of the Charlottesville Transit Service and the Charlottesville/Albemarle Convention and Visitors Bureau. We want additionally to express our gratitude to Foras na Gaeilge, Dublin, and its deputy director, Deirdre Davitt, for funding that supported discussion and research essential to the development of this book's chapter on the Gaeltacht. And we offer special thanks to CEO Chris Little at Dominion Digital, the company that created the project's ongoing Web site, www.re-imagining-ireland.org.

Additional support for key elements of the project came from Gropen Signs and Displays, with special thanks to Neal Gropen; The FUNd at the Charlottesville Albemarle Community Foundation, with special thanks to Greg Graham; the Forum for Contemporary Thought, with special thanks to Robert Kretsinger; the British Councils of Scotland, Northern Ireland, Ireland, and the United States; Marty and Richard Wilson; the Honorable Blanka Rosenstiel and the Rosenstiel Foundation; Caterpillar Corporation; Peter Sutherland; the Northern Ireland Bureau, Washington, with special thanks to cultural affairs officer Ann Ryan Hanafin for her always optimistic counsel; the Milwaukee Irish Fest Foundation, with special thanks to director Ed Ward; RBC Dain Rauscher; ServerVault; Keswick Hall at Monticello; the Irish American Cultural Institute; Anna L. Lawson; Monticello, the home of Thomas Jefferson, with special thanks to Dan Jordan; Charlottesville's Vinegar Hill Theatre, with special thanks to Ann Porotti and Reid Oeschlin; the Barnaby Council for Celtic Studies; J. W. Sieg and Company/Guinness; Marie Moriarty; Anna Magee, and Mary Jo Herriman.

I am personally grateful to former VFH board chair Richard T. Wilson III, who was a vital source of strategy, encouragement, support, and metaphors as we built the financial "house," one brick at a time, working to get the "bumblebee to fly." My warm thanks also go to the entire VFH board, especially former chair Elizabeth L. Young, VFH president Robert C. Vaughan, current chair the Hon. L. Preston Bryant Jr., and Anna L. Lawson. I will always appreciate Rob's and the board's vision for the Foundation as a statewide, national, and international programming agency and their willingness to commit staff time to undertaking a multiyear, multipart project during a precarious period in our country's political, psychic, and economic history.

A project with so many elements has required the commitment and ongoing partnership of many institutions, organizations, and agencies. Principal among these has been the Irish Museum of Modern Art (IMMA); its former director, Declan McGonagle; and Catherine Marshall, senior curator and head of collection at IMMA. Catherine and the museum's staff, among them Marguerite O'Molloy, have been extraordinarily generous collaborators, supporting our efforts at all phases of the project, particularly in organizing the exhibition Irish Art Today. The University of Virginia Art Museum and museum director Jill Hartz also offered extraordinary support, working with us as flexible and committed partners and friends to bring the full range of Irish creative life into play, both for the "Re-Imagining" program and art enthusiasts throughout Virginia and the country. Also generously assisting in ensuring that the full range of Gaelic art and culture would be brilliantly represented at the conference and in this book was the Gaelic Arts Agency, Proiseacht nan Ealan, on the Isle of Lewis in Scotland. Many thanks go to Director Malcolm Maclean and his deputy, Mairi S. MacLeod, for enabling us to offer a North American preview of The Great Book of Gaelic, as well as for supporting its representation in this volume.

VFH also greatly appreciates the creative and logistical support of the Irish Film Board/Bord Scannán na hÉireann and its former director Rod Stoneman; the Cork International Film Festival and director Michael Hannigan; Poetry Ireland and director Joseph Woods; the Irish Traditional Music Archive and director Nicholas Carolan; the Irish Centre for Migration Studies and director Pieras MacEinri; Glucksman Ireland House at NYU and director Joe Lee; the UVA Department of Drama and chair Robert Chapel; the UVA Rotunda and administrators Carolyn Laquatra and Leslie Kelly; and Robert Brickhouse and the staff of UVA News Services. Additionally, my special thanks go to Joseph Mooney, Sister Albertus, Tomoko Hamada, Frankie Gavin, Kathleen Wilson, Tim Hulbert, and Richard Herskowitz for their kindness, encouragement, counsel, and essential assistance throughout the project.

The Re-Imagining Ireland documentary film moved us onward to the completion of the book and contributed to the project's award-winning profile. My special thanks go to Paul and Ellen Wagner and their team at Paul Wagner Productions, whose assistance was vital in planning for the documentary. Working in partnership with VFH, they superbly coordinated all of the filming, conducting the interviews at the conference, and also consulted with us during the postproduction process. I am grateful to editor Neil

Means, who was with us for the wild ride to the St. Patrick's Day deadline. His technical support was critical, and he made important creative contributions throughout the assembly and sweetening process.

VFH greatly appreciates the generous support of Radio Telefís Éireann, RTÉ, Irish national television, which, through the RTÉ Archive, provided rare and brilliant public affairs footage to illustrate the film and also offered production support and advice throughout the project. Many thanks go to director general Cathal Goan and RTÉ's commissioning editor for factual programming, Kevin Dawson, for their interest and commitment. I personally appreciate the collegiality of—and the creative and logistical support provided by—David McKenna, RTÉ's executive producer for music and arts TV features, at every stage of production. Special thanks also go to RTÉ assisting producer Niamh Ni Churnain for her essential archival research.

The conference itself posed logistical challenges still daunting to contemplate. Operations manager Tori Talbot took a winger and joined us to apply her organizational genius and extraordinary capacity for focused work to help make it all happen. Tori's dedication and brilliant contributions to the project were indispensable to the success of "Re-Imagining Ireland." Amy Marshall's initiative and assistance were also essential throughout the organizational and implementation process, as well as in preparing the review manuscript for the Press. And my thanks go to Tamara McCandless for trailblazing administrative support at the earliest stage of the project.

My gratitude goes also to VFH staff members Nancy Damon, Kevin McFadden, and Jon Lohman for stepping in to manage key conference venues with grace and aplomb. The VFH came together as it always does to make good things happen. Among the many on deck at key moments were Roberta Culbertson (to whom I am also grateful for her encouragement and conceptual insights in planning the overall project), Sheryl Hayes, Sarah McConnell, Sean Tubbs, Gail Shirley-Warren, Susan Coleman, David Bearinger, Andrew Chancey, Ann Spencer, Lynda Myers, Althea Brooks, Jeannie Palin, Judy Moody and Franz Canon. They and many other temporary assistants and volunteers—among them, Jim Benedict, Pippa Brush, Polly Ewell, Elizabeth Kiem, Sarah Stovall, Jennifer Wise, Anthony Zabukovek—pitched in to make the dream a reality. I owe many thanks to all of them, as well as to Kevin Donleavy, Mary Lyons, Myra Horgan, and the good folks at the Irish Cultural Organization of Charlottesville.

The task of editing and assembling the book itself has been eased by the assistance of three able associates at the VFH. Special thanks go to Lydia

Wilson, who diligently worked to style and compile the final manuscript; and to Katherine Greiner, who energetically tackled the endnotes, making them all consistent and checking out anomalies with precision; and to Maura Walz, whose expert editorial skills at the copyediting stage smoothed the road to completion. I am especially grateful to Boyd Zenner, the book's acquisitions editor at the University of Virginia Press, who offered much-needed counsel throughout—encouraging, advocating, urging, and helping us to make good things happen and to get it all right; to Press project editor Mark Mones for clarifying and assisting us in negotiating stylistic conundrums; to Susan Brady for her enthusiastic, meticulous attention to the copyediting process, and to managing editor Ellen Satrom, for her graceful aid and support as we finally brought the ship into port.

There is only one person left on the acknowledgment list: my partner in life and work, Susan Bacik, my wife. Susan, above all others, conspired and joined with me to make the imagined "Re-Imagining Ireland" what it finally became. She suggested the architecture of this book and helped to select the contents. She provided essential creative support as a writer and associate producer for the project documentary. She co-curated the Irish Art Today exhibition, wrote the catalogue essay, designed the "Re-Imagining Ireland" logo, and assisted with many other conference activities. She read and edited all the key publications and the proposals that brought in our funding. She offered strategy, counsel, sympathy, and unconditional support as we ran the race and made our way to the finish line. I thank her for her faith and will always be grateful for her willingness to extend her energy and love in these and many other ways.

The Irish are a very fair people. They never speak well of each other.
—Samuel Johnson

Notes from the Notice Box

An Introduction

FINTAN O'TOOLE

Reading Henry James's *The Portrait of a Lady* recently, I was struck by a passage that hadn't seemed remarkable to me before. Describing his heroine Isabel Archer, James writes that, "It may be affirmed without delay that Isabel was probably very liable to the sin of self-esteem; she often surveyed with complacency the field of her own nature . . . she treated herself to occasions of homage." What leaps out, in the early twenty-first century, is of course the notion that self-esteem is a sin. For us now the greatest sin of all is to undermine or diminish self-esteem, a concept that has replaced the rather more stringent idea of self-respect in our working model of personal integrity. Yet like Isabel, Ireland is often guilty of the sin of self-esteem and has a tendency to treat itself to occasions of homage.

I am not especially ancient, but I grew up in a lost world, before we had Mr. Spock on the television or Dr. Spock in the nursery. It was a world of small houses and big Catholic families, where children could be arranged in family photographs like the steps of stairs and self-esteem was still a bad thing. And in that world one of the worst things you could be was a "notice box." A notice box was a child who was forever seeking attention, who never learned that small people, like all small things, are meant to be beyond notice. For parents harassed by tribes of youngsters, it was important to inculcate the notion that a good child was one that knew how relatively uninteresting it was to most adults most of the time.

It is perhaps a memory of those times that makes me slightly embarrassed at Ireland's status as an international notice box. Ireland, to be frank, gets far too much attention. There is something deeply immoral, for example, about the degree of international importance accorded to the conflict in Northern Ireland, which took fewer than four thousand lives over thirty years, in contrast to the developed world's relative indifference to the conflict in the Congo, which has taken a thousand times as many over ten years. Irish writers, living and dead, are often wonderful, but the main reason they get so much notice, compared to, say, Danish writers, is that most of them happen to write in a language that has become, for extraneous reasons, the dominant international tongue. As an example of the way a small country could navigate twentieth-century modernity, Ireland is a relative failure, compared, again, to Denmark, with which it shares a great deal in terms of scale and circumstance.

Ireland's wildly disproportionate place in the world is not, moreover, entirely to its advantage. In the messy aftermath of the groundbreaking Belfast Agreement of April 1998, which constructed a framework for peace, many commentators began to complain, with some reason, of the "helicopters-on-the-lawn syndrome." Local politicians seemed so addicted to international attention that they found it impossible to sort out any problem without at least two prime ministers, a high-level U.S. envoy, and an army of television crews rushing in to create the necessary air of global crisis.

This tendency to lose a sense of proportion has deep roots. The conflict itself was partly driven by mutually reinforcing exaggerations. The ability to inflate one's own sense of self-importance, to make the intimate epic, the banal heroic, has fed into what Freud famously called "the narcissism of small differences." The Irish magnifying glass has tended to make real and intolerable injustices look uniquely monstrous, creating what the Belfast wits called the MOPE (Most Oppressed People Ever) syndrome—a self-pity which, for both sides in the conflict, justified extreme violence toward the other. The sense of being specially chosen by a malevolent God for the torments he felt were too harsh for Job has been deeply embedded in Irish historical consciousness, even though, over the course of the twentieth century, the island was a relatively lucky place, free of concentration camps or gulags, famines or epidemics, rape camps or killing fields.

Meanwhile, the slippery, ambivalent position of the Republic in the wider world, its odd mix of underdevelopment and hyperdevelopment, of insularity and globalization has often sanctioned outrageous comparisons with Africa or the old Eastern Europe. Some aspects of Irish experience in the twentieth century can certainly be illuminated by reference to the great historical traumas of the rest of the world. Words like "torture" and "slavery" can usefully be applied, if only as a rebuke to self-righteousness, to the imprisonment and abuse of children in the Republic's church-run Industrial School system, which ended only in the 1970s. The scope of literary censorship in the Republic from the 1930s to the 1960s has something in common with the control of literature in the Communist world. Aspects of the relative poverty and underdevelopment of the Irish economy until the 1990s can be analyzed within frameworks that are more usually applied to the developing countries of Asia and Latin America. A term like "death squads," borrowed by Irish Republicans from El Salvador and Guatemala in the 1980s, and applied to Loyalist sectarian murder gangs, had some purchase on the reality that was experienced by vulnerable Catholics. A word like "apartheid" has some rhetorical justification when applied to the way the contemporary Irish health system treats rich and poor.

But these analogies are also misleading, especially in the scale of horror that they imply. They should be placed in the context of an island that avoided the worst of what even the history of privileged Europe had to offer in the twentieth century. No Irish city has been besieged for two-and-a-half years during which 750,000 of its citizens died, as happened to Leningrad (now St. Petersburg) between 1941 and 1944. In no Irish city has virtually the entire female population been threatened with a sustained experience of mass rape like that of Berlin was in 1945. For all the systematic discrimination against Catholics in Northern Ireland, no Irish ethnic group in the twentieth century has been subjected to a serious and largely successful campaign of utter annihilation in the way that the Nazis tried to exterminate Jews or even to the less structured campaigns of genocide that faced Armenians, Gypsies, and Bosnians in Europe.

The effects of the Irish civil war of 1923 still shape politics in the Republic, but it was a minor skirmish in comparison with the horrific Balkan civil wars of the 1990s. The authoritarianism of Irish governments, north and south, real as it was, would have represented astonishing freedom for many Europeans during long periods of the century when Ireland was one of a small handful of surviving democracies. Some images of Ireland in the twentieth century (the hollow ruins of central Dublin after the 1916 Rising, for example, or the paratroopers with machine guns in the front yards of houses in West Belfast in the 1980s) recall the devastation of the wider continent in the 1930s and 1940s, but no Irish city has been flattened, divided by a wall, or had its nationality changed and changed back according to the contingencies of power. Ireland had no war in which 10 to 20 percent of its total population was wiped out, as happened to the Soviet Union, Poland, and Yugoslavia in World War II. In World War II, Europe as a whole lost around forty million people, and no more than a few thousand were Irish. Holland, a small country that did not actively engage in the fighting, lost about three hundred thousand people in those six years, ten times as many victims as the Irish Troubles.

Even the language of Irish discourse often tacitly acknowledged a nagging sense that, however awful things could be in Ireland, the real epics of human tragedy were unfolding elsewhere. The very term "the Troubles"—used for both the interlocking struggles of 1916–23, from which the Republic and Northern Ireland emerged, and for the North's civil conflict of 1968–98—suggests, even in the midst of great personal suffering, an understanding that Ireland occupies a footnote in the long book of the century's immense cruelties. There is even a note of bathetic comedy in the Republic's official term for the Second World War, in which it managed to stay neutral: "the Emergency."

I mention these rather obvious facts merely because in much discussion of Ireland, they are not obvious at all. The sense of special victimhood so nicely captured in Frank McCourt's wonderfully sardonic opening to *Angela's Ashes*—"Worse than the ordinary miserable childhood is the miserable Irish childhood, and worse yet is the miserable Irish Catholic childhood"—tends to prevail. The irony is that nothing is more common, especially to small nations, than the belief that your tribe has forged a unique destiny from unique sufferings.

Irish people like to see Ireland as an exceptional place. Our suffering throughout history is unparalleled. Our monks saved civilization in the Dark Ages. Our religiosity is incomparable. Our literary achievements are unique. Our struggle for freedom inspired the peoples of the world. Our sense of fun is unmatched. The complexity of our dilemmas is unsurpassed. The leap we have made from premodernity to postmodernity is faster and therefore stranger than that of any other society. And because Ireland occupies a place in the world grossly disproportionate to its population, this sense of our own uniqueness is often reflected back on us from the outside.

All of this may suggest that the conference which this book recalls was just another of those occasions of homage which tempt the recidivist Irish yet again into the sin of self-esteem. I think it is true, indeed, that many of the Irish participants did feel somewhat shamefaced at the disproportion between the extraordinarily generous interest in Ireland taken by the Virginia Foundation for the Humanities and their own almost unadulterated ignorance of Virginia. In hosting the gathering at all, the VFH might be accused of adding to the self-importance of a culture that could perhaps benefit from being reminded that it occupies a small corner of the privileged world, protected, to a very large extent, from the catastrophic disruptions and cataclysmic disorders that ought to command the world's attention.

For all that, though, there are some ways in which Ireland is modestly but genuinely interesting. The very disproportion between its scale and the attention it receives is an eloquent expression of a deeper imbalance: the disparity between the island's population of 5.5 million, on the one hand, and, on the other, a global Irish Diaspora ten times that size. In its scale and duration, Irish emigration to North America, Britain, Australia, and other parts of the old British Empire is truly remarkable. And in the complex, shifting, but nonetheless real sense of Irishness that is continually being invented by the descendants of its exiles, Ireland has become one of the touchstones for the kind of multiple identity that many people feel they need in the contemporary world.

There is, too, the human tendency to be overwhelmed by massive events and numbed by enormous tragedies. It is sometimes easier to see and feel the ebb and flow of history in a little cove than in the great ocean. The great Irish essayist Hubert Butler, contemplating the relative lack of interest on the part of French historians in the fate of the thousands of children sent to Auschwitz from the transit camp at Drancy, north of Paris, in 1942, wrote that:

> I believe we are bored because the scale is so large that the children seem to belong to sociology and statistics. We cannot visualize them reading Babar books, having their teeth straightened, arranging dolls' tea parties. Their sufferings are too great and protracted to be imagined, and the range of human sympathy is narrowly restricted. Had four or five children only been killed and burnt, and had it happened outside the booking office at the Gare d'Austerlitz, we would have responded emotionally . . . and the names of their murderers would be remembered forever.[1]

Something like this may perhaps apply to Ireland as well. The relatively small scale of its conflicts allows their cruelties and sufferings to remain within the narrow range of immediate human sympathies. The image of the family of Jean McConville, a widowed mother of ten children murdered by the IRA in 1972 and secretly buried by them, waiting over thirty years to find out if her bones had been found at last, has a dramatic power that surpasses somehow the deadening sight of a field of skulls in Cambodia or Rwanda. When the sister of Robert Hamill, a young man kicked to death by a Loyalist mob in 1997 for the crime of being a Catholic, speaks of how some of her neighbors laugh in the street while they jump up and down imitating the attack in which he was killed, the nature of hatred comes home more clearly to us than when we try to contemplate the overpowering massacres at Srebrenica or the Twin Towers.

There is, too, the sole civilizing virtue of that disgraceful Northern Ireland conflict: its reminder that atavistic political brutality is not the unique possession of people who look and speak differently to the white Christians who form the mainstream of the rich world. As in some respects the tail end of the religious wars that engulfed Europe after the Reformation, the Troubles belonged to all the societies shaped by those events, a list that certainly includes North America and most of Europe. That it took so long for either the United States or the European Union to make any really constructive contribution to their solution adds to the feeling that Northern Ireland was the embarrassing love child of a wider Christian culture whose dark secrets it threatened to reveal. In that sense, the conflict did have a larger international significance than the blank statistics of dead and maimed might indicate.

And if this is true of its unforgivable protraction, it is also true of the eventual efforts toward a solution that culminated, on Good Friday 1998, in the Belfast Agreement. The promise of that deal has yet to be fulfilled, and it may well take some years for the democratic institutions it envisages to be fully established. But the continuing failures and frustrations are in some respects less remarkable than the intellectual achievement of the agreement itself. While different parties may wish to see changes, everyone tacitly or explicitly accepts the framework it has established. And that framework contains some of the most genuinely radical ideas ever embodied in a formal international treaty: that sovereignty is open-ended and contingent; that a nation and a state are not necessarily coterminous; that multiple national identities are not just permissible but perhaps necessary; that a people can exert its right to self-determination not just by asserting its claims but by giving them up; that a nation is not a piece of territory but the active, human search for agreement and consent; that what people can live with is more important than what they're prepared to die for.

These notions are fruitful, not just in the Irish context, but around a world where there is no shortage of deeply ingrained conflict in which competing political, religious, and ethnic allegiances form a knot that appears impossible to disentangle. And, if anything, the international importance of the Belfast Agreement has grown with time. In the late 1990s, it was just one of a number of seemingly successful peace deals that generated a sense of global optimism. Now, in spite of its incomplete state, it is one of the few examples of relative success. It has, too, a particular resonance in the world after September 11, 2001, where the question of how to defeat terrorism has risen to the top of the agenda. It reminds us that where military solutions, at least on their own, failed, the complex political engagement of re-imagining the problem might in the end be more successful. If, as seems likely, the IRA, one of the most effective terrorist organizations of the last fifty years, eventually puts itself out of business, something of real global significance will have been achieved.

There is, besides the Irish Diaspora and the Peace Process, a third respect in which Ireland has an international significance beyond its own self-importance. It pertains not to Ireland's imagined uniqueness but, on the contrary, to its extreme position within a process that affects everyone on earth: globalization. In April 2004, the latest edition of the annual *A. T. Kearney/ Foreign Policy Magazine Globalization Index* placed Ireland, for the third year in a row, as the most globalized nation on the planet, "due to the country's deep economic links and high levels of personal contact with the rest of the world." Using data for 2002, the compilers of the index noted that Ireland in that year defied the downward investment trend throughout most of Western Europe, registering its highest-ever FDI (foreign direct investment) inflow of $24.7 billion, including notable new investments in the high-growth IT and pharmaceutical sectors. Intel, for instance, announced that it would spend an additional $2 billion in Ireland over the coming years to manufacture new-generation semiconductor wafers. However, Ireland's lead over other countries shrank in 2002, as portfolio capital investment dropped by a quarter from 2001. Nevertheless, a strong showing in noneconomic facets of global integration helped sustain the country's top position. For example, Ireland once again proved to be a leader in technological connectivity, ranking seventh worldwide in the number of secure servers per capita.

Ireland's consistent position at the top of this particular tree suggests that it is extremely globalized, both at the structural level of the economy and politics, and at the personal level of human contact. Two aspects of this situation are important. One is that Ireland's small and relatively intimate scale makes it possible to see the amorphous and often invisible set of forces that we call globalization at work in a way that might be more difficult in a larger society. The other is that Ireland's arrival at this position has been sudden and largely unexpected. Even fifteen years ago, when the Republic was an economic basket case characterized by very high levels of unemployment, negative growth, mass emigration, and political corruption, and Northern Ireland was mired in an apparently interminable conflict that made economic progress virtually impossible, the transformation of Ireland into a poster child for the ideology of globalization would have seemed fantastical.

For much of the twentieth century, the growth of output per capita in Ireland was the lowest among twenty-three European countries, with the single exception of the UK. Ireland's economic performance was far worse than almost every comparable Western European country. In 1913, Ireland was just 8 percentage points below the typical Western European level of per-capita production, but by 1987 the gap was 35 percentage points.

The opening up of the economy began in 1958 with the publication of "The First Program for Economic Expansion." In broad terms, then, the integration of Ireland into the global economy has been underway for over forty years. But the pace and scale of the process increased beyond recognition in the 1990s. In 1990, Ireland imported €15.8 billion worth of goods and exported €18.2 billion. By 2002, the respective figures were €55.3 billion and €93.7 billion. The effects of this massively increased trade were dramatic. Between 1986 and the fourth quarter of 2000—little more than a decade—the unemployment level went from 17.4 percent to 3.9 percent. At the same time, the ratio of external debt to Gross Domestic Product—the best measure of how solvent a state is—fell from 120 percent to less than 50 percent. In 2001, Ireland was exactly twice as rich, measured in real terms, as it was in 1990.

It is not just that the change in the Republic happened quickly but that it happened in an unusually monolithic and in some respects extraordinarily traditional culture. The overwhelming dominance of Catholicism, the strong commitment (in public at least) to conservative social values, and the general adherence to a nineteenth-century conception of nationalism all suggested that this was a society which would find it extremely difficult to adapt to such radical change. How could a consumer boom sit with the antimaterialism of Catholic teaching? How could the permissiveness of consumer culture and the flood of competing images of the good life be reconciled with the old hierarchies? How could the nationalist quest for self-determination survive when the most important decisions affecting the daily lives of Irish people were being taken in corporate headquarters in Seattle or Chicago? How could the authority of bishops and politicians not come into conflict with a young, well-educated, confident, and prosperous population? How do you get away with laws limiting contraception and banning divorce when the world's supply of Viagra is manufactured in Cork?

The answer to these questions would seem to lie most obviously in bitter social conflict, and there were indeed deep divisions in Irish society over issues like divorce and abortion. Yet the real story is how easily an apparently conservative society adjusted itself to a radically altered landscape, and how suddenly the apparently formidable authority of the Church collapsed as dark stories of abuse and hypocrisy began to emerge from the shadows. The way all of this happened is a fascinating case study in the cultural effects of globalization, and one that suggests that simplistic notions of the obliteration of old traditions by rapacious new forces have to be tempered by a realization that sometimes globalization may do no more than speed up an already inevitable process.

An interesting question in the current context is whether it is possible to find a new Blasket Island myth in Irish literature, one that draws on the traditional resonance of the islands but reconfigures it to take account of all that has happened since: the transformation of the Ireland of which the islands were an imaginary microcosm in the 1920s into the state which has now itself become a microcosm for the process of globalization. There is in fact such a literary myth. It is appropriately bizarre and, also appropriately, not written by an Irish writer. It is a sometimes ludicrous but also weirdly prescient science fiction novel, Fred Hoyle's *Ossian's Ride*.

Fred Hoyle, who died in 2001, was a leading English astrophysicist of the mid-twentieth century who contributed significantly to the development of radar and to theories of the evolution of stars. *Ossian's Ride* appeared at an interesting time. It was published in 1959, the first year of the globalization of the Irish economy. Irish economic nationalism had just collapsed under the weight of mass emigration, mass unemployment, poverty, disillusion, and a dwindling population. The radical decision had been made to take down tariff barriers and invite foreign investment, principally from American transnational corporations. For an English observer like Hoyle, especially one with a speculative turn of mind, there was now the possibility that sleepy, predictable, rural Ireland was going to be transformed into a modern economy that could actually compete with Britain.

The novel is a strange mixture of science fiction and John Buchan–style English adventure story. It is now 1970. The narrator, Sherwood, a young English mathematician, is summoned by what appears to be British Intelligence and sent on a mission to penetrate the headquarters of I.C.E., the Industrial Corporation of Eire, a fictionalized version of the actual IDA (Industrial Development Authority), which was given the task of attracting foreign investment to Ireland. The nature of I.C.E. is explained to Sherwood:

> I.C.E. . . . came into being some twelve years ago. A small group of very able scientists approached the Government of Eire with what seemed an entirely straightforward proposition. Their proposal was to establish an industry for the extraction of a range of chemicals from the organic material in peat—turf as the Irish call it . . . Within a short time, I.C.E. was producing an amazing range of valuable chemicals, ostensibly from turf as raw material, although whether this was really so is open to doubt. At British chemical concerns, there were many red faces.[2]

I.C.E, like the companies attracted by the real IDA, has been given a ten-year tax holiday by the Irish government. After its fourth year, however, it makes an immensely profitable breakthrough. It invents the contraceptive pill, which it apparently manufactures from turf. After this, I.C.E. switches from chemistry to physics. Ireland becomes an industrial, and potentially a military, superpower. The Old World powers need to know what is going on, and Sherwood is sent as a spy.

Laughable as all of this undoubtedly is, the shape of the story is eerily prescient. The foreign scientists and the government tax breaks were already a reality in 1959. But parts of the fable make a peculiar kind of sense in the light of what happened in the mid-1990s. Ireland did not, in fact, discover how to make contraceptive pills from turf, but its economy is now stiffened by Viagra, which is manufactured in County Cork by the multinational chemical corporation Pfizer. In Hoyle's potted history of I.C.E., the discovery of the contraceptive pill in a famously Catholic country undermines the power of the Church by leaving it open to mockery. When Sherwood asks why the Church didn't stop it, his handler replies: "Ridicule, my boy. . . . Think of it, contraceptives from turf! For decades the Church had fulminated against their use, while, all the time, outside every cottage, there'd been piled a whole mountain of the stuff" (10).

In its own way, this tells what would become an obvious truth. The globalization of Irish society through the influx of multinational capital did in fact slowly undermine the authority of a Church whose hold on power weakened as other sources of authority gained strength.

What Sherwood sees on his trip to the then future, now past, Ireland of 1970 is a similar mix of the outlandish and the metaphorically accurate. He sees in Dublin a "city [which] was being systematically demolished and rebuilt" (36). But he also witnesses the arrival of television, and Hoyle summarizes remarkably well the impact that it would actually have in Ireland a few years after his book was published: "It seemed as if two different worlds had come into sharp conflict, and yet why not? . . . Here were two people, apparently isolated in a remote spot, who by the flick of a knob could now find themselves immersed in the maelstrom of human affairs" (64).

Sherwood also witnesses the conversion of the Irish countryside into an industrial, high-tech landscape, with the fabulous new city of Caragh constructed by I.C.E. outside Cahirciveen. While the vast Intel microchip-fabrication plants outside Maynooth, County Kildare, in the real contemporary Ireland may not have Caragh's futuristic beauty, the sense of transformation of an agricultural topography into a space-age landscape is not all that far from Hoyle's wild imaginings.

It turns out, in any case, that I.C.E. has sealed off the southwest corner of Ireland—Kerry, West Cork, and Limerick—as its own territory. And its holy of holies, the inner sanctum where the head scientists are based and from which they organize their futuristic enterprise to make Ireland the center of the modern world, is the Blasket Island of Inishvicillaune. For the contemporary Irish reader, this is almost too absurdly appropriate. For, though it was uninhabited when Hoyle was writing, Inishvicillaune is now owned by Charles Haughey, the corrupt Taoiseach (prime minister) of the 1980s and early 1990s who saw himself as the architect of Irish industrial modernity and father of the Celtic Tiger boom economy.

The Inishvicillaune architects of I.C.E. are, of course, aliens who have taken human form. They came to the Blaskets from a distant, imploding planet, bringing with them the knowledge accumulated by their vastly more advanced civilization. For Hoyle's original British readers there may have been a certain reassurance in knowing that the witty Irish scatterbrains couldn't really work all that complicated mathematics and technology on their own. Yet here, too, there is a metaphorical ring of truth. The transformation of Ireland over the last forty-five years has sometimes felt as if a new world had landed from outer space on top of an old one. Because Irish development was externally driven, its relationship to the society in which it happened was far from organic. In a way, therefore, Hoyle's sometimes ridiculous book is the myth of globalization that Irish writers did not manage to create. His re-imagining of the Blaskets of Tomas O Crohan and Peig Sayers as the hub of a high-tech invasion is a strangely eloquent image of the tectonic shift in Irish culture.

Yet the very fact that we have to look to an obscure English science fiction novel to tell this story suggests the problem of Irish culture in this new globalized age. What is left that can be regarded as authentic? Is there any viable notion of a workable tradition? But perhaps we might, in the best Irish fashion, answer the question with another question. Was there ever a simple, workable standard of authenticity in a culture that has been shaped by the globalizing forces of invasion, empire, and emigration?

If Ireland is interesting for the way it has coped or failed to cope with the consequences of opening itself up to the world economy, it has also become interesting to those who have a political stake in global ideologies. On the one hand, the raw economic data make Ireland an apparently formidable example for free-market global capitalism. In North and South America and in the emerging states of central and eastern Europe, Ireland is very frequently cited as proof that right-wing economics—low corporate taxes, minimal government interference, and a determination to attract investment at all costs—offer the solution to the world's problems. Its transformation seems to suggest that the woes of postcolonial societies are essentially their own fault, and that all they have to do is to stop whining and follow the Irish model. The shrinking of government, the cutting of taxes, and the reduction of public expenditure created wealth, even in a country that had previously been an economic black hole. By embracing the global market and following the rules laid down by neoconservatives, Ireland prospered. And even if the rich did best, everybody benefited. Wages rose, unemployment shrank, emigration turned into immigration, and we all had the best years of our lives.

On the other hand, though, this very insistence makes the Irish model worth examining both for what it is and what it has and has not achieved. It is in fact rather more complex than any simple free-market model might suggest. It was driven in large measure by precisely the kind of institutions that the neoconservative movement despises: an interventionist government, activist public servants and planners, the social democrats of the European Union who helped to fund it out of a sense of solidarity, and the trade union movement who bargained relatively low and predictable wage increases for some degree of social progress. Even in strictly economic terms, the role of left-wing movements like feminism, which created the climate in which women could remain in or rejoin the workforce, was crucial.

And whatever its origins, the results of the Irish boom are not quite as unequivocal as many conservatives would like to think. While wealth has increased, so has inequality. By adopting an American model of economic development, Ireland has ended up with a social structure that is also remarkably American. The United Nations Development Program's annual *Human Development Report* ranks countries not just in terms of raw economic wealth but according to the larger goal of a healthy society. On one of its indices, ranking countries for a combination of poverty and inequality, there is a list of how well the seventeen most-developed countries are doing. At the bottom, nestled rather uncomfortably together, are Ireland and the United States. Even at the height of the Irish boom, one in every four households and one in every five people in Ireland was living in poverty.

The way in which Ireland has become more American in the last decade is one good reason for trying to re-imagine Ireland in America. But there is a more profound reason why a conference like "Re-Imagining Ireland" made so much sense. It is that the three large forces of change that give Ireland some genuine claim to the world's attention—the Diaspora, the Peace Process, and the economic boom—interact with each other in a way that is hard to appreciate without the kind of removal from the everyday life of the island that the Virginia conference offered. In and of themselves, these three big forces, with all their attendant ramifications, are hard to grasp. What makes them even more difficult to pin down, though, is that they have bounced off each other in all sorts of complex ways.

To take the Peace Process as an example: It is not really possible to understand how it became possible if it is treated as a discrete development. Economic change in the Republic has been crucial in breaking down the old stereotypes of poor, rural, and romantic Catholics versus prosperous, urban, and hardheaded Protestants. Those clichés, of course, were always crude and stupid, but they had enough truth within them to be credible and therefore open to political abuse. The transformation of the Republic into an economic success story, with wealth to flaunt and a per capita GDP higher than that of the UK, has killed off the stereotype for all but the most recalcitrant bigot.

This shift in turn has affected one side of the sectarian equation: The opening up of Irish Catholicism and the collapse of the political authority of the Church hierarchy are both causes and consequences of the economic boom. Had the grip of traditional Catholicism not already been weakening, the economic boom would have stalled because married women would not have joined the workforce, thus depriving a rapidly expanding workforce of the labor it needed. The boom, in turn, with its new values of individualism and materialism, has further weakened the authority of the Church.

On another level, the influence of the Irish Diaspora has been important, not just in the mechanics of the Peace Process, but in opening up notions of multiple identity that have been crucial to the Belfast Agreement. On the one hand, the Diaspora has shown, both to Protestants and Catholics, that identity is extraordinarily resilient and is not quite so dependent on political and geographical continuity as traditional notions of nationalism assumed it to be. On the other, the fact that millions of people seem reasonably comfortable with a hyphenated identity has offered a reassurance that the idea in the Agreement that people born in Northern Ireland can be "Irish or British or both" is not, in practice, all that weird. In the context of globalization, it may even become the norm.

Or consider a direct issue that affects both Northern Ireland and the Republic today: immigration and racism. As Ireland becomes, for the first time in its history, a significant destination rather than a point of departure for people looking for a better life, it faces genuinely new challenges. While there have always been immigrants, and while emigration will always continue to some extent, the island's magnet has been essentially turned around, exerting a force of attraction rather then repulsion. And here, the experience of generations of Irish emigrants, who often encountered the abuse and lies that are the migrant's lot, can, if it is properly re-imagined, provide a crucial bulwark against the rise of racism and neofascism. In this sense, the historical work of American scholars like Noel Ignatiev and David Roediger on the transformations and manipulations of notions of Irishness and race is as directly relevant to contemporary Ireland as the latest sociological data.

These connections are vital to an understanding of Ireland and its place in the contemporary world. But they are often difficult to make in the separate worlds occupied by academics, artists, journalists, economists, and politicians, let alone the separate worlds of the homeland and its Diaspora, of the

Republic and Northern Ireland. In bringing these worlds together, Andrew Wyndham and his colleagues at the Virginia Foundation for the Humanities created a unique context for a new kind of conversation to begin. That context is one that starts with the recognition that there are many Irelands and the hope that they have nevertheless enough common ground to communicate with each other. If Ireland could be a little like this conference, it could be imagined as the kind of open space where the passion required to speak and the curiosity required to listen are held in some kind of creative tension.

NOTES

1. Hubert Butler, *The Children of Drancy* (Mullingar: Lilliput, 1988), 186–87.
2. Fred Hoyle, *Ossian's Ride* (London: Heinemann, 1959), 9. Hereafter citations to this work appear parenthetically in the main text.

What Is the Celtic Tiger?

HELEN SHAW

In 1962, Nobel Prize writer John Steinbeck took an anonymous trip around America to rediscover his own nation's soul. He wrote, before the trip, that consumerism was destroying his country's moral health. "If I wanted to destroy a nation, I would give it too much and I would have it on its knees, miserable, greedy and sick," he told Adlai Stevenson. Over forty years later, Irish writers, thinkers, politicians and policy makers are exploring the impact of a sudden burst of "too much" to both the Irish psyche and nation.

So what is or was this phantasmal beast, the "Celtic Tiger"? It is a mythical creature created by an economist, Kevin Gardiner, who used it in a report for his employers, the bankers Morgan Stanley, in 1994. It took three years for the phrase and idea—that Ireland would be a booming high-tech economy—to take off. The boom might have more accurately been tagged the "Irish Wolfhound" since we've about as much experience with tigers as with snakes, and calling the Tiger Celtic is about as accurate as calling it the Pict, Firbolg, or Viking Tiger.

But very quickly everything good or bad about the economic take-off was attributed to the claws and paws of the Tiger. It became a muddled metaphor for the changing social, economic, and cultural world of the late 1990s in Ireland, and as early as 1998 people were writing passionate pleas to kill off, not the boom, but the phrase "Celtic Tiger."

By mid-2000, Oliver O'Connor of *Finance* magazine wrote in the *Irish Times* of the phrase "Celtic Tiger," "It's a metaphor that serves not to clarify an idea but to mish and mash what could be useful discussions." Every clichéd nuance of the Tiger has been employed by the media, from the *soft belly* to the *shadow of the beast.* Soon traffic; housing prices; lack of staff; our inability to get a plumber, carpenter, builder; the influx of refugees; our loss of manners and hospitality—everything was laid firmly at the foot of the fantastical Tiger.

In a trawl through the archives, you see the list of ills blamed on the booming economy and sudden wealth—from a spike in underage drinking and smoking to car rage and suicide. John Waters leaped on the news that the Irish had gained a stone (14 pounds) in average weight in the 1990s to stretch the analogy that the Irish, now fattened, were sacrificing the fat cow—the bringer of the Tiger—C. J. Haughey himself. All our sins of excess and greed were blamed on the speed of economic growth rather than being seen within the context of overall change in Ireland from the 1970s, perhaps lulling people into thinking that it was money that is the root of all evil, rather than a composite of multifaceted changes across our society. My favorite twist on the hackneyed Tiger comes from the *Irish Times* subeditor who titled Andy Pollak's article on the increase in births and marriages in 2000: "The Sow That Eats Her Farrow Has Become a Celtic Tiger Bearing Cubs."

So was the Tiger more a Cheshire Cat that keeps appearing and disappearing and leaves just a grin and a tail behind? What are the forces which are making and creating modern Ireland, and how do we sift out the chaff and find the true grains that feed our transformation?

At the heart of the debate are the questions, what caused the Irish boom, and how profoundly is it linked to real change within Ireland? One side sees Ireland moving into the land of light—becoming a modern, tolerant, liberal democratic European nation—leaving the dark repressed days of the 1950s behind us. The other sees Ireland slavishly following the U.S. corporate model, selling our national soul, our history, and our heritage to become a subsidiary of either the United States or a federal Europe. One version sees the Celtic Tiger economy as the result of state intervention—an economy made ripe for the high-tech take-off—drawing on an educated English-speaking workforce, with a low corporate tax regime. Another sees us as a boat going full-tilt in a global wind—happy to sail, but equally likely to sink in the tidal waves of global economic change as high-tech moves east.

So for us the issues are, what does the "Celtic Tiger" represent—the evolution of a postcolonial nation into one which now takes its place within Europe and the world, or a short-term unsustainable boom that has allowed us to ignore the social problems of exclusion, racism, and poverty? What kind of Ireland are we creating or building—a new social and economic model, drawing on the lessons of both Europe and the United States, or one where we are importing the failures of hyperconsumerism and the market, just as we built the Ballymun Flats in the 1960s, when the high-rise social housing model was already seen as flawed?

Today, we're still looking at those flats, which are only now being demolished. Let's hope that we can build and construct *this* model, which eastern Europeans talk approvingly of as the "Irish Model" rather than the Celtic Tiger. Let's hope we have the courage to make our own way, holding onto the social and public values of our past—rather than ultimately seeing the marketplace as the venue of all wisdom.

If we do have the courage to truly envision a transformed society, we may then become more than a footnote in economic history and provide a living model of a successful small nation, able to answer the question, *"What is ours?"* Our challenge, if we face it, is to make this a transformational rather than a transitional change process—one which envisages the future rather than allowing global events to dictate it.

Poverty in the Midst of Prosperity

PETER McVERRY

Some time ago, a nine-year-old boy was found sleeping on the streets of Dublin. He was filthy, covered in lice, and was not attending school because, he said, the other children were laughing at him being so dirty. When a social worker was contacted, she stated that she had instructions *not* to take the boy into care, as there were no places available for him.

This occurred twelve years after the Child Care Act of 1991 was signed into law by the president, an act which guaranteed that every homeless child would receive adequate care and accommodation.

I have worked for the past twenty-five years with young homeless people in Dublin. In all that time, I have never known the problem to be as bad as it is today. During the years when the Celtic Tiger was at its strength, the numbers of homeless people in Ireland doubled, to 5,580. Most of the increase was in the earlier years of the Celtic Tiger. This was not an unforeseeable by-product of the Celtic Tiger—it was a direct consequence of it.

Due to the Celtic Tiger, the cost of private housing soared obscenely. Many people living in public housing who would normally save for a mortgage to enable them to access private housing were no longer able to afford a mortgage. They have found themselves stuck in public housing, thereby preventing others from entering. The number of households on the waiting list for public housing has, as a consequence, soared during the past six years and now numbers almost fifty thousand. During the years of prosperity, we did not even build sufficient public housing units to meet the numbers of *new* entrants into the public housing market. Homeless people, particularly single homeless people, are at the bottom of the housing queue, which is just getting longer and longer.

There are many other examples of poverty amidst the Celtic Tiger economy. Among them:

Over four hundred schools are in urgent need of renovation; some of them have leaking roofs, dangerous electrical wiring, or are rat-infested, overcrowded, and lacking adequate sanitary arrangements.

A succession of very damaged homeless children has worn a path to the High Court to seek the accommodation to which they are entitled in law by the Child Care Act of 1991. Children with special needs—for example, autistic children—have also found that the only way to secure their right to education and care has been to go, at enormous cost and effort on their parents' part, to the High Court.

Adults with intellectual disabilities are still accommodated in psychiatric hospitals, some of which are in appalling physical condition. Many poor families are reluctant to seek a doctor's attention until a crisis arises, due to the fact that they are ineligible for free medical care. A government commitment to extend the Full Medical Card scheme was not implemented, due to lack of resources. The increasingly inadequate public health service has been repeatedly highlighted—problems include long waiting lists for elective surgery, overcrowded casualty departments, and a very inadequate supply of hospital beds.

Each year, four thousand children leave school with no qualifications, and some schools in deprived areas report up to one-third of pupils absent each day. A total of twelve places in a therapy program exist for four hundred sex offenders.

The list goes on and on.

How can we understand the contradiction between our wealth and what we as a society provide? We have managed an economy but we have not adequately cared for the most vulnerable of our people. An attitude appears to exist among our political decision makers that those who directly, through work, contributed to wealth-creation and increased productivity should be rewarded and those who were unable to do so, for whatever reason, cannot expect to share in the benefits.

While we have never had it so good economically, there are good reasons for being very concerned about the direction in which our society is going. Many have more money in their pockets, bigger cars, and can enjoy foreign holidays. But in a society in which home ownership is a key value, today many double-income families with good jobs can only dream of owning their own home; those lucky enough to manage a mortgage have less time with their children as both parents must earn an income, work long hours, and commute long distances. Suicide is the major cause of death of young males aged fifteen to twenty-five. Our consumption of alcohol has increased dramatically, in contrast to other EU countries. Drink-related violence has become a major cause of concern, and binge drinking is the recreation of choice of many schoolchildren.

Many are asking, What is the meaning of all this frantic activity? but cannot find an answer. The old religious truths and social mores that bound us together have disintegrated, but we have nothing to replace them except a rush to find our security in accumulating wealth. Many say that we have become more self-centered, greedier, less caring, and that our young people are increasingly driven by the desire for self-gratification.

Who is asking the question, Where are we going? The car has been traveling down the road at a faster and faster speed, and all the attention has been given to making it travel faster, more efficiently, more successfully. But what is the destination at which we seek to arrive? What sort of society are we creating?

I don't want to go back to the past, yet I feel that nobody is steering the car as we speed into the future. While the engine is constantly being retuned and refined, and the oil replaced—so the car can go faster, with less fuel—who is asking the basic question: Where are we going, and why?

Celtic Tiger

Social and Cultural Implications

LIZ O'DONNELL

I value the opportunity to take stock of where we have come from as a people and where we are going after a period of unprecedented economic and cultural change. Ireland today is successful, wealthy, vibrant—the fastest-growing economy in the developed world; more successful than at any time in our history as an independent state. Did this happen by chance? No. In my view, it was the culmination of a series of domestic political choices and policy decisions made over a period of, say, thirty years. There were many critical intersecting factors at play.

Economic reform was bringing lower taxes, stable public finances, and deregulation. Our population was young and well educated. The Irish baby boom happened in the 1960s and 1970s, twenty years after America's. There were plenty of people available for work also because of high unemployment, at over 15 percent at the start of the 1990s. There was also considerable scope for more participation in the labor force by women—at the start of the 1990s, women's participation in the labor force was 36 percent; it is now 49 percent. We had a proven, successful strategy for attracting foreign direct investment, and between the United States and Europe foreign direct investment boomed, in both directions, in the 1990s. We have been very well placed to take advantage of this: Our population has grown to 3.9 million, up from 3.5 million in 1990. GDP growth reached 10 percent or more in successive years between 1995 and 2000.

But perhaps the most important factor of all was our membership in the European Union. Joining the EU in 1973 transformed Ireland in more ways than one. It turned the country's face outward and beyond our nearest neighbor and market in the UK. It opened our minds and liberated us from an insular isolationism, allowing us preferential access to the world's richest markets. We enjoyed substantial financial transfers from the EU in farm supports and infrastructural investment. We are now strategically placed as a bridge between the United States and the European Union. In 2004, with the accession of ten central and eastern European states, even more opportunities opened up on that front.

The statistics which say it all for me, as a practicing politician, are that we have moved in a relatively short period from mass unemployment to full employment, from mass emigration to net inward migration. Since 1990, the number of people at work has increased from 1.1 million to 1.8 million. That is 700,000 more people at work in Ireland, an increase of 63 percent. Most of the additional jobs came in the second half of the decade: 445,000 between 1996 and 2001, compared to 158,000 from 1991 to 1996. Unemployment in Ireland has been brought down from more than 15 percent to less than 5 percent now. The phenomenon of long-term unemployment—being unemployed for more than a year—has been virtually eliminated in Ireland. Fewer than 25,000 people are currently counted as long-term unemployed. And forced emigration, so long a feature of Irish life, has been brought to an end.

The social implications of a full-employment economy are tremendously positive. We have seen many of them already: a real improvement in reducing poverty; greater participation in economic life of all age groups and among women; increased revenues from taxation; the ability of the government to pay higher pensions, and so on. Most important, there is a huge sense of relief that we are now educating our youngsters for jobs in Ireland rather than to emigrate, with all the human disappointment, separation, and despair that was our lot for too many years.

Ironically, some people claim that Irish people are unhappier now after achieving greater wealth and economic growth. They say that the problems of traffic, excessive drinking by young people, crime, and rising costs have made us question, "Is it all worthwhile?"

This point of view is often advanced without research other than anecdotes. I tend, like President McAleese, to take an unapologetically positive attitude to our economic success. I do not accept that we were happier when poor. I believe we should embrace the challenges of newfound wealth with enthusiasm, not pessimism and foreboding.

Maintaining full employment, or as close to full employment as possible, remains a social imperative for Ireland as well as an economic one. Our society could not possibly be better off if we accepted permanently high unemployment again. The best poverty beater is a real job.

We can remain confident, or we could slump back to cynicism and despondency under a wave of self-doubt and hand-wringing. Some people are casting doubt on whether Ireland will be a civilized society in a globalized world. The suggestion is that riches have made us crass and materialist, devoid of cultural content, mere consumers in a capitalist economy, and a mere four million, at that, among the world's five billion.

I would hate to think that we had to endure high unemployment and emigration in order to be a decent, civilized, culturally rich society. I do not believe we have lost our soul. Notwithstanding increased secularization and modernization, Irish people remain essentially a spiritual race with a strong moral compass. We have a long tradition of solidarity with the poor in the developing world; of a compassionate response to humanitarian disasters, man-made and natural; of peacekeeping at the UN. Ireland is now a leader in the donor league of aid to the poorest countries and is making rapid progress toward the UN target of 0.7 percent of GNP on overseas aid. Only five developed countries have achieved this.

To our credit, we are mindful of the dangers of new wealth and consumerism. We are grappling with the social challenges of lawlessness, intoxication, despair, and exclusion. Our hearts are, I believe, still in the right place as a people. The challenge now for us is to sustain our success, and not, as they say at home, "lose the run of ourselves."

Between Europe and America

PEADAR KIRBY

I want to put the emphasis not on Europe or America but on the other word in the title, the word "between." For, if Europe (or "Berlin," to use the term in which the debate has taken place in Ireland) stands for the social market model of social democracy, and America (or "Boston," in the terms of the Irish debate) stands for the liberal market model, then the debate about which of these models applies to Ireland is missing the point. Models are coherent things, growing either out of consistent policy orientations fostered by bureaucratic and political elites, or from deep-rooted social values and political instincts (such as the debates in the United States preceding independence, which saw government as the source of tyranny and division and saw society as being naturally virtuous if allowed to be so, thus informing what we now think of as the liberal market model). Placed in this context, it has to be said that Ireland has not so much achieved success through fashioning a coherent model as had success thrust upon it. Since the recognition of the economic boom, much intellectual effort has been expended on trying to understand how it happened. It is this retrospective analysis that has seen us as being pulled in two different directions.

On the one hand, our productive economy is largely based on maintaining low tax rates, particularly on corporate profits, as a competitive advantage to attract U.S. foreign investment. On the other hand, we aspire to European levels of social provision and infrastructure and have expected the EU to contribute substantial funds to help us achieve these. More and more, the contradiction at the heart of this approach is annoying our European neighbors. Our political and business leaders are touting a low-tax approach to development that contradicts essential features of the European model; they are strongly resisting moves to tax harmonization in the Union and are using tax levels to undercut other countries' efforts to attract foreign investment. Yet they expect high levels of social transfers to Ireland. This "in-betweenness" has allowed us to avoid the difficult dilemmas facing the European model—how to combine growth with equity. Instead, Ireland has prioritized growth while obscuring increasing and deeply entrenched levels of inequality in a fog of benign rhetoric about equality. With EU enlargement to the east, these fudges are no longer going to be sustainable: Ireland will lose much of its competitive advantage for U.S. investment into the EU, while it will also become a net contributor to social funds for eastern European countries.

In understanding this "in-betweenness," this lack of definition, I have found another America that bears great resemblances to Ireland and helps throw light on our situation; that other America is Latin America. Like Ireland, its colonial past has left it grappling with the *problematique* of development. It too has had numerous economic booms, but it has never managed to translate these into a sustainable model of developmental success. At the cultural level, the Mexican writer Carlos Fuentes has remarked on a feature of Latin America that bears resemblance to Ireland. He wrote that it is through artistic and cultural endeavors that Latin Americans express themselves, while their intellectual output remains essentially imitative and lacking originality. Even more is this true of Ireland.

Living in Chile for the academic year 2001-2, I found a lot of similarities with contemporary Ireland. Since the late 1980s, Chile has achieved high rates of economic growth and job creation comparable to those of Ireland and for a longer period. Yet it is the social costs of this success and the challenges it raises for society that I find most instructive and that pose major problems for the quantifiable and evolutionary view of social change that dominates policy discourse in Ireland. By this I mean the view that we have achieved a lot in Ireland, that much remains still be to be done, but that we must avoid damaging our achievements in the process. For the Chilean example draws attention to the social costs of economic success, particularly the social destruction unleashed by intense competitive pressures. Success was also achieved through taming civil society, at great political and personal costs (Chile has internationally very high rates of mental illness), and it resulted in a severe weakening of Chileans' sense of belonging, of their "identity," amid atomization and alienation. This has been richly documented and analyzed in the 2002 Human Development Report for Chile of the United Nations Development Program (UNDP), entitled *We the Chileans: A Cultural Challenge* (PNUD, Santiago, 2002).

We have nothing at all comparable available for Ireland. This experience challenges us to a more complex understanding of the nature of social change, of the actors who help bring it about, and of the possibilities that can be created. These take us way beyond the evolutionary, managerial approach, alerting us to its inadequacies as it fails to acknowledge the exclusionary processes at work amid economic boom and the social and even cultural legacies of these.

What we need to aspire to therefore is not Boston or Berlin, nor Buenos Aires, Brasilia, or Bogota, but to face the dilemmas, contradictions, and social strains of our present situation rather than minimize or deny them. We need to imagine society anew, to foster the solidarities underpinning it, and to release its many latent energies. We need to aspire to do in our times what Thomas Jefferson and his fellow revolutionaries did in theirs.

Finding Identity
in a Global Context

13 Ways of Looking at the Question

THEO DORGAN

1

Muros, Galicia. The fishermen, snug up to the bar, are complaining about the Irish fishery patrol boats. Los Diablos. They hate them, enforcers of European Union law. Simon, from the Mayo Gaeltacht, looks at me, an eyebrow raised, as we stand on the threshold. We order in Spanish, go sit by the fire; the fishermen, silent now, watch us in the bar mirror, strangers in from the sea. We speak together in Irish, the fishermen relax; unaccountable foreigners, stormbound sailors, we are of no further concern to them.

2

Giordaí Ó Laoghaire, a musician from Cork, goes off to Nicaragua in the 1980s, to work on a coffee brigade. I meet him soon after he gets back, in a café run by a Dutch couple on Paul Street. He tells me, in Irish, that from now on, where possible, he will only speak Irish.

What brought this on? One night, after a hard day's harvesting, a campesino had asked him why he always sang in English. Because that's what we speak in Ireland. But don't you have your own language?

3

London, the mid-1970s. A number of us, mostly from Cork, are living in squats in West Hampstead. Two of the lads, we have noticed, disappear every Wednesday night, won't say where they go. One night we follow them to Elephant & Castle, and find them playing country-and-western music. Despite, or because of, this worrying discovery, we are all of us in the height of good humor in the Tube going home. The carriage is almost empty. A pale-faced City type, brown pinstripe, *Financial Times,* horn-rim glasses, grimaces to himself as the hippies pile on. Opposite where we are sitting, a mother and her twin teenage daughters, glowing with good humor.

One of us makes them a flowery compliment, in Irish. I am surprised to discover he speaks the language. The women respond to the import if not the meaning. I join in, they respond again, we affect not to understand English. Now they are making ribald remarks about us, choosing possible night companions, commenting on our merits and demerits, as one after the other the seven of us discover that we all speak Irish. Our end of the carriage is bathed in smiles when the City type gets up to leave. He stands with his back to the doors, and as they hiss open, having somehow snared our attention, he says: "Ah bhaineas an-sult as an gcraic, lads. Níor chualas an oiread sin Gaeilge líofa blasta le blianta anuas" ("Ah, lads, I thoroughly enjoyed the crack [good-humored talk]. I haven't heard so much fluent Irish for years"). He steps back, still looking at us, and the doors close. Spontaneously, we all seven stand and applaud him. As the train gathers pace again he bows from the waist, acknowledging our applause. The three women are utterly mystified.

4

On the Antrim Road in Belfast, 1972, my first visit north. The RUC station is heavily armored in green metal cladding, festooned with barbed wire. Soldiers in the observation oriels watch us through telescopic sights as we walk past. I think "Fort Apache," I think "I am an Indian." That was the winter I read *Bury My Heart at Wounded Knee.* I was very young.

5

Queen's University Common Room, I am having a pint with some English Literature graduates. It is 1990 and I have been meeting them on poetry business. "Have you got your pesos for the return journey, eh?" one of them asks. The others, there is no other word for it, snicker. I get it all then, the backward Republic, grey skies, priest-ridden, the works. It comes to me that in the previous twelve months I have been in Paris, twice, London, also twice, Moscow and New York. I speak three languages. "Is that French? I don't speak French." "Is that Irish, I don't speak Irish." It's getting ugly, and I'm being childish, I know. They have never been outside Northern Ireland. Not one of them, ever. Self-planted.

6

I have been traveling north for more than thirty years now, up and down, up and down. Each time the train leaves Newry going south, closing with the border, my breathing deepens and steadies. Even now, in the wake of the Agreement.

7

Mullaghbawn, South Armagh. In the hospitable and cosmopolitan house of the singers Pádraigín Ní Uallacháin and Len Graham. There has been a night of music and poetry with, among others, Ciaran Carson, just home from reading his poems in Japan. It's late, the whiskey is going around. The conversation touches on an old song, its provenance. I am mesmerized as, for the best part of an hour, my three table companions meticulously track the song from its origins nearly two hundred years ago to its present form. They follow it from Pomeroy in Tyrone over to Sligo, down into North Cork, up and down across the island, naming the succession of singers and carriers, dissecting the changes and metamorphoses the song has undergone in its travels. For the first time I understand that oral history is as meticulous and exact as written history, perhaps more so: the entire discourse is egoless, three men with a common and fierce interest in getting it right. As they speak on, and the night deepens, I feel my country deepen beneath me, swell in the dark outside the window, its rich freight of memory, its sustaining music.

8

Educated by the Christian Brothers, I have been a remorseless anticlerical since the age of fourteen. My Nigerian friend came to Ireland because he was so impressed as a boy by the large-hearted, generous, and thoughtful Irish missionaries.

9

The boys in hoodies, jeans, trainers, are about nine or ten years of age. Parnell Street, in the heart of Dublin. O'Casey country. Two are, at a guess, Ghanaian, one Korean. I ask for directions to a Thai restaurant that I know is somewhere nearby. Shrugs, they shift from one foot to the other, look at each other blankly. As I walk away, I hear, in pure Dublin accents: "What did yer man want?" "Dunno, couldn't understand him." "Yeah, bleedin' culchie [person from the country]."

10

Midwinter, driving rain on O'Connell Street. A gaggle of young girls coming toward me—denim jackets, tee shirts, bare pierced midriffs. Tottering on high-heeled boots. Television. They think they live in Australia, California. In any real sense, they do. I turn to watch them go past the statue of James Larkin. His hands raised to high heaven.

11

I have been asked to write 1,000 words for a Microsoft localization CD-ROM. Their Dublin office is handling this for Europe. I assemble the information, put it in order, write it out in plain, bare English. Forty-three telephone conferences later, they still can't agree on the final wording—every night, it seems, there's a new bit of jargon in from Redmond in the e-mail that they want to use. Never the most patient of men, I finally give them twenty-four hours to sign off on this.

We meet in the offices of X-Communications, the company to whom they have subcontracted the business. The Microserfs are personable, well-fed young men. They have the strange, braying mid-Atlantic drawl of the new South Dublin. I bully them into agreeing a final text, then we sit back and have coffee.

The great thing about working for Microsoft, they tell me, is that you don't have to wear a uniform. Marie Redmond, X-Comm's MD, is a wise and witty woman: she makes a great effort not to catch my eye. I examine these new techno-Irish: each is wearing Timberland boots, Gap shorts with cargo pockets, a letter tee shirt (University of Utah, MIT); they have surfer hair cuts, evangelical dentistry, and the slightly crazed smiles of true believers everywhere. For badness I ask them what they think about the forthcoming General Election. Election?

12

Italia 90, the World Cup. The Irish perform heroically, lifting the hearts of an entire nation. I have never seen such mass enthusiasm, nobody can remember anything like it. Grannies in bus queues are earnestly discussing the finer points of the game with bankers, postmen, and punks. We progress from game to game. Hubris is in the air but she passes over us. We know it can't go all the way but we are enthralled, we want to see how long this can continue. Finally, we crash and burn to a single goal from the never-to-be-forgotten Toto Schillachi, Italy's star striker. No matter. The country is a sea of joyous tricolors, the foreign press is in love with the traveling Irish supporters, "the best fans in the world." We feel very pleased with ourselves in an eerily good-humored way.

The hero of the nation is Paul McGrath, our indomitable defender. McGrath's father was Nigerian, his mother a Dubliner. The chant everywhere you go is: "Ooh, Aah, Paul McGrath."

Three hundred thousand people gather in Dublin to welcome the team home, ten thousand at least in Dublin airport.

Two planes are approaching the airport simultaneously, one carrying the team, the other bringing Nelson Mandela to receive at last the Freedom of the City of Dublin, conferred on him years before when he was still a political prisoner. Protocol demands that President Mandela land first, but the crowd doesn't know this.

The plane taxis up to the red carpet, the doors open, the band strikes up, and Mandela steps out, accompanied by Kader Asmal, minister in his government and, until his return home, the heart and soul of the Irish Anti-Apartheid Movement. The huge crowd is taken aback for an instant, then an enormous roar: "Ooh, Aah, Paul McGrath's Da!" Utterly spontaneous, followed by long volleys of heartfelt, deafening applause. Mandela, taken aback, bends down to Kader for an explanation. He straightens, looks around him, beaming, then slowly raises a triumphant fist in the air. He just about dances at the top of the steps. I have never heard a crowd roar as they roared then.

13

Sometimes the best way into a large subject is through the small, unexpected door in the corner. I had spent days grappling with the historical-philosophical dimensions of this question of identity before I had to put it aside and go to London on business. Rummaging in a drawer for my passport I found my whole train of thought shunted sideways, I found myself on a different track entirely.

Nowadays, entering Britain, one simply strolls past the officials, one's passport getting no more than a cursory inspection. It wasn't always so. I have, as many of my coevals have, some bitter memories from the 1970s and 1980s— of attitudes varying from rudeness to paranoia, from aggressive interrogation to grudging acceptance that one wasn't, probably, a mad Irish bomber.

It was quite an experience, to land in Britain during those years; to be braced for, tensed for, a whole raft of questions, negative attitudes, and suspicions, all based not on any knowledge of who *you* were but on a culturewide assumption which might be simply rendered as *they're all the same.* That could be, that often was, a bruising encounter with being Irish. That could be and often was an unsettling instance, too, of that curious form of alienation we experience when our comfortable *I* is brutally overwritten into a catchall *they.*

Over the years, my many experiences of confrontation with the outer manifestations of the British State came to constellate around the passport itself. Every time I reached into the drawer for my passport I would experience a small premonitory anxiety if I were on my way to Britain; if I were going anywhere else at all it would be a different kind of moment. The anticipation of a faint but unmistakable pleasure.

It used to be more pronounced, but it still happens. At Charles de Gaulle, for instance, flying into Paris, when you proffer your Irish passport there's a moment's hesitation, then the briefest of nods from the gendarme, an acknowledgement of something it's very hard to put a finger on. You notice this as you notice the passengers on either side of you, if they're not Irish, get an impassive look. You go through, feeling like distant but acknowledged family. You've crossed into a country where it is a good thing to be Irish.

You ask yourself, what is it he thinks he's acknowledging? What is it he's trying to convey?

I've held a passport for thirty-three years, since I was seventeen. I remember that first passport vividly, the glazed canvas cover, a dark matte green, the gold harp stamped on it. That harp, it always seemed to me, was a talismanic stamp. Border guards everywhere (except in Britain) would soften a little when they saw the harp. They'd look at it for a moment, flick through to the page with your photo and your details, then flick back to regard the harp again for a second or two. Nowadays, with the common European Union passport, where most people at a checkpoint hold theirs open at the business pages, as it were, I always flash the harp first, before a sharp flick of the thumb presents the photo pages. Almost always this elicits a brief nod from the official, often a faint smile, a tiny gesture of welcome.

I have stored up, I realize, a whole stack of such moments, from frontier posts all over the world. Sometimes when I've just boarded a plane and am preparing myself for the null space of a long flight, I play these moments back, calling up now this face, now that, from a long litany of border guards over the years. There is the faintest possible feeling, faint but unmistakable, that in one narrative thread of my life I have been passed on from one to another in a long string of such handings over, at way stations in a pilgrimage through the world, through time, through this life. What is remarkable in this story is the sense that one is approved of because one is Irish. As if all these guards, down all these years, have a common idea of what it is to be Irish, a common sense of—what else to call it but kinship?

I remember, on my first trip to Moscow, a young lad in the green-peaked cap of the KGB Border Guard at Sheremetyevo, his sudden broad grin surprising himself as much as me, the salute as he handed me back my documentation. I watched him for a while after I'd passed through, saw he saluted no one else, all grim business. I wondered about that, the way you do.

What might it be about us that they think they know?

Well, the thirty-year war in the North notwithstanding, we come from a nonbelligerent nation, that might have something to do with it. We coast in the slipstream of the Anglophone countries but our armies are negligible, we have no empire to live down, such foreign service as our soldiers have seen has been in the peacekeeping forces of the UN, where indeed they appear to have distinguished themselves for human sympathy, professionalism, and tact—rare qualities in an army.

And then, ours was an early twentieth-century example of a war of liberation, and no matter the complications as seen by ourselves, the hedgings and qualifications and redefinitions of that struggle in our own minds, in the postcolonial world at large that still counts for something. The Ireland paradigm, as seen by others, is essentially a benign one. Perhaps that gendarme had a happy holiday here, an Irish lover, a good night out in an Irish bar? Maybe that Greek policeman enjoys our relaxed attitude to delays, our habitual air of informally adjusting to prevailing circumstances? Maybe that Border Guard is having a passionate affair with a young Irishwoman from the Aer Rianta Duty Free? Who can tell?

I simply want to put on record that I have never except in Britain hesitated to produce my passport, have formed the habit based in experience of expecting a positive response when I do. These days, in post–Peace Process Britain, with the exception of a few die-hard ex-squaddies now working in "security," their regimental badges tattooed on their forearms, one encounters, is greeted with, usually, a benign weariness—just like everyone else.

Does this tell me anything about Irish identity? Insofar as identity is a negotiation between subjective formation and external construction, yes it does. The moment when you produce a passport is a defining moment. It is a claim, sometimes an admission, of identity. It is not simply a statement of personal identity, since all passports are unique, identify a person as unique. It is a statement also of a larger identity—the passport says, I am of Ireland, I am Irish. When the policeman smiles, nods, indicates that he or she takes a benign view of me, it is not so much me that is being acknowledged as my nation.

At every frontier I come to there is this realization: I have a nation. I should of course record here that one has sometimes the negative experience, one meets the policeman whose paranoia bristles when confronted by the harp, the one who reaches for the internal phone without taking his eyes off your face, who taps something mysterious into his computer terminal, who scowls in—disappointment, is it?—when forced to acknowledge one's blamelessness. Nevertheless, even the negative experience prompts the realization: I have a nation.

I grew up with the identikit 1950s Irish identity impressed on me: to say Gaelic, Catholic, Nationalist is of course a gross oversimplification, but those were the cardinal points ("me" being the fourth) that one used for orientation on those odd occasions when the question of identity might briefly arise. The question of identity as a philosophical question arose for me at the same time as I began to travel, so that who I think I am is inextricably bound up with who or what others think I am. I think this has now become the norm in Ireland, a country where 90 percent of the population holds a passport. It has, in fact, become something of a joke with us that there is nowhere one could imagine going where one could be sure of not running into an Irish person. A remarkable fact when you think of it, given there are only about five million of us on the island.

It has become something of a joke with us, too, that the most unruly and pugnacious of boozers became saintly ambassadors for dear old Ireland when traveling to support the national soccer team, but it is nevertheless observably true that, having been told they were the best-behaved supporters in the world, the Green Army, as they liked to style themselves, did in fact become just that. You know something odd is happening when you can contrast the stoic, gentlemanly, and sportsmanlike behavior of the Irish in defeat with the depravity, no other word for it, of the English hooligan abroad, win or lose (and yes, of course, I know there are many decent English fans, I know, I know). Old paradigms are being elided, old stereotypes scrubbed out. In the new world narrative, somewhat to our surprise, it is often a very positive thing to be Irish.

I think it may be that, acknowledging ourselves in the various welcomes we find abroad, or at least in the benign indifference we experience when we encounter Officials Abroad, we have expanded our own sense of ourselves beyond the tribal, defensive, essentialist confines that previously prevailed here. At a time when questions of identity provoke anxiety in so many countries, it seems to me that Irish people, by and large, are pretty comfortable with and relaxed about being Irish. It's a good thing, you might say, but no big deal. Scale alters fact: we are too small a nation to want to lord it over anyone, to proclaim with any conviction that to be Irish is to be, in some sense, of God's anointed—as so many Americans, if I may say so, still do. We are no more immune to essentialist boasting than anyone else is, but I do sense that the odd bit of flag waving and tribal boasting is for many people, not all of course, sadly, no more than pro forma: keeping one's end up as it were.

How long this will last, I can't say. It may be already breaking down. The new immigration will pose, is already posing, difficult questions, Bloom's answer to the Citizen notwithstanding: "What is my nation? Ireland. I was born here." One of the more grotesque anomalies of the new Ireland is that a child born here is automatically an Irish citizen, is entitled to a passport, right of residence, all the benefits of citizenship—but her or his parents, one or both of them, may be deported if they do not satisfy the Byzantine requirements of the asylum and immigration laws, if they are not citizens prior to the birth of the child. Such deportation necessarily involves the deportation of the child citizen as well.

It may be we'll get fed up of being nice wherever we go, it may be we'll get fed up of ourselves, it may be that the relentless erosion of civil society here

THEO DORGAN ෴

under the pressures of a globalized economy will turn us sour and make us unloved. It may be that our new (to my mind precarious) economic security will make us insensitive, arrogant, unlovely.

It is likely that some of those whom we have so ignorantly deported from our shores will, in the fullness of time, become border guards themselves in their own or in other countries. It will be interesting to see how these men and women react to an Irish passport. Perhaps our brief period in the sun of the world's affections is already over.

Here I would simply like to record that at this moment in history, as many a CIA or FRS agent well knows, when you're standing in line at a frontier post it is a reasonably good and secure feeling to be carrying an Irish passport. Not everywhere and always, of course, as recent events in, for instance, occupied Iraq have shown. There will always be those whose contempt for human life cannot be charmed away by a harp on a passport, just as there will always be those who will exploit for their own dark purposes the passport of a relatively blameless country, as a consequence putting all its genuine citizens at risk. There is no sovereign remedy against all harm, but as protective talismans go, I repeat, the harp on the passport is still reasonably good magic.

Ireland and Britain

COLM TÓIBÍN

I grew up in the town of Enniscorthy, in the Southeast of Ireland. Every year in the summer we held a Strawberry Fair, and every year, too, the elders of the town would meet to select a Strawberry Queen. One year, they asked a contestant what she would do with the prize money if she won. "I'd feck off to England," she said.

I was a youth then, and the words stuck in my mind when I heard them, confirming everything I had suspected. England appeared before me as a haven of freedom and pleasure. I longed for England.

I was nineteen, however, before I set foot there. I remember going, as soon as I could, to see Bertolucci's film *Last Tango in Paris*, which was banned in our great little Republic, and sitting in the cinema in Leicester Square, watching two people on the screen alone with each other, with no context, two people devouring each other in an almost empty apartment.

And then there was the great city of London, the world outside the cinema as rich and strange as the world on the screen. The pure exhilaration of being out of Ireland, of being sure that you could meet no one you knew on the street, no one who would suddenly appear and know all about you. You could do anything you liked in London.

I remember during that first trip finding cheap record shops in London. The magnificent recording that Janet Baker made of Elgar's *Sea Pictures*. The wonderful recordings of Kathleen Ferrier. And just as watching a banned movie leads you to muse, half whimsically, about the freedom that the English won for themselves and how comforting that freedom is to an outsider, so too the music leads you to consider the strange configurations that have existed between the two islands.

When my grandfather, for example, was interned in Frongoch in Wales after the 1916 Rising, the Enniscorthy prisoners discovered, to their consternation, that their guards were speaking Welsh, and they were speaking English. Almost every time you begin to deal with the relationship between the two islands, you operate in areas of irony and contradiction.

I was led back into what is an older culture in Ireland not by politics but by music, by the singing of Maighréad Ní Dhomhnaill and her sister Triona, by the singing of Joe Heaney and, later, of Lillis O Laoghaire. So that it was easy to live in Dublin to search for all the records and then CDs of Janet Baker and appreciate in her voice certain English qualities that arose not only from the English choral tradition, and from the stability of English life, qualities I might want to call honesty and integrity, which I can hear in her voice and in the voice of Kathleen Ferrier. These are different from the qualities I notice most in the singing of Maighréad Ní Dhomhnaill, qualities mainly of sweetness and melancholy and beauty.

Mick Moloney, a musician whom I admire greatly, has spoken eloquently about music that is older than we are, greater than we are, bigger than we are. He spoke about being in Lorient in Brittany and listening to a great assembly of Irish traditional musicians, and others from Scotland and Wales and Brittany and Galicia, and feeling, he said, more Celtic than ever before. I don't think I have ever felt Celtic in my life, and I think it is too late now to begin. But, since all these matters come bathed in the healing waters of their very opposite, I have to confess that I enjoyed music in Scotland not long ago. I traveled to Scotland specifically to hear it. I suppose, on a generous day, you could call it Scottish music, because it was the Scottish National Opera's production of Wagner's *Ring*. And among those in the audience for "Siegfried" was a politician I greatly admire, David Trimble.

I don't think Mr. Trimble or myself had a Celtic bone between us that night, even though we were, in our own different ways, Irishmen in Scotland. It was not as though, by being there, we were doing a joint walk along a musical Garvahy Road in protest against anything. It wasn't as though we were seeking to be more European by listening to the music. We loved the music for itself and the drama, Siegfried's dilemma, the waning power of Wotan, Erde's warning. It was the notes that held us and made all the difference.

All of us who live in the Republic of Ireland or Northern Ireland, or in two rooms full of books which belong to no state, or in Scotland or Wales or the great free city of London, or in England, must be alert to the constant state of flux in our identities, the irony we must unleash every time we wish to define ourselves. Music becomes one of our ways to juggle with this, so that, when we are quiet, reading or listening to music, when we are most ourselves, national identity does not cost us a thought.

And yet when I think about Northern Irish Unionists seeking to have their British identity preserved, and taking that as a fixed and recognizable identity, I have to ask myself what I would feel if Ireland were to be reunited with the British crown and I was to carry a UK passport, there being no Irish passports anymore, as there are no Scottish ones now. I would be against this, even if it were in my economic interest. I have benefited hugely from the skills and largesse of the great English publishing house of Macmillan, who rescued writers like Sean O'Casey and Patrick Kavanagh when Ireland had no place for them. I have published with Jonathan Cape, who also published *A Portrait of the Artist as a Young Man* when nobody else would. Thus becoming English might be in my interest, even if those two companies are now owned by German multinationals. Yet I would resist it; it would keep me awake at night; it would come as a profound shock to my system.

There remains with us a strange shadowy identity, often hyphenated and gnarled, which is hard to define, or hardly worth thinking about unless it comes under threat. It is an idea that we belong to a place greater than our family or the streets we know. This has become for many a place of longing, a place they know only because they miss it. For others, it has become a haven of security. But the words which govern it constantly slip and fail, and the emotion surrounding it can lead to dangerous fanaticism or pure foolishness or both. Nonetheless, I would not wish to lose it.

Scotland, viewed from Dublin, even when it gives us great Wagner productions, remains puzzling. It is hard not to ask them, and the asking can sound like goading or teasing, if they would not like to have a Scottish voice with equal power in Brussels as the Irish voice, equal partners with other European countries. Would they not take pleasure, as Garret FitzGerald did as Irish foreign minister, when Dublin was the first English-speaking capital to host the presidency of the EU? He wrote in his memoirs:

> We were determined, as the first English-speaking country to hold the presidency, not to weaken the hitherto exclusive role of French as the working language of political co-operation at official levels . . . Incidentally, our decision to retain French as the working language forced the British to follow suit in 1977. Later on we were told by a Foreign Office official that some of the tension between Tony Crossland and his Permanent Secretary had derived from the Secretary's insistence that they must follow *our* precedent, which was de-

scribed as "an unwarranted break with the tradition of Palmerston, to establish the practice at the Foreign Office of transacting all business and communication in English."

That idea, still, of the Irish setting the precedent and breaking a long and sacred tradition which the British rulers held dear, gives me mischievous pleasure. I would love to tour Scotland asking them why they don't want to do this too. And I know they will tell me that Ireland and Scotland are different, that Scotland's Industrial Revolution and energetic role in the empire made a fundamental difference to its heritage and set of loyalties. And yet when I listen to Jean Redpath singing the songs of Robert Burns all argument melts away. I am Scottish too.

The differences between our places on these islands, between all the little nations we live in or imagine, between the North of England and the South of England, between the lowlands and highlands of Scotland, between the islands and the mainland in Scotland, between west of the Bann in Northern Ireland and east of the Bann, between south Armagh and north Armagh, between the West of Ireland and the East of Ireland, between the Republic and the North, between Welsh-speaking and English-speaking Wales, come to us with strangeness and with irony, but are sometimes very real and stark. It is not as though they do not matter, or that somehow the globe and the World Wide Web have taken over. We are not all Europeans now. It is not quite like that. As we walk out of the cinema into the crowded freedom of Leicester Square, having fecked off to England, we are both nobody and a nation. The space in between, almost funny and no joke at the same time, remains unsettled.

Between Ireland and America

FRANK McCOURT

There's been relatively little written about the Irish in America in fiction. And even up to fifty years ago, very little Irish American history written. I started thinking about this whole difference between the Irish and the Irish American. And for the scholar, it's a virgin area; I don't think it's been examined at all. One of the things that triggered this was a question that was asked me when I started teaching in Staten Island, McKee Vocational Technical High School, which was a very tough school where the kids gave you no quarter whatsoever.

When I started teaching, I had to deal with this powerful question, "What's Irish?" I'm standing up at the board threatening to teach grammar. I was so flattered because I thought that they were interested in me. What happened was this is my first week of teaching, and things looked bleak. So they have tricks, adolescents have tricks. "Yo, Mr. McCourt, you Scotch or somethin'?" "No, I'm Irish." "Well, yo, what's Irish?" And that was a powerful question. All these kids are Italian. A lot of them had Irish mothers, because the Irish marry Italians in order to get fed.

So I had to deal with this powerful question, "What's Irish?" Even though I had arrived eight or nine years earlier, spent my time working on the docks and in hotels, being in the United States Army in Germany for two years— training dogs, and chasing Fräuleins, and drinking beer—the Irish question didn't come up that much.

But now this question comes out. "What's Irish?" I didn't know, I thought everybody knew. They didn't know—they had no sense of geography, for one thing. And I made a rough map of Europe on the board with chalk, and I made this little island out in the middle of the Atlantic: that's Ireland. That didn't mean anything to them. I had started teaching in March, early March, and St. Patrick's Day was approaching and they were sure that I wouldn't come into work that day. They despaired when I showed up on St. Patrick's Day.

So this is the thing, and I had to deal with it. I wasn't prepared for this. I knew about all the Irish stuff, and St. Patrick's Day and the rest of it, but they kept asking me questions—I'd like to think they developed an interest in Ireland. But, no, it was just to keep me away from the parts of speech.

But the question started me thinking. Because I had grown up in Limerick, and we didn't worry too much about the Irish thing, except we had spasms of pride from time to time—when we saw images, or when we were told in school that Ireland had a long and glorious history, mostly of suffering. That we were always on the verge of victory, but that in our midst there was always an "informer"—the dirtiest word next to Cromwell in the Irish language. It wasn't an education; it was brainwashing, and it was conditioning, it was bullying. But we were never encouraged to ask a question.

We'd go over to the Lyric cinema on a Saturday afternoon, and we were imbued with certain images of Irish America. There was our hero: Cagney. We all wanted to be Cagney. You knew there was a Cagney movie playing at the Lyric cinema when you saw us swaggering out, and talking tough, and riding on the balls of our feet, and saying, "C'mon, Sucker!" We were ready to go to America, like Cagney, and be executed like him. This was our hero, this was our Cuchulain in America. Then, of course, we knew that the Irish were responsible for great football at Notre Dame. These were our images. And of course the First World War was won by the "Fighting 69th."

We needed these distant images of Cagney and Pat O'Brien, and Spencer Tracy, and so on, in America, fulfilling dreams. Because in the back lanes and the back streets of Limerick, that's about all we had—the dream—and Hollywood fulfilled it. The other outlet for our dreams was, in a strange way, the Church, which is in such poor repute nowadays. But the Church was our window on Europe. The Church was our only window on European culture; we had no other: the liturgy, the music, the robes, the mystery and wonder and awe of the Mass and the sacraments in general, the ritual of confession.

When I came to New York, I tried to muffle my accent, or to get rid of it completely. I tried to use an American accent—it wouldn't work. And I had a friend, when I was teaching, from Roscommon. He got rid of his Irish accent completely. So he was able to move through life like an executive from IBM, or something like that. And nobody said, "Oh, you're *Irrishe*." Because you have to deal with it—you're stopped in your tracks. "Yeh, I'm Irish." And then they look at you expectantly. And I don't know what to say to their expectations.

So this is what saved me in the classroom, because they found that brogue a bit exotic—a teacher who's different. If I had been a Greek, or something like that, I don't think they would have been that impressed. But Irish: they had the images, the stereotypes of the Irish. And you know what the stereotypes were. You know if you saw *The Quiet Man* what the stereotypes were— the wild drinking Irish, and so on. We're mercurial and we're poetic.

The wild, mercurial, poetic Irish—where did that come from? When the Irish came to America, they might have been wild when they drank, they might have been mercurial, but there are very few traces of poetry left. Ireland is a seeding ground for poetry, but there are very few major Irish American poets. There's one major Irish American dramatist, O'Neill. And he always wanted to be like O'Casey; he wanted to have one of the characteristics of O'Casey which is always applied to Irish writers: *lyrical*. We're all lyrical. When I published the book, I said, "Please God, I hope nobody will say it's lyrical." But they did.

So here I am, stumbling along, trying to be a teacher and trying to deal with this thing of being Irish, this thing of being American. I was *born* in New York, so I could say, "I'm American!" They didn't believe it. I had the brogue, and I had all these images from growing up in Ireland. So I had to make my way. When I was teaching, which I did for thirty years, I really didn't live in an Irish world. I would teach all day and then go home and fall down on the floor from exhaustion.

The main thing is that I had to appear before 165 adolescents every day. And they all have questions. They have questions about everything about Irishness, and sex, and music and everything. *Music*—that saved me! They resisted poetry, which I wanted to teach. So I thought I'd sneak it up on them through music. And I xeroxed these Irish songs, like "The Rocky Road to Dublin," and then I'd lead them into narrative poetry, and then maybe what you'd call the more challenging poetry. But I used my Irishness. I used Irish music. And you can imagine the class—Korean kids, Chinese kids, African American kids, all singing "Weela, Weela, Wallia" and "The Rocky Road to Dublin." And that takes me back to the relationship between the Irish and Irish Americans.

The Irish in Ireland were thunderstruck when Joannie Madden, and Seamus Egan, and Eileen Ivers, and Michael Flatley and people like that were going over to Ireland and dancing Ireland into extinction, and singing, and playing the flute. What's going on here? The Irish Americans, whether you agree with this or not, have felt maybe intellectually, or maybe poetically inferior to the "real Irish," who have the "tabernacle." They have the secret; they have the chalice—because they're the ones who have suffered most: the eight hundred years of suffering. You can't compare Irish American suffering with Irish suffering! Because the Irish came over here and they exploded— they took over everything, except maybe the arts. But they exploded in politics and in journalism, especially in politics.

What was it—maybe their facility with the English language—that they were able immediately to move into positions of power? People like Richard Daley out in Chicago, and Curley of Boston, who's a giant figure, one of the greatest rogues that Irish American politics has ever seen. And brilliant. They're never given credit for their brilliance—Croker, and Murphy, and Kelly in New York: they were all brilliant men. I became interested in them because I wanted to find a door to American history. And the door for me was the Irish experience here. And I went back to my reservoir of images, to Cagney and the rest of them, and poor old Barbara Stanwyck in *Union Pacific*.

And I became fascinated with the Union Pacific and how the Irish built it on one side, and the Chinese are building the Central Pacific. And about the day they met in Ogden, Utah, and the golden spike was driven. And when the picture was taken, *you don't see any Chinese.* Only the Irish—we did everything! But the Chinese set a record for laying track; they beat the Irish. This is not generally known, and I don't want you to feel inferior because of it.

This fascinating narrative part of Irish history led me into American history. And what I needed to feel, I suppose, I needed to feel comfortable somewhere—because I didn't know for a long time where I belonged. You think well, what the hell, Limerick, I grew up in Limerick. And that, in many ways, was a miserable place, but it was a very rich place, in many ways, because we were on the streets all the time. We never talked about what we watched on television; we talked about what we did in the streets. We made up our own games. We were adventurous. And there was one word we never heard in Limerick, or in Ireland in general, and that was "boredom." Nobody was ever bored. We made up our own stories. And maybe this is the source, one of the sources, of this eloquent, poetic, and *lyrical* race, the Irish.

Forgetting to Remember

LARRY KIRWAN

I've spent most of my life writing music—Celtic and otherwise. At one time, I believed that creativity was divine, something doled out to the lucky ones by the gods. It took me many years to realize that most art springs from experience. And the overriding experience in my life has been emigration. Some people emigrate to forget, others to remember. It seemed that I had to forget in order to remember.

I was raised by my grandfather in Wexford town. Thomas Hughes was an Irish Republican. In other homes, the pictures of the twin Johns—the twenty-third and Kennedy—blithely gaped down from artless walls. The green-framed signatories of the 1916 Uprising, however, glared unrepentantly from ours. Pádraig Pearse was top center, and to his left, appropriately, James Connolly. Unconcerned with status, Sean MacDermott peered out from the bottom. Sixty years after his death, this secretive man—chief recruiter for the Irish Republican Brotherhood and the straw that stirred the revolution's drink—was still a pivotal figure in my grandfather's life. Outsiders think of Republicanism as a political or armed movement. It's more like a religion, a spiritual path, even a cult, and my grandfather initiated me into it. On long winter nights before the coal fire, he loved to recall and thrash out the nuances of our long and painful national history. His firm belief was that we in the South had abandoned the Nationalist population of the Six Counties to a sectarian and politically repulsive state; and that it now behooved each following generation to resolve this matter.

All well and good, until I reached the age of fifteen or thereabouts, and discovered two other equally strong movements—sex and rock and roll. Being a good Jansenist Irish Catholic, Thomas Hughes didn't even acknowledge the first (although he had sired seven children); as for the second, he dismissed it as "auld English dance music" (Elvis and James Brown appear to have passed under his critical radar). Our house became tense and argumentative over these issues; meanwhile various other national and historical chickens were also coming home to roost. The Troubles had flared up again across the North, and with the will to resolve them absent in London, Dublin, and Belfast, the armed struggle resumed. Unwilling to relive my grandfather's past, I packed my guitar and emigrated.

I arrived in New York determined to put Republicanism and, indeed, many other forms of Irishism behind me. Hemingway rhapsodized about being young in Paris. He would have died for New York in the 1970s. The Lower East Side was a hedonistic republic unto itself with CBGB's as the center of world music. I formed a band that gained a following in the glass-strewn streets of Alphabet City, landed a record deal, and was well on my way, as I thought, to becoming another David Bowie. The best-laid schemes of mice and Irishmen, indeed! Still, the nights were long and the days short, rents miniscule, the ladies' dresses even shorter, and I even sported a green lightning streak in my hair. And yet, I could feel an odd emptiness rattling around inside of me: I didn't like what I'd become—didn't believe what I was singing. In short order, the band broke up; I went full-time into the theater and put music behind me. Again trying to forget, but with still so much to remember.

My grandfather died, and in the careless ways of youth and those times, I even missed his funeral. But the past has a way of catching up. Like many Irish Americans, I was deeply moved by the sacrifice of Bobby Sands and the other hunger strikers. Floundering around, looking for some purpose, I began to hear whispers of the old man's voice; while late at night, shards of our marathon fireside conversations began to prickle both my conscience and consciousness. And so I wrote *Mister Parnell,* a musical drama about the life and divorce case of the Uncrowned King. This led me to research the music of the 1880–90s, and to my surprise, I knew all the parlor songs—courtesy of my grandfather—wonderful melodies most of them but calcified in a staid and static Victorianism. Yet when I stripped these tunes down and matched them with beats and contemporary lyrics, they soared as they must have when first written.

It was common knowledge that, in the middle of the nineteenth century, African American and native Irish musicians had played together in the "she-beens" of the Five Points. Charles Dickens himself had even cocked his nose at the sight of this unholy alliance. Irish melodies had once worked with black rhythms and beats—why couldn't they do so again? And so I mixed tradi-tional and original Irish melodies with the rap of the Bronx and the reggae of Brooklyn. At that time, most Irish American musicians were getting cricks in their necks from gazing back sheepishly, and even reverently, at Irish players. To me, that was just another form of cultural colonialism. Why imitate out-siders? In New York City, we had the finest of rhythm sections, greasy to the core. We had the jazz, the funk, the blues, the rap, the reggae. We had Miles Davis, James Brown, Lou Reed, Public Enemy. We could take Irish music to a different plane, if only we dared. We could transform our Irish roots and make them truly palatable to American youth.

And so I formed Black 47 with Chris Byrne, a New York City policeman, and we set out to re-imagine Irish music—not as something that should be consigned to museums or sessions in back rooms of pubs, but as a vehicle that would alert young Irish Americans to their background, their political her-itage, and their duty to effect a solution to the ongoing problems in the North of Ireland. We reintroduced them to heroes like James Connolly, discarding the mawkish ballad that misrepresented him and instead revving him up and showing him for what he was: an international socialist. We explored Michael Collins, Countess Markievicz, Bobby Sands, Father John Murphy, and on the way we exposed the youth to their own American heroes such as Paul Robeson, Bobby Kennedy, the San Patricio Brigade, Father Mychal Judge. We didn't lay down a party line—in fact we refused to endorse any politician; but we did ask Irish Americans to re-imagine their heritage, their percep-tions, and their communal past. We demanded that they take control of their future by asking questions, not following leaders (including us), rejecting easy solutions, demanding answers both from themselves and those in au-thority. We also advised them not to get stuck in the past—Connolly, Sands,

Robeson, Collins, Kennedy, et al. were all visionaries. Each one dreamed of changing the world for the betterment of those living in it.

The island of Ireland is fine. It can look after itself. True, its newfound wealth has cost it a part of its soul. But its writers, poets, and musicians will attend to that. That's what art is about. Anyway, it's really not my concern any more. I look out for the descendants of the Diaspora, be they in North or South America, Britain, Australia, New Zealand, or Europe. That's where the future lies. That's where my work is. That's what my re-imagining is all about.

Re-Imagining Ireland

An Eclectic Retrospective

LENWOOD SLOAN

Amazing grace! how sweet the sound
That saved a wretch like me!
I once was lost, but now am found,
Was blind, but now I see.

Thank you for singing with me. I'm Lenwood, fourth-born of six children of John and Isabelle Sloan of Pittsburgh, Pennsylvania. You know it takes amazing grace for an oppressed people to continue . . . to make such sweet sounds throughout so long a period of despair. It also takes a great amount of grace to move off your comfort zone about a question of identity.

I have come along to ask you, "Is Ireland defined by its latitude and longitude?" Is it geography and topography—flora and fauna, terra firma? Is it the annual census? Or is Ireland a state of mind that embraces its full Diaspora? Forty million people worldwide who claim Irish heritage are eager and willing to join in this conversation.

Between 1820 and 1860, thousands of Irishmen were hijacked into the Caribbean and forced into indentured servitude for six to ten years. After entering the United States through its gulf port of New Orleans, they met many Irish immigrants who had traded their body weight as ballast for ships bound for New Orleans. Still others, known as "Kaintucks," took rafts and flatboats down the Ohio and Kentucky rivers, on a one-way ride to the mighty Mississippi and a new life. They lived and mixed with blacks and Native Americans. Their offspring and extended families are found throughout the Mississippi River region.

This was the route of a man named Jim Oakley from Kilkenny. He arrived in New York a bit of a renegade as a result of the unrest surrounding the 1848 uprisings. Oakley was immediately spirited away to Minneapolis, Minnesota, a stronghold of Irish sentiment. The name, Jim Oakley, was traded for that of his maternal grandfather. Thus, Jim Oakley was left behind in Minneapolis, as Thomas Moore sets off on a flatboat for Carthage, Arkansas. In Carthage, Moore had a son whom he also named Thomas Moore. The son married or bonded with a black Indian and had ten children including my father's mother, Molly.

Thomas Moore's family grew, blending with the three cultures of the region. Throughout the South, before 1890, one could still find communities where indentured servants, Native Americans, and freedmen lived together in tolerance, if not mutual benefit. My father states that, as early as he can remember, his people traveled far and wide in family work groups looking for a day's wages or a season's contract, always returning to Carthage at some interval that only they understood. Each time that they set the mixed families on the road to find work, the numbers had increased.

Early in the 1860s, George Custer wrote to the president of the United States that "a formidable power would shift if Blacks, Irish and Indians ever consolidated their struggle against the dominant culture which keeps them in servitude." He encouraged the powers-that-be to do "everything within their ability to keep these three people at odds." It appears to have worked.

Thomas Moore started his migration north after the Separate Car Act of 1890. My grandmother states that the train stopped somewhere in the South. The conductor could not distinguish a difference in the faces of the riders but was required to ask her father if she was a white child. Her father answered elusively under his breath, and she was required to move to another car. Sitting alone for the remainder of the journey, she realized for the first time that there was something different between the families that would set them apart forever.

In 1900, the "hollowed masses" lived on the hillsides along the three rivers in Pittsburgh. Thomas Moore's mixed-blood band of thirty families joined this cacophony of identities, including African Americans, Jews, Irish, Polish, Germans, Swedes, and Italians. They were ready to enter the mines and mills with their usual "one for all and all for one" attitude toward survival. However, supremacist organizers used the labor forces against each other to keep the masses divided. The pressure was too great for the band of families, and we evaporated into the world of "difference," dissolving our world of "sameness."

Some passed for white and disappeared; some considered themselves already white and joined the mudslingers on the picket lines. Some kept their secret lineage to the grave. The core who were darker went about silently working to bring the other black and mixed-blood families from Carthage. Those on the edges of manhood kept the family fires for the elderly and those less fortunate.

Thus, I inherited the job of shoveling coal, building fires, and cleaning grates for the old white-haired, blue-eyed Irishman who lived at the back of the field beyond my parents' house. I never got paid for it either, a fact I did not understand since my parents demanded that we get paid for our labor.

When Thomas Moore passed away, my parents mysteriously mourned. The men stood around on the steps of his house while the women packed most of his belongings into the attic of my Grandmother Molly's house. Nobody even asked a question about his or her strange behavior. Life went on. Years later, on a long rainy afternoon while raiding grandmother's trunks, I discovered that Thomas Moore was her father—my great-grandfather—an Irishman.

I lay no claim on your land and status. And I'm not coming home to find my roots. But the conversation about what is Irish is beyond our ability to control now. You are in us and we are in you. But you already know that, don't you? I can see it in your eyes.

The sons of my father wear the green on St. Patrick's Day. My father heads a house and sets a table that would be the envy of any patriarch depicted by Eugene O'Neill or created by James Joyce. I am a black Irishman, and it's your turn to embrace me as you have asked the world to shelter, harbor, and embrace you for more than two hundred years.

We're aliens and we'll never be Irish enough, even though we speak the
Irish language and my father says we're more Irish than the Irish themselves.
—Hugo Hamilton, *The Speckled People*

Beyond the Pale

Race, Ethnicity, and Irish Culture

LUKE GIBBONS

Two recent images of race and multiculturalism in Ireland, North and South,
highlight the contrasting fortunes of immigrants and foreign nationals in the
era of the Celtic Tiger and the Peace Process. The first, a remarkable short
film, *Yu Ming Is Ainm Dom* (*My Name Is Yu Ming*, directed by Daniel O'Hara,
2003), begins in China, showing the disgruntlement of a young man, Yu
Ming (Daniel Wu), with his menial job in a store, which turns his thoughts
to emigration. These opening sequences are shot in a rich, green hue, and, as
if taking a lead from his tinted environment, the young man's finger alights
on Ireland when he spins a globe to choose his destination. Knowing nothing about the country, he consults an encyclopedia, where he discovers,
among other things, that the official language is Irish. With a diligence that
would put many Leaving Certificate students to shame, he undertakes a self-
taught, crash course in Irish to prepare him for his new life abroad, only to
discover on arrival in Ireland that no one understands a word he says.

As he checks into a student hostel, the Australian at the counter pre-
sumes Ming is speaking Chinese when he asks for a bed in Irish, and he fares
no better when he enters a pub looking for a job. At this point, he at last
gets a break when Paddy (Frank Kelly), one of the customers propping up
the bar, answers him in Irish, which leads to an animated discussion between the two over a pint. Paddy explains that the everyday language of Ire-

land is in fact English, which leaves Yu Ming even more mystified than before. He is not the only one at a loss: the bartender is also mystified at one of his long-standing customer's newly discovered linguistic proficiency, and says to his co-barman: "Here—did you know 'oul Paddy could speak Chinese?" The film ends with a tourist bus wending its way through the Gaeltacht, the Irish-speaking district of Connemara. We expect to see the benighted Yu Ming among the customers who stop off at a local bar for refreshments, but it is in fact the young Chinese man who is serving behind the bar, feeling at home at last in his country of adoption.

A contrasting image of the reception accorded to Chinese immigrants in Ireland is found in a report in the *Sunday Tribune,* January 11, 2004: "Ulster Will Fight, and Ulster Will be White: Why Chinese Are the New Taigs" (a derogatory term used to label Catholics). This is accompanied by a photograph showing a scrawl of graffiti on a gable wall of a house in a Loyalist estate in Belfast, displaying a crudely drawn swastika, the initials KKK (Ku Klux Klan), and C18 (from the racist British nationalist group Combat 18). In the background, there is a Chinese restaurant. In the adjoining article, Susan McKay relates how the resistance of Chinese immigrants in Belfast to Loyalist intimidation and protection rackets led to an attack on one couple in their house during Christmas, leaving the woman, eight months pregnant, badly beaten and her husband in intensive care in hospital. As Yinmei, the expectant mother, described it: "It was about 7:30 in the evening. I was resting and my husband was watching television . . . Two men, a fat one and a thin one, broke down the front door and the inside door. The thin one said something we couldn't understand, then the fat one smashed a brick in [her husband] Hua Long's face." Yinmei tried to get between the men and her husband, who was bleeding heavily. The intruders punched her on the head.[1]

Police statistics reported 212 racist incidents—mainly in Loyalist areas—in the eight months before Christmas, 2003, making Northern Ireland the most racist region proportionately in the United Kingdom.[2] This, clearly, is no country for immigrants; but as is often the case historically, it was no country for natives either, at least where the imperatives of colonialism were concerned.

Race and "Progressive Amnesia"

It is often tempting to fall back on a time-honored balancing act, pointing out, as a character puts it in the film *Cal* (directed by Pat O'Connor, 1984),

LUKE GIBBONS ∞

that "there are bad bastards on both sides," and that anti-Chinese sentiment is far from absent in the Republic as well. In a notorious incident in January 2002, a young Chinese man, Zhao Liulao, was beaten to death in a late-night fight in a Dublin suburb, after being taunted by racist youths. This death occurred against a background of reports of increased attacks on immigrants in the north inner-city area of Dublin, in an area designated in media accounts as "Little Africa." The tendency here is to counter every story of racist abuse on one side of a historical colonial divide with an example from the other, as if both are equal on the scale of oppression and intolerance, and racism simply arises in societies of its own accord. But there is, of course, a distinction, reflecting the profoundly different historical formation of both cultures. Around the corner from the racist graffiti directed at Chinese immigrants in Belfast is another Loyalist mural depicting a grim reaper, with an injunction: "Kill all Taigs." As the links with Combat 18 suggest, these are the ideological death-pangs of empire, the remnants of a White Anglo-Saxon and Protestant supremacy whose global reach once extended from Connemara to China, but which has now fallen into a state of abjection. It is tempting to ascribe such crude racism to the resentment of an underclass divested of the privileges it enjoyed under empire, but this is to disregard the wider cultural milieu in which such views are fostered. As Polly Toynbee wrote in relation to similar attempts to sequester "degenerate" notions of British patriotism within the fringe element of football hooliganism: "So where does this empty pride and false patriotism come from? Who stokes it up? Who poisons the air with the daft idea that to be British is best? Who pumps the bellows of belligerent nationalism? Our own rightwing press, from the posh end of the Euro-hating *Telegraph,* to the xenophobia of the *Mail,* right down to the flagrant loathing of foreigners in the *Sun.*"[3]

The official discrediting of such residual imperial fantasies in recent decades has much to the do with the recoil from racist thinking and eugenics that followed the revelations of the Holocaust and the full extent of Nazi atrocities in the aftermath of World War II. It is important to remember, however, that this about-face was not simply the benign outcome of the West's wrestling with its own conscience: decolonization and national liberation movements were central to this challenge to white supremacy, with the dismantling of the British Empire taking a preeminent role in such emancipatory struggles.

Moreover, as the initials of the KKK in the Belfast graffiti remind us, the persistence of old regimes and mentalities was not just something that happened "elsewhere," in remote corners of the earth, but precipitated the rise of civil rights movements in the metropolitan center—in the United States and, of course, Northern Ireland. Upholders of white privilege in the southern states saw themselves not just as the stentorian guards of Manifest Destiny, but—as the (misappropriated) Scottish tag of "clan" indicates—in so doing, they were following the lead of their Ulster Scots forbears in Northern Ireland and Scotland. Inspired by the strident Anglo-Saxonism of Thomas Carlyle and others, proponents of Aryan racial supremacy at the end of the nineteenth century had no doubt that in terms of steadfastness and righteousness, the Lowland Scots and, above all, their Ulster confreres, were God's frontiersmen. In the eyes of Dr. Isaac Taylor, as formulated in his *Origin of the Aryans* (1889), Lowlands Scotland and Ulster were, in a sense, more Anglo-Saxon than England itself:

> Now that Christianity has spread over Europe, it is divided into two opposed camps—the Catholic and the Protestant . . . In the [latter], individualism, willfulness, self-reliance, independence, are strongly developed; the second is submissive to authority and conservative in instincts . . . The Lowland Scotch, who are more purely Teutonic than the English, have given the freest development of Protestantism. Those Scotch clans who have clung to the old faith have the smallest admixture of Teutonic blood. Ulster, the most Teutonic province in Ireland, is the most firmly Protestant . . . In Galway and Kerry it has no footing.[4]

As the closing sentence makes clear, Gaelic, Catholic culture is at the bottom of this racial ladder and has no claim at all on such delusions of superiority. Though easily overlooked from the standpoint of the long twentieth century, it is often forgotten how much Aryan race theory, in its powerful White Anglo-Saxon Protestant variant, defined itself against the savage on its native shores, the Gaelic, Catholic other in Ireland.[5] It is not the historical record as such, but the implications of this for rethinking the relations between race and multiculturalism in Ireland—and among the Irish Diaspora abroad—that concern me here.

In recent years, the association of racist prejudice with Nazi ideology has correctly drawn critics and historians to in-depth historical investigations of how systematic barbarism could have been produced in the heartlands of European civilization. Conveniently, given the historical determination of imperial powers to stamp out indigenous cultures and anticolonial resistance, nationalism—and particularly the romantic nationalism of allegedly atavistic "premodern" peoples attempting to throw off the shackles of empire—has been seized upon as the origin of this virulent species. The trail here leads back to the "counter-Enlightenment" writings of German thinkers such as Herder, the first systematic theorist of cultural romanticism, and in the hands of Daniel Goldhagen, this penchant for racism, xenophobia, and authoritarianism was projected onto the German people themselves and the phantom of German national character.[6] The fact that it is not nationalism per se (whatever that would mean) that fosters such delusions of racial or cultural supremacy, but rather such versions of nationalism as aspire to *dominance*, global or otherwise, to political expansion and worldwide control of markets, escapes the scrutiny of such indictments. There is nothing peculiarly German about the logic of extermination under imperial modernity: Belgian imperialism was responsible for the deaths of up to ten million Congolese in pursuit of rubber profits,[7] and, as Mike Davis has powerfully demonstrated, late Victorian Britain presided over a market system that introduced starvation and death for the first time on a mass scale in history.[8] These were not, of course, systematic, calibrated blueprints for genocide of the kind drawn up by the Nazis; but neither were such policies pursued, as Sir John Seeley famously claimed of the British Empire, in a fit of absent-mindedness. They were predictable and, in many cases, the desired outcomes of the spread of white, Teutonic civilization, a by-product, as Anthony Pagden notes, if not of absent-mindedness, then of the progressive amnesia that accompanies the victors of history.[9]

Racism has little to do with national character; still less is it a product of premodern mentalities, or the kind of backwardness that has to be brought kicking and screaming into the modern world. In keeping with attributions of racism to the "counter-Enlightenment," much of the debate around the recent resurgence of racism in Ireland has located its origins in xenophobic nationalism, as if it emanates from "Irishness" itself rather than from the uneven historical integration of Ireland into colonial modernity and, more recently, into a union with European powers only two generations removed from their own colonial pasts. The extensive restrictions of the EU against refugees and asylum seekers, decided upon at the Dublin convention in 1997, were the product of Fortress Europe, not just the backwoods mentalities of those in rural Ireland who refuse to become modern. Rather than lagging behind the metropolitan center, the growth of racism and related forms of virulence may be signs that Ireland is catching up with its advanced European neighbors, and so displaying (at however a rudimentary a degree) the kinds of cultural fissures and conflicts that have long been part of advanced industrial societies with mass far-right political parties and lingering imperial nostalgia. For this reason, issues relating to the emergence of racist sentiments in "traditional" cultures—for example, whether racism existed in nineteenth-century Irish society—are not so important as the question of how fear of the unknown, parochialism, ethnocentrism, prejudice, or even inflated national sentiments are converted into overt and self-conscious forms of racism.

In his discussion of Irish class and racial formation, David Roediger notes that before the mid-nineteenth century, "abolitionists noted little popular racism, and much sympathy for the plight of the slave, in Ireland," an observation borne out by Frederick Douglass's experience of traveling through Ireland in the 1840s.[10] This had less to do with the moral virtue of the Irish national character than with the fact that the conditions for racism were not present in Ireland—if, that is, one ignores the racism "from above" directed at Irish people themselves. The relative absence of racism in Irish culture at home stands in stark contrast to the readiness with which the Irish espoused racial views in the United States. "It was not in Ireland you learned this cruelty," Daniel O'Connell remonstrated, but, as Roediger points out, in the entirely different socioeconomic structures of the New World, the disjunctions of race and class were such that it was in the perceived interest of the Irish to identify with whiteness, compromised and questionable as their allegiance may have been. In this, their experience of assimilation was not unlike that of other European diasporas: "Whiteness was a dramatic and American choice. At a time when immigration history missed the drama of the European immigrant's learning of race relations in the United States, [James] Baldwin tellingly observed that Norwegians did not sit around in Norway preening themselves about how wonderfully white they were."[11]

Racism in the fully articulated sense is thus a product of dislocations within modernity itself. It is derived from the structural incapacity and psychological consequences of a world system that cannot ensure that all boats will rise, and *can long sail*, on what Yeats called the "filthy modern tide" of progress. This structural incapacity and the uncertainties that accompany it provide a justification for the superexploitation of recalcitrant or simply different peoples, a form of planned human obsolescence in which whole societies are discounted and lose out in the scramble for wealth and power. Such peoples, in one of the most ominous developments of social Darwinism, were regarded as belonging to "doomed races"—the members of whom, even if they did survive, were destined to be the hewers of wood, and the drawers

LUKE GIBBONS ᏯᎣ

of water, of empire. Preeminent among these, and providing a trial run in the early modern period for much of what would come later in the outposts of empire, was Gaelic society, with its own language, customs, land system, legal codes, trade routes, and—perhaps the source of its greatest threat—the potential to chart its own distinctive path to modernity. The closing off of such alternative routes to modernity brought with it the many "unintended consequences" of famine, depopulation, and mass emigration which characterized the incorporation of Ireland into the British imperial economy. This points to one of the historical ironies of *Yu Ming Is Ainm Dom*—the fact that the laughter provoked by his inability to negotiate his Irish environment through language is at the expense of Irish people themselves, who lost not only their language in the previous century but even the consciousness of that loss. It is one thing for the Australian in the student hostel to misrecognize Irish: it is another thing for an Irish barman to fail to recognize it or, indeed, for a customer to possess fluency in the language but never to gain an opportunity to speak in his local pub.

It may be, following Ernest Renan's injunction about the need to forget in founding a nation,[12] that such amnesia might be seen as part of the success story of modern Ireland, a clear demonstration of the facility with which the Irish people jettisoned all baggage surplus to the requirements of entering the modern world. But there is no modernity without tears: the Irish did not simply lose a language but also much of the "habitus" (in Pierre Bourdieu's phrase) that went with it, the forms of life and horizons of meaning that constitute a culture. Hence the "paralysis" of post-Famine Ireland diagnosed so unflinchingly by James Joyce, in which the forces of both Church and State combined to fill the void created by the collapse of an entire pre-Famine moral ecosystem. Under the aegis of a powerful, centralized educational system, adopting English was not simply an exercise in linguistic proficiency but a matter of buying into (at least where not actively resisted) the values, aspirations, and habits of authority that went with the acquisition of English in the heyday of British imperialism. In his analysis of the Irish in Victorian Britain, Roy Foster emphasizes the importance of the phenomenon of "Micks on the make"—the social mobility of certain sections of the immigrant Irish and their all-too-apparent readiness to accommodate themselves to a British way of life.[13] Nor was this confined to the middle classes; the Catholic missionaries who operated under colonial rule, the hundreds of thousands who thronged the streets during Royal visits to Ireland, and perhaps even greater numbers who joined the British army, bear witness to the conflicting loyalties of what Joyce called "the gratefully oppressed." Even the language of Revivalism and much of Nationalist propaganda was permeated by newly emergent racial discourses of Celticism and the attendant fears that Gaelic culture itself may be one of the doomed races of the Western march to modernity.[14] Whatever is made of studies such as the Rev. Ulick Burke's *The Aryan Origin of the Gaelic Race and Language* (1875),[15] it need hardly be added that, as in the case of Norwegian racism above, myths of Aryan origins were not the stuff of fireside conversations in the West of Ireland (though, with the rise of anticolonial Nationalism, the search for affinities between Ireland and India may not have seemed so strange after all).

The lack of precision in many recent discussions of racism in Ireland is nowhere more evident than in the tendency to equate the history of anticolonial resistance to British rule, and the cultural processes of decolonization, with racial prejudice. Attempts to link Irish resistance to the Protestant Ascendancy and imperial domination with Irish pogroms against Jews of the kind that took place in Limerick in 1904 or recurrent discrimination against the Travelling community are misguided. Bryan Fanning writes: "Protestants, Jewish people and Travellers became the focus of racializations which, in each case, served as justification for their exclusion within Irish society. The concept of racialization refers to political and ideological processes by which groups come to be defined with reference to real or imaginary characteristics and where 'race' or ethnicity is used to define boundaries between groups of people."[16] The extraordinarily wide brushstrokes in this picture ignore questions of *power* and *domination*, virtually construing decolonization itself as a form of racism. In keeping with this, Fanning cites Nationalist determination to regain ownership and control of land—namely, a remark in one parish by a farmer on regaining land that "'tis grand we got it back"—as further evidence of Irish racism.

On this reading, campaigns by the Aboriginal peoples of Australia or by Native Americans for land entitlements would be racist, not to mention Palestinian struggles to regain control of the occupied territories. Nor is this simply a case of reacting against political domination. In the Philippines at present, the Chinese account for 1 percent of the population but account for as much as 60 percent of the wealth, a situation that is bound to generate intense hostility and ethnic conflict.[17] But it by no means follows that this is racism, any more than similar campaigns to regain control of economic resources from elite Protestant ownership in Ireland were motivated by the same kind of hostility directed at less powerful groups in society. Nor was it surprising that Nationalist claims to civility and self-esteem tended to be couched in the available discourses of race (however loosely conceived) and cultural prestige, for, as Steve Garner points out in his more nuanced analysis of Irish racial discourse, such were the conditions of recognition and negotiation in the international community at the onset of the twentieth century.[18] The Catholic Church and constitutional Nationalism were at one in straining to avoid giving offense to empire, and it would, perhaps, have taken a conceptual revolution in politics equivalent to that of Joyce in literature to break out of these dominant imperial frames. The ingredients for such a postcolonial paradigm shift were indeed present—in the writings and political agitation of figures as diverse as Patrick Ford, Michael Davitt, George Sigerson, Frederick Ryan, James Connolly, Constance Markievicz, Roger Casement, and Liam Mellowes—but clearly their nonracial conceptions of Irishness or "rooted cosmopolitanism" (in Timothy Brennan's phrase) did not win out.

The Transatlantic Irish

There is little doubt that an upwardly mobile identification of the Irish with the dominant culture of whiteness in the United States also encouraged a related amnesia, militating against solidarity with their erstwhile coworkers on the lowest rung of the labor market: African Americans in the East or—to take up the opening observations about Irish-Chinese relations—Chinese immigrants in the West. Yet, as Matthew Frye Jacobson demonstrates, immigrant status itself, and the barriers of anti-Catholicism and anti-Celticism, made this more problematic than identifying with a dominant "common" culture.[19] Republicanism was undoubtedly a major attraction of the American polity to the immigrant Irish, but the persistence of the hegemonic WASP element within whiteness produced conflicting modes of assimilation, one in which the Irish tried on the one hand to be more white and patriotic than the Americans themselves (through, for example, military service, Catholic-led anticommunism campaigns, or, indeed, espousals of racism) or else devoted their energies to radical countercurrents that encouraged cross-ethnic rather than cross-class alliances, establishing new modes of solidarity with other immigrant groups, blacks, and Native Americans. Once more, it is not a matter of lining up Irish activists on both sides of the racist divide—for every John Mitchel on the side of slavery, there is a Patrick Ford or John Boyle O'Reilly in implacable opposition to it—but rather of looking at the ideological formation of the racist frame of mind, and understanding how subaltern groups buy into such ideologies.

It is in this sense that Irishness can be seen as an essentially contested zone in comparativist, postcolonial, or wider cultural debates on race and ethnicity. Ireland's recent ascendancy to the status of an advanced Western economy sits uneasily with the legacy of an unresolved colonial past, and it is this contested, ambivalent inheritance that the Irish brought with them into the modern world, and more particularly to the American Dream. The irony here is that the affinity with black culture expressed in the much-quoted lines from Roddy Doyle's *The Commitments*—"The Irish are the blacks of Europe . . . Say it loud, I'm black and I'm proud"—is taken by some critics to be undermined by the very success of the film, whose projection onto the world stage clearly indicates the integration of Irish popular culture into the orbit of the Hollywood system, with its concomitant whiteness, corporate power, and globalization. Such a success story sits ill at ease with memories of underdevelopment, or, as some revisionist critics would have it, with pretensions toward Third World or "postcolonial" solidarity. Such critiques of Irish identification with the underdogs of empire see the Irish more as sinners than sinned against—as racists in the draft riots in America (strangely underplayed in Martin Scorsese's *Gangs of New York*), Catholic zealots at home, or as the shock troops of empire in the British or American armies. In the era of the Celtic Tiger, in which Ireland for the first time acts as a host country for immigrants, refugees, and asylum seekers, the Irish are seen as showing their true color, as it were, in reports of racial abuse and intolerance toward immigrant minorities.

It is for this reason that some critics have discerned in Ireland's "in-between" status an alibi for a new guilt-free whiteness, a born-again version of liberal America, bleached of the original sins of the Founding Fathers. Hence the suspicion that behind Irish claims to postcolonial status lay an example of what Diane Negra describes as "a general invigoration of whiteness through the discovery of ethnicity."[20] Ethnicity or identity politics, from this point of view, may act as a camouflage for the injuries of race, seeking to introduce an undue complexity into what, after all, are master narratives of whiteness and Western supremacy. As Negra argues, in the aftermath of the Cold War and with the increased homogenization and Americanization of global markets, it became increasingly difficult to identify a foil to the American way of life, an "other" it could define itself against: "In the absence of other cultural territories to encroach upon, we naturally turned inward. In

LUKE GIBBONS ᘛ

mid-1990s American culture, popular fictions were very much shaped within a crucible of barely disguised 'white panic' and one way to detour around the problematic status of whiteness was to take evasive action by claiming ethnicity."[21]

Clearly, this search for an alien other has become less difficult since the attacks on the World Trade Center, and the identification of an "axis of evil" against which all friends of freedom must defend themselves. As if unwittingly bearing out Negra's analysis, moreover, the post–September 11 political climate has been declared less hospitable for expressions of ethnicity, particularly as it bears on Irishness and whiteness. Thus, for example, the forecast of an imminent decline in Irish studies in the United States, given that underneath the vogue for things Irish lay a culture in which terror, both official and unofficial, was still part of the unfinished business of Irish history. "When, after September 11, the words 'IRA' and 'terrorist' began to be used in the U.S. in the same sentence, it was a disturbing first in the mainstream U.S. media. This juncture and the recession could become a genuine liability for Irish matters within the academy."[22] Behind the reassuring whiteness of the Celtic Dr. Jekyll, it would seem, the shadow of Mr. Hyde was still visible.

Race and Ethnicity

It may be, however, that instead of obfuscating questions of race, we need to introduce *more* ethnicity into whiteness, if by that is meant a salutary bringing to the surface of the often submerged cultural, nationalist, or religious values underwriting its political alibis. For Richard Rorty, the all-embracing civic category of Americanness stands as a neutral, transcendent identity above the cacophony of multicultural claims to ethnicity and religious diversity, but this is to deny the hegemonic, often fervid, WASP culture that animated much of official American ideology.[23] The kind of American patriotism mobilized during war is far from being a neutral abstraction but taps into some of the deepest—and most troubled—narratives of the nation, drawing more on the Western, Gothic, and gangster genres than the lofty, transcendental ideals of civic republicanism. Many of the doubts cast on the patriotism of Irish Americans—the original target of the put-down tag "hyphenated Americans"—and their commitment to their new host culture, lay in their persistent questioning of the equation of Americanness and whiteness with Anglo-Saxonism and Puritanism. By insisting in the early decades of the twentieth century that being American was not incompatible with (other) ethnic filiations, both the Irish and Jewish Diasporas opened up many of the spaces that other struggles for greater cultural diversity were to avail of later in the century. As noted above, it may have been precisely this alienation from Anglophone Americanism which permitted such cross-cultural solidarities as the Irish managed to forge, whether with African Americans, Native Americans, Mexicans, Asians—or, indeed, with radical, dissenting strands within Protestant culture itself.

In the twentieth century, the most eloquent and visually evocative expression of the alternative spaces opened up by the Irish on the American political landscape is to be found in the films of John Ford, with their complex inscriptions of diasporic and Native American identities on the frontier and the wilderness. Ford was not questioning Americanism as such, for like successive waves of Irish emigrants before and after him, he looked to the United States as a republican experiment which sought to give political expression, however imperfectly, to the ideals of a truly diversified political Enlightenment. What Ford was questioning, however, was the fatal association of these ideals with slavery, genocide, and expansionism which, as Reginald Horsman has shown, owed much of their persistence to the hegemonic, Carlylean Anglo-Saxonism that vitiated the American body politic.[24] This strident Americanism, grounded in notions of Manifest Destiny and white supremacy, needed to be rescued, in Ford's eyes, from its own essentialism, just as the biological conditions of whiteness, blackness, or, indeed, gender need to be extricated from their hidden cultural contraband. Diane Negra is wise to express caution with regard to attempts to render palatable the power of whiteness through an emphasis on ethnicity, but there is a danger at the other end of reifying pigmentation, as if there is no possibility at all, in Jacobson's phrase, of "whiteness of a different color," thus retrieving emancipatory projects for alternative political futures.

Deconstructions of racist discourse may take different forms, but crucial to any such task is the need to expose the manifold cultural preconceptions and projections of "otherness" masquerading under the guise of color. Hence the importance of paying careful historical attention to the ethnographic demands *beyond visual difference* which, for example, the Irish, Slav, and Jewish peoples presented to Enlightenment ideals of progress and civility. Considered on these terms, the "Irish other" is a historical anomaly, at once white and Anglo-European (after a fashion), but yet at odds with much of the cultural capital that constitutes the hidden contraband of race. As John Ford memorably expressed it, catching the contradictory forces that led to his sustained reworking and interrogation of the American Dream: "More than having received Oscars, what counts for me is having been made a blood brother of various Indian nations. Perhaps it is my Irish atavism, my sense of reality, of the beauty of clans, in contrast to the modern world, the masses, the collective irresponsibility. Who better than an Irishman could understand the Indians, while still being stirred by the tales of the U.S. cavalry? *We were on both sides of the epic.*"[25]

What is of interest here is Ford's own take on what it means to *understand*—in the sense of a lived critical engagement with—another culture. In Ford's westerns, there is a recurring critique of a certain kind of armchair anthropology which purports to understand another culture on the grounds of knowledge alone—particularly as interred within the covers of books and texts. (It is in this light that we should interpret his lumbering his scriptwriter Frank Nugent with over fifty books before setting him down to write the screenplay of *Fort Apache*. When Nugent inquired what should he do when he had worked through this library, Ford replied, "Forget them!") In Ford's eyes, it is not *ignorance* of other cultures that is the problem, but often knowledge itself, particularly of the detached, instrumental kind that can be used against the cultures it purports to understand. Understanding another culture is not just something to be gleaned from a Fodor's guide or—as Yu Ming finds out on coming to Ireland—an encyclopedia. Nor is it simply a matter of picking up another identity, like Yu Ming spinning the globe at random. Rather, it involves a prolonged engagement with another culture, its language(s), and—equally important—the social rituals and symbolic practices that make sense of those languages. Structures of feeling are not overnight sensations, but that is precisely the point: cultural diversity is not simply willed into existence but is part of a protracted, mutual process that resists absorption or assimilation by either side.

Irishness and Ethnic Options

Given the increasingly threadbare texture of social life in the United States—variously diagnosed as "bowling alone," or, more ominously, "bowling for Columbine"—it is not surprising that ritual and the performative elements of identity have made a startling comeback in recent decades under the rubric of multiculturalism, the reclamation of group/cultural rights, or the affirmation of what Mary Waters has described as "ethnic options." As Diane Negra summarizes these trends: "Conceptualizing ethnic identity as a matter of flexible consent, rather than rigid descent, is for many Americans, as Mary Waters has observed, 'increasingly a matter of personal choice of whether to be ethnic at all, and, for an increasing majority of people, of which ethnicity to be.'"[26]

The facility with which Irishness lent itself to cultural longings and ethnic options at the end of the twentieth century was no doubt helped by a subtle shift from *nationality* to *class* as a badge of identity. For all the emphasis placed by the Irish Diaspora on a rich cultural inheritance, the emphasis switched from history and, indeed, riches, to poverty, adversity, and the foul rag-and-bone shop of a deprived upbringing. Instead of the heraldic shield and the "once-were-warriors" ethos of the emigrant family romance—the belief that though fallen on lowly times, all the O's and the Mac's were once chieftains and of "high ancestral fame"—ethnic pride now derived from tracing genealogy to its more likely actual base: the lower end of the social spectrum, among the great unwashed of the Irish laborers and servant girls who made their way across the Atlantic.

Several cultural developments in the 1990s aided this heightened awareness of a once-discarded past: the digitalized accessibility of family and local histories; the official sanction given to the renewal of interest in Irish roots by President Mary Robinson's explicit outreach to the Irish Diaspora; the acknowledgment of the legacy of the Famine induced by the various commemorations in the mid-1990s; and, not least in the United States, the extraordinary success of *Angela's Ashes,* most notably captured in the scene of the wives' reading group in *The Sopranos,* where they wonder if this grueling story applied to Italian communities as well. But underlying all these developments is the corporate coming of age of the Irish themselves in America, for it is only from this vantage point that the acknowledgment of despised origins is possible. As in the case of the Celtic Tiger in Ireland, which provided the comfort zone to look back in anger at the Magdalene Laundries, the injustices of the Northern Ireland conflict, and the corruption scandals of the Haughey era, so also distance allowed disenchantment with the view of romantic Ireland that had once sustained Irish America. In a form of reverse nostalgia, the past was becoming more miserable as present-day Irishness was transformed into an ethnic option, a cure for the woes of de Valera's Ireland.

To convert culture into an option, however, or tradition to the heritage industry, is to remove ethnicity itself to the lost-belongings department of everyday life. The replacement of attachment to the homeland by Disney-land is nowhere more evident than in Ireland, with the transplanting of New York–style St. Patrick's Day parades to Dublin, bringing it all back to a home it never left in the first place. In a comic interlude in the 1970s film *The Flight of the Doves*, two children on the run from their captors in Dublin seek refuge in a St. Patrick's Day parade, hoping to blend in with the marchers. Instead of fitting in seamlessly, they in fact stand out, for the parade is a ver-itable assembly of the United Nations, with a colorful array of the world's peoples marching Coca-Cola style to the tune not so much of "I'd Like to Teach the World to Sing" but—closer to home—"You Don't Have to Be Irish to Be Irish." At best, this episode gives a welcome preview of increasingly diversified forms of Irishness in the 1990s and the first decade of the twenty-first century; at worst, it suggests that for this to happen, Irishness itself has to be hollowed out into the commodity form to extend a welcome to the Other.

The film was made before the "recovery of roots" phenomenon which took on a new lease of life in the United States in the 1980s and 1990s, and, of course, before the projection of a new global Irishness onto the world stage in the 1990s, fronted by *Riverdance*, U2 and Irish rock music, the Frank McCourt phenomenon, the prominence of Irish leading males in Hollywood, Roddy Doyle's fiction, and the wider cultural resonances of the Celtic Tiger. Invigorated by these developments, and with identity becoming indistin-guishable from "lifestyles," Irishness assumed a new vogue for many in search of a rich cultural genealogy, as if it could be simply picked off the shelf, like a souvenir at Shannon. This is the mentality Sean Thornton (John Wayne) brings to Ireland in John Ford's classic *The Quiet Man*, as if he has only to will his Irishness into existence for it to appear, like the apparition of Mary Kate Danagher (Maureen O'Hara) and her sheep. But as locals keep reminding him, this version of Innisfree may be more a product of his own heat-oppressed brain, forged in the furnaces of Pittsburgh, "so hot a man forgets his fear of hell," than of the Ireland to which he has returned. Sean Thornton's reclaiming of his identity is not a matter of his own volition, but of *becoming eligible* to be considered Irish. Ethnicity does not depend on fate, still less on biology; but neither is it a product of multiple choice, as if it can be picked at will. Were this the case, everyone could apply for minority rights, affirmative action programs, or, indeed, for membership in Native American communi-ties. Choice and decision are integral to cultural identity, but the logic of eth-nicity is not that an individual selects a culture: rather, the community itself has a say in the process, and the gift of membership is partly of its own making. In *The Quiet Man,* Sean Thornton has to undergo the rituals of apprenticeship to *earn* as well as lay claim to membership of a society. This is not to say, however, that it is a one-way transaction, taking everything at face value and leaving all the values and customs of a society intact. Sean accepts the dowry system, for instance, only to question it, or at least to dispose of the elements that involve the subjugation of women. In the last shot of the film, the "nice stick to beat the lovely lady with" is thrown away, as if both Mary Kate and Sean have learned from the collision of cultures.

For an example of such cross-cultural interaction in practice, we might turn again to the ritual of the St. Patrick's Day parade, this time as enacted on Michigan Avenue, Detroit. In the 1990s, the New York St. Patrick's Day parade became a flashpoint for precisely the kind of questioning of Irish attitudes toward sexuality exemplified in *The Quiet Man,* as Irish gay rights groups sought inclusion in the parade. When told that they could march as individuals, they quite rightly contested this on the grounds *of their Irishness,* insisting that Irishness for them had to be reclaimed for a set of expansive and enabling attachments, rather than a closed exclusivist identity. Such alternative versions of Irishness were already part of St. Patrick's Day parades elsewhere, as described by John Hartigan in his account of the parade in the racially diverse environment of Detroit. Pointing out that many neighborhoods once characterized as Irish have now become inhabited by Mexican, Maltese, and other ethnicities, the parade still wends it way down Michigan Avenue, past Tiger Stadium:

> As a slice of the racial formation of Detroit, the parade presents a stunning picture: Its content is only partially ethnic; in between the lines of floating scenes of Irish history or demonstrations of Irish culture march all-black bands from the city's high schools or junior highs. On a frigid day in March, I stood with the other huddled spectators, white and black, watching the "ethnic" parade as it rolled down Michigan Avenue with its dozen or so bands from the city schools. For the white spectators I spoke with, the presence of black high school bands presented no disruption of the ethnic nature of the event, even if only one of the bands performed a traditional tune such as "Danny Boy." These whites seemed to be intrigued by the seamlessness with which blacks moved in this performance of "ethnicity," as if it confirmed the fundamentally ironic nature of ethnic identity in the United States. Nor were the black spectators that I talked with perturbed by the presence of whites in

this "black metropolis." People of both races were fascinated by the ability of this parade to unfold yearly with its heterogeneous racial content.[27]

Hartigan proceeds to point out that far from emptying out the vitality of Irish culture, the music and dance ran late into the night in the Irish American clubs but were in no sense compromised by the more public enactments of identity on the street. Correctly, he points out that the full potential of such cross-cultural currents was not fully resolved or realized but remained "on the cusp of some unarticulated threshold, waiting for something to be made of it." But such realizations do not come from theory or political pronouncements: they come from the practices themselves, and the notion that as performative processes, rituals are *creative* as well as consolidating forces in the lives of those who look to them for meaning.

In 1760–62, Oliver Goldsmith published one of the foundational satires of modern travel writing and anthropology, *A Citizen of the World,* in which the customs and mores of the "advanced" West—more particularly Britain—are subjected to the scrutiny of a visiting Chinese philosopher, Lien Chi Altangi. It was not the first time the device of a seemingly uncomprehending stranger was used to cast a critical gaze on the values of a culture that prided itself on its normality, but in Goldsmith's case, the Chinese visitor was not just a foil to Western self-criticism: he also brought with him values that left their imprint on the host culture, turning the visit into a two-way transaction. Concerned originally with the mid-eighteenth-century craze for irregular Chinese gardens, the vogue for things Chinese in the mid-eighteenth century developed into far-reaching inquiries into the boundaries between artifice and landscape, nature and culture, that prepared the ground for the new Romantic sensibility that was to sweep Europe. In learning about others, Goldsmith implies, a culture extends the horizons of its own self-knowledge—even aspects of its identity that it may be hiding from itself. Likewise with that contemporary citizen of the world, Yu Ming, and his entry into the Ireland of the Celtic Tiger. At one point in the film, Yu Ming is shown struggling with a knife and fork, eating his dinner before deciding that life is too short for such niceties: he converts the handles of both knife and fork into an improvised set of chopsticks, and proceeds to finish his meal. Sometime later, in a seemingly unrelated throwaway incident, he reaches out for his pint of Guinness as soon as it is placed before him on the counter, while Paddy, his Irish-speaking friend, stops him with a gentle wave of his hand to let the pint settle. Not a word is spoken: communication is left only to the gestures of a shared, everyday ritual. Yu Ming takes his lesson to heart, for in the final scene of the movie, we discover he has become a bartender. The bus full of tourists that Yu Ming serves in the Connemara Gaeltacht may have come directly from the nearby "Quiet Man" country, but the moral of the tale may well be that it is not only outsiders who are tourists in Ireland. In a world of ethnic options, Irish people themselves have been so estranged from their own pasts as to become tourists of their own culture. The lesson of Yu Ming's cultural apprenticeship in Ireland is that through an encounter with "the other," and an openness toward the stranger, Irish citizens might end up learning more about themselves—and the worlds they have lost.

NOTES

1. Susan McKay, "Ulster Will Fight, and Ulster Will Be White: Why Chinese Are the New Taigs," *Sunday Tribune* (Dublin), 11 January 2004.

2. Dan Keenan, "Belfast Man Was Told Not to Rent to Immigrants," *Irish Times* (Dublin), 10 January 2004; Dan Keenan, "Belfast House Attacked Hours after Pakistani Family Moved In," *Irish Times* (Dublin), 9 January 2004.

3. Polly Toynbee, "The Press Gang," *Guardian*, 17 June 1998, quoted in Vron Ware, "Perfidious Albion: Whiteness and the International Imagination," in *The Making and Unmaking of Whiteness*, ed. Bridget Brander Rasmussen et al. (Durham: Duke University Press, 2001), 188. It is striking that the emergence of a tabloid press in Ireland in the 1990s (often Irish editions of British titles), the expansion of Sky television, and related globalization of Irish media coincide with the rise of the new racism.

4. Dr. Isaac Taylor, *The Origin of the Aryans: An Account of the Prehistoric Ethnology and Civilisation of Europe* [1889], cited in J. M. Robertson, *The Saxon and the Celt: A Study in Sociology* (London: University Press, 1897), 93. I deal with Aryan Anglo-Saxonism at greater length in *Gaelic Gothic: Race, Colonialism, and Irish Culture* (Galway, Centre for Irish Studies: Arlen House, 2004).

5. For the powerful countertradition of Protestant critiques of colonialism from the Elizabethan to the modern period, see Christopher Hodgkins, *Reforming Empire: Protestant Colonialism and Conscience in British Literature* (Columbia: University of Missouri Press, 2002), chaps. 5–6.

6. Or, as Goldhagen euphemistically describes national character, "the deep roots" of "the cultural cognitive model of German society." *Hitler's Willing Executioners: Ordinary Germans and the Holocaust* (New York: Alfred A. Knopf, 1996), 74–75.

7. Adam Hochschild, *King Leopold's Ghost: A Story of Greed, Terror, and Heroism in Colonial Africa* (Boston: Houghton Mifflin, 1998).

8. Mike Davis, *Late Victorian Holocausts: El Niño Famines and the Making of the Third World* (New York: Verso, 2001).

9. Anthony Pagden, "The Rise and Fall of the British Empire," *New Republic*, 26 May 1997.

10. David R. Roediger, "Irish-American Workers and White Racial Formation in the Antebellum United States," in *The Wages of Whiteness* (New York: Verso, 1994), 134.

11. David R. Roediger, *Black on White: Black Writers on What It Means to Be White* (New York: Schocken, 1998), 21, cited in Ware, "Perfidious Albion," 207.

12. Ernest Renan, "What Is a Nation?" in *Nation and Narration,* ed. Homi Bhabha (London: Routledge, 1990).

13. R. F. Foster, *Paddy and Mr. Punch: Connections in English and Irish History* (London: Allen Lane, 1993).

14. See Brian O' Conchubhair, "Degeneration and the Irish Language: From Revivalism to Postcolonialism," paper presented to Keough Seminar, University of Notre Dame, January 2002.

15. Rev. Ulick Burke, *The Aryan Origin of the Gaelic Race and Language* (London: Longmans, Green, 1875). The use of the word "Aryan," of course, did not carry with it the racist connotations that followed its adoption by Nazi propagandists. The division of Aryan races between Teutonic and Celtic elements, however, introduced some of the sinister implications of later race theory, not least in the internalization by Irish scholars and language activists of the dying or "doomed race" theory. (I am indebted to Brian O'Conchubhair for discussions on these points.)

16. Bryan Fanning, *Racism and Social Change in the Republic of Ireland* (Manchester: Manchester University Press, 2002), 51.

17. Amy Chua, *World on Fire: How Exporting Free Market Democracy Breeds Ethnic Hatred and Global Instability* (New York: Doubleday, 2003).

18. Steve Garner, *Racism and the Irish Experience* (London: Pluto Press, 2004).

19. Matthew Frye Jacobson, *Special Sorrows: The Diasporic Imagination of Irish, Polish, and Jewish Immigrants in the United States* (Cambridge: Harvard University Press, 1995).

20. Diane Negra, *Off-White Hollywood: American Culture and Ethnic Female Stardom* (London: Routledge, 2001), 137.

21. Negra, *Off-White Hollywood,* 140.

22. Christina Hunt Mahoney, "Funds, Faculties, and a Nostalgia Gap," *Irish Times* (Dublin), 12 April 2003. Mahoney goes on to note, "Americans tend to be Anglophilic as a rule, and there is some genuine Hibernophobia."

23. See Richard Rorty, *Achieving Our Country: Leftist Thought in Twentieth-Century America* (Cambridge: Harvard University Press, 1998) and "Rationality and Cultural Difference" in *Truth and Progress: Philosophical Papers,* vol. 3 (Cambridge: Cambridge University Press, 1998).

24. Reginald Horsman, *Race and Manifest Destiny: The Origins of American Racial Anglo-Saxonism* (Cambridge: Harvard University Press, 1981).
25. Cited in Joseph Curran, *Hibernian Green on the Silver Screen: The Irish and American Movies* (New York: Greenwood Press, 1989), 84.
26. Negra, *Off-White Hollywood*, 166. The Waters quotation is from Mary Waters, *Ethnic Options: Choosing Identities in America* (Berkeley and Los Angeles: University of California Press, 1990), 147.
27. John Hartigan Jr., "Locating White Detroit," in *Displacing Whiteness: Essays in Social and Cultural Criticism,* ed. Ruth Frankenberg, 188–89 (Durham: Duke University Press, 1997).

Green Yodel No. 1

RODDY DOYLE

In July 1930, the American country singing legend Jimmie Rodgers, "The Singing Brakeman," went into a studio in Los Angeles. With him was Louis Armstrong. Together, they recorded a Rodgers song called "Blue Yodel No. 9." Despite the title—it is, after all, the ninth blue yodel—this was a unique and thrilling occasion, and the recording is a fascinating, glorious piece of music, years ahead of its time. A mix of rural country and urban jazz; the blues sung by a white man, country-and-western played by a black man. Country meets jazz. Rural meets urban. White meets black. For two minutes and thirty-eight seconds.

"Blue Yodel No. 9" was the result of individual and creative courage. Two men chose to ignore the world outside the studio and created a piece of music that both defied that world and celebrated it. They made new rules, broke old ones. And they made a very good record.

Dublin in 2003 is not Los Angeles in 1930, but much of that creative opportunity is there, and a lot less courage is needed. The opportunities are hopping in front of us, to invent new stories, new art, new voices, new music. Irish-born artists and newly arrived, working together and alone. New slang, and new accents. Follow a Nigerian around Dublin and you'll walk a new geography—meeting places, church halls, lanes, supermarkets, corners to go to or avoid. Follow a Latvian in north County Dublin, and you'll see men and women, bending down in the muck, picking potatoes. Follow a Chinese student walking home—observe his fear. Follow a young Ethiopian family walking through Arnott's department store—observe their excitement. Look at the expressions on the faces of the people they pass. Look at the couple in the Forum Bar, African and Irish, trying to understand each other, wanting to. New love stories, family sagas, new jealousies, rivalries, new beginnings and new endings. We live in exciting times, if we want them.

A father in an Irish play has three daughters. Do all three have to be white? I recently saw a play for children, a version of the Lear story, by Marina Carr. One of the daughters was played by a young black woman. It made sense, and added to the humor and power of the piece. One big daddy—in this man's world, there's no mention of the mammy or mammies. In an operatic production of my own book, *The Woman Who Walked into Doors,* which was produced by a Belgian company, the part of Paula, a working-class Dublin woman, is sung by an African American soprano, Claron McFadden. Her voice is the character, and it is glorious. Do we ignore her skin? Of course not. It's beautiful. She's a woman, telling the story of how she lost and took back her life.

The question, "What's it like being Irish?" could come from a Guinness commercial or a *Bord Fáilte* promotion, but, in fact, it is one of the most exciting, if unanswerable, questions that artists working in Ireland today can ask. It demands more questions, strange answers, images, hilarious and depressing, consoling and dangerous. And it probably leads many of us to the conclusion that brainy people hate: "I don't know." But, as a writer of fiction, I'm quite fond of those words "I don't know," especially when I add the word "but." BUT is the invitation to write, the door slowly opening. "What's it like being a woman?" I don't know, but . . . "What was it like in the General Post Office in 1916?" I don't know, but . . . "What's it like being Irish?" I actually don't know, BUT.

For some years I've been writing episodic short stories, bringing together characters living in Dublin, born there and recently arrived. In one, a young woman brings her African boyfriend home to dinner to meet her parents. "D'you have spuds like them in Nigeria?" the father asks. It might not be the most profound line ever written, but I enjoyed writing it. In another, a man from Zimbabwe, as he turns on the tap in his bed-sit and listens to the plumbing, sings, "The pipes, the pipes are calling." In another, a group of young people, from Russia, Spain, Dublin, Nigeria, the U.S.A., Romania, and Roscommon, form a band and call themselves the Deportees. They sing the songs of Woody Guthrie, the songs of the Dust Bowl. In one I've just started, the narrator has been in Dublin for just three months. He's getting to know the place, the dangers, the prejudices, the accents. It starts:

This morning, I stand at the bus stop. I have been in this city three months. I begin to understand the accent. I already know the language. How do you do? Is this the next bus to Westminster? I have brought my schoolroom English with me. There is no Westminster in this city but I know what to say when the next bus goes past without stopping.

—Fuck that.

People smile. One man nods at me.

—Good man, Bud, he says. —Making the effort.

I smile.

I understand. This word, Bud. It is a friendly word. But I cannot say Bud to this man. I cannot call him Bud. A man like me can never call an Irish man Bud. But I can say, Fuck that. The expletive is for the bus, the rain, the economy, life. I am not insulting the bus driver or my fellow bus stop waiters. I understand. My children will learn to call other children Bud. They will be Irish. They will have the accent. If I am still here. And if I have children.

It is Spring. I like it now. It is bright when I stand at the bus stop. It is warm by the time I finish my first job. Early morning is the best time. It is quiet. There are not many people on the footpaths. I do not have to look away. Eyes do not stare hard at me. Some people smile. We are up early together. Many are like me. I am not resented.

What's the narrator's name? I don't know, but I have a short-list of good ones. What happens in the story? I don't really know. The narrator will go through a rough time, but I do want him to fall in love. Will it end happily? Yes, it will. It's in my hands, and I'll make this one end happily.

A Traveller's Story

MICHAEL COLLINS

I might just start off with a bit of background history to our extended family Collins—Joyces, McDonoughs, and the Keenans. Our family would have been the midland Collinses and originated from Mayo, and for about four generations they have traveled the midlands, Offaly, Kildare, Cavan, and West Meath. In the 1950s and 1960s, they would have made their living through tinsmithing and chimney sweeping, by buying and selling horses, and by making, painting and selling wagons, or begging and hawking.

I was born in the mid-1960s, and at that time big changes were coming into Travellers' lives. The old traditional ways were dying, like the tinsmithing.

The old tents, wagons, and the horses were all going out, and motor cars and trailers were starting to come into the country and replace the traditional ways.

I was born in the mid-1960s, and my mother and father were camped just outside of Kilbeggin. At the time, the story goes from my father and mother, they were stopping in a camp outside of Kilbeggin, and my grandfather and grandmother and a couple of other Travellers were with them. My grandfather was known as auld Mick Collins, and he was better known to other Travellers as the Puck Collins.

When my Mammy went into labor with me, my father ran six miles to the priest's house to get an ambulance because they were camped outside the town. In those days it could be six to ten miles away to the nearest house. The ambulance came down for my mother and headed to Mullingar hospital, as it was the nearest. On the way, a tree fell down on the middle of the road, and I was born in the back of the ambulance. I always tell the story of when I was born in the back of an ambulance and say I am always going somewhere but never getting there on time.

My earliest memories of the old traditional ways of life, which are long gone now, were when we were stopping with my grandfather and grandmother. They had been living the old traditional Travellers' living, in the barrel-top wagons, and they had traditional tents. We also had an old wagon and tent, and my Daddy had an old mare and a horse, and my grandaunt, which would have been my Daddy's Aunt Biddy.

I remember one time Mick was coming back from the country in the flat which is known as a four-wheeler. Travellers would have used them when they were going off, and dragging the wagon around the place; they would have had the four-wheeler and maybe sticks and water and then come back. And I remember him coming back one day and taking off the harness, and giving out and cursing. And I said, what's wrong with ya? Mick, he said, the noise of that yoke is driving the horses mad. I remember hearing a few miles up the road a GRRRRRRR, and it was either bikes or motorbikes that was driving the horses mad.

But I remember him saying to me, go down and ask Biddy Doyle for a *geansai,* so I went down and ask her, and she gave me a geansai—a geansai is what some people call a jumper [sweater]. So I went back up with the geansai, and when he was finished taking the harness and all off the horse, he put a rope round its neck. And I remember him putting one sleeve of the geansai round one of the horse's legs and the other sleeve round the other leg. And I says to him, Mick, what are you doing? He said, well, if you tie the two legs for when they're grazing, so when they are grazing and the horse has to move, he has to move two legs like a hop. So they don't move too far, so they don't stress themselves, so they always stay close by, because if he goes into a farmer's field, the farmer call the Guards, and the Guards come up and move them on.

I remember around the time of the old fire, the campfire, me and Mick sitting down and maybe for a day or two making a load of buckets and tin ware. And I used to go and get the stick, and he used to amaze me. He was only about five foot five or six, but he would bring back a bundle of sticks that would be three times the height of him and three times his weight. But he used to have a technique of carrying them and tying them and bringing them back. But I used to be amazed at him walking through the fields and the ditches and bringing them back. The whole thing around that time was the sticks and water—you made sure you had the sticks and water.

Black Biddy

One of my earliest childhood memories is that of what can only be described as a colorful character named Black Biddy. She was my father's grandaunt, and she wore a long black skirt, a black shawl, and she smoked a pipe and wore a pocket. I am not sure why she never married and never had any children of her own, but in a way she owned us all, as she would look after us.

Biddy, small Black Biddy, as she was called, would beg the houses, and when we saw her coming home, we knew that we were getting something off her, maybe sweets, food or fags for the older ones. She saw it as her job, but it wasn't really her job, but she knew she had to bring something back for everybody. She would come home from the country—you could always hear her coming before you could see her because she would be giving out and arguing with her mule. She be saying, if I had knowing that you weren't going to do what I tell you, I'd have got a bigger stick to beat you with. In the evening she would put on a big pot of spuds in the skin, and when they were boiled, she would get the spuds and poured them on top of a flour bag—the bag had holes in it—and she used it to strain the spuds, then smother the spuds in butter. We would all go up to her for food, but before we could sit down, she would have to coax her little black-and-white mongrel dog called Spot.

Because he didn't like children, she would give him a bit of tobacco to chew and tell him to sit down at the fire and leave the children alone. It wasn't just us that loved Biddy—she would have all the settled children at the fire, feeding them.

That is one of my earliest memories as a young child: sitting at an outside fire, waiting on our spuds and looking over my shoulder at the road that we were camped, the old barrel-top wagons and the tents with the cover up and the straw falling out at the site of what would be our bed that night—auld Mick at the fire, where he was making a bucket, throwing a stick on the fire, and watching the sparks climbing up into the air. That was the old way of life that Travellers talk about now, and I have to say that I am very privileged to be able to live and remember that.

Moving to Dublin

When we moved to Dublin, we moved to the back of the site, and we were living in a trailer. And I remember my Daddy—how we got the trailer up there was, he had a big American car and this was a big huge car, and it used loads of petrol, so we only used it when we were towing the trailer. That would have been in about 1973–74, so we were there in the back of the field for about two years, and at that time our Martin made his Holy Communion. And there was a boys' reformatory school behind us, and at the time my Mammy had six of us under seven years age—Martin was seven, and the rest of us were under seven, including the two twins.

Sister Luke and the Convent

I remember our Martin going over to the convent behind us, which was a reformatory for young boys who got into trouble. And he went over and met this nun and asked, had she a bit of grub. And he would say three Hail Marys for her. What she did was, she gave us three cans out, with spuds in one, vegetables in the other, and another one with a dessert in it. And then we start going back over every day, and I have to say, only for that convent, we would have been dead today. It was what kept us alive, because in the 1970s and 1980s was very hard for everybody, and not just Travellers. So that's what happened. And people would know us on the site from getting things from the convent, and when we would get the soup or anything that we didn't need, we would give it to other Travellers around.

Moving into the Hut and Early School

Then after that we got one of the huts, and me Uncle Tom lived in that, and he was known as Horse Tom. And we moved into that hut, and all it had was a range and a bedroom and a sink and a table. And outside that, was three bedrooms. There was no electricity or toilet, but it had three bedrooms, and we used to sleep in that.

Me and our Johnny and Martin started school. And we went over and started school, and we went to St. Joseph's school in Finglas. But we went in a prefab which was at the back of the school which had different ages of Travellers and mixed between boys and girls. And there was a girls' school, and they had a big playground, and we weren't allowed to play in that playground. And actually, I remember when I left school. I was at it from about six till I was twelve—till we made our confirmation. And I remember school was kind of grand, because I remember not doing anything between seven and twelve picking spuds. And we didn't go to school, and we would go to the houses on Thursdays and Fridays begging, and Saturday. And nobody ever bothered us.

When I say we would go begging houses, my Mammy would bring me, Johnny, and Martin out, because we were the three eldest. And say there were forty houses, you would go to the forty. And say six houses gave you something, you would go back to them—called "call backs"—and they knew you and would bring you in for a cup of tea and give you a sandwich or breakfast. And before you go, they would give maybe eighty pence or a pound, or four grain of sugar. But if you went to strange houses to get stuff, you would say: How ye, missus? Would you have a grain of sugar, or a bit of bread, or a sup of tea, and we'll say three Hail Marys for ye, and God bless ye? And that's how we would say it and that. And that lasted between school and after school, but after we left school we started doing seasonal work and that, picking spuds and onions. In summer it was lovely, but not in winter. And you would often cry with the pain in your fingers, and then, when it would thaw out, it was lovely, and you would look forward to the cup of tea.

So we did that for a couple of years, and then we started working the dumps, like, collecting scrap and holding it. Our Martin got engaged at sixteen years of age, and we were looking forward to the wedding. So we were out doing the dumping and collecting scrap, and me Mammy was out begging and that, and we were still going to the college and getting fed every day, and saving for the hotel. And Martin got engaged at fifteen and a half, and

Martin was married in 1993. And in the meantime, I was matched off. I was matched off to a first cousin of mine who lived in Clare. And I remember meeting the girl, and she was a very nice girl, and was saying thanks for the jewelry, and thanks for that. And I don't remember sending down anything, but what was happening was, me Mammy was sending down things and writing to her. But when I met her, we didn't click, so I called off the wedding. And my Mammy went mad and my Daddy made a leap for me, so I had to run out and jump over the wall into the field and kip there for a day or two. But anyway, they got over it.

Meeting John O Connell

I suppose the next big step after that was the dole office, and turning eighteen years of age, and turning up at the dole office and signing on. But maybe it was a summer's day, and a couple of boys playing football, and lighting a fire, and me and a couple of Collinses, and this man and woman came up to the fire. And they were talking about this course, it was a personal development course, and they said they were trying to get a mixture of twenty-four—twelve men and twelve women to join this course. So, at the time we were on the dole, so we were trying to find out, do you get an extra couple of quid for it? And I remember John O Connell saying, yeah, you get an extra couple of quid, and you get lunch money, so it comes to about twenty quid extra. And we said, fuck it, sure we'll give it a go. So me and Martin went down, and bread Mickey, Mickey McCann. And we were the first ones in the door, and all these Travellers came in, and we didn't know them, and they didn't know us, and there was a kind of excitement and energy, and it was all boys and girls, and we kind of got ourselves registered and settled.

I remember going down to the dole office, and I said to the woman, and I said, I want to sign off. And she said, what's your name? And I said, Michael Collins. And she said, what do you mean Michael Collins? And she said, oh right, and you live in Villa Park, and you want to sign off, and why are you signing off? And I said, what do you mean, why do I want to sign off? And she said, you're a Traveller, and Travellers don't work. And I said, look I'm doing a course. And she said, well, do you have any identification saying that you are Michael Collins? And I said, yeah, I have my dole card, and I want to sign off. And it was kind of, she didn't want me to sign off, so I went up to John O Connell for a letter, and I went back down with the letter and I signed off.

I remember one time in one of the groups, and it was about eighteen or nineteen Travellers sitting around in the group. One of the things that came up was, John O Connell said, was anyone here ever discriminated against? And we all looked at each other and said, no, not at all. And he all looked at us, because he would have talked to us before, and he knew we all were. So he said, can I put this a different way? And so we were looking at him and as well.

We didn't know what the word discriminated meant, and we all say. And he said, were you ever put out of a shop, or put off a bus, or called names? And everybody put up their hands and and, by Jesus, all the stories came flooded out, see, in Finglas, Clondalkin, Coolock, Northside, and Southside. And they were all giving their stories of how they were put out of places and discriminated against, and one of the first words we learnt about was discrimination. And over the course of time the training was, at that time was, absolutely brilliant. I haven't seen anything like it since, and I suppose it's one of the things that came out of that course that people who are running the courses now came out of that one—Johnny McCann, Martin Collins, Catherine Joyce, and other people.

And the other type of thing was finding out what kind of words the government use and what affects Travellers. Travellers at the time was discriminated in education, social welfare, employment, accommodation. And as time went by, and you were learning, and you were learning about what happened in South Africa and segregated school and the blacks in America and civil rights in America and the segregated schools, and black and whites for toilets, and separate toilets, and all that kind of stuff. And then I started thinking about my education, and they wanted to know who could read and write, and all I could tell was all I could write was my name. And then we started learning about South Africa, and then I started thinking about school.

Acting

When I went into acting there was this writer writing about native Travellers, and he wanted to get it right. He used to write it in Gaeltacht language, and it was his first one in the English language, he came to us and asked us to come along and improvise the show. One of the most difficult things for me as a young Traveller was, there were really two things: leaving the traveling community and go and live and work with the settled community and not having very much experience of it and trying to live up to their expectations and standards and watch what you say and eat and do. And so we done it, and the play, and I thought the play was brilliant. But then we started doing workshops, and in the workshops, myself and Liam Heffernan would do the workshops, they were very difficult. And even though they were about Travellers and settled people, in the settled-people scene it was about family relations and employment and emigration. But in the traveling, it was about discrimination and match weddings and family values, and it kind of always concentrated on the Travellers.

And the way our workshops were around Travellers and the things they would say about Travellers would actually hurt me, and my stomach would actually go very tense. They were saying that Travellers were dirty and smelly and they didn't know how to wash themselves and they never contribute to society, and they don't pay taxes and when there is a funeral they close down pubs for them—I know Travellers who come into my shop and I wouldn't serve them.

But when you say to the young settled people—I'd say, well, you are saying this about Travellers, well, do you know any Travellers, have you met any Travellers? No? Well where would you get your views from? Well, at that time it would have been in the media and from their mothers and fathers. I remember meeting with Liam, and I remember I said, I can't take this anymore. There has to be a let out. I don't want to be getting angry with the people, because if I do, this just brings me back as far as ever, so I remember we can up with this thing.

We would say, there is a Traveller in the class, and who was it? And nine times out of ten they used to pick Liam Heffernan because he had the long hair, and he was shabby dressed, and he was saying, how's it going, and blah blah blah, real tough, rough, in a big Louth accent. Where I was playing a real teddy boy, with the hair slicked back, real cool. And I would say, no, I am the Traveller. And then you would see the expression on their faces, and you would see them going, Oh Jeysus, maybe I shouldn't have said that. And I would go, look it, we are all entitled to our opinion. I mightn't agree with it, but I'm here to tell you about Travellers and what we're doing, and open up a new avenue for you to learn about Travellers. And sometimes you would have people coming up to you and saying, I'm sorry about what I said, and you did change my image of Travellers.

Gangs of New York

NOEL IGNATIEV

How we look at the past reveals a great deal about us in the present. Consider a recent look at the past, Martin Scorsese's film *Gangs of New York,* and the critical response to it.

The climactic scene in the film depicts the so-called New York Draft Riots of 1863. I say "so-called" because the riots, although they were triggered by the draft, were the result of forces that had been operating long before. Their underlying cause was the opposition by Irish unskilled laborers to a war they feared would result in their being forced to compete with black workers in a free labor market. In order to prevent that, they attacked symbols and representatives of the federal government, fought with the police, tore up railroad tracks, and destroyed telegraph lines and port installations. In the course of their weeklong insurrection, they killed hundreds of black people, in many cases setting them on fire and perversely mutilating their bodies, and burned the Colored Orphanage. They did all these things at a time when armed forces of the enemy were a hundred-odd miles away, making clear they understood what they were doing by running up and cheering the enemy's flag. The film depicts the events, more or less. Although a few reviewers criticized Scorsese for fiddling with the record, compressing time and so forth, many hailed the film as an epic. The *Boston Globe,* noting the high level of violence, praised it for showing the "savagery" at the heart of the American experience. The *New York Times,* praising "Mr. Scorsese's bravery and integrity," compared it to John Ford's films, which make up a "myth of American origins," and to D. W. Griffith's *Birth of a Nation. America* says it could be called "The Birth of a City."

Neither the violence nor the minor deviations from actual events and details bother me; after all, that is what an artist is supposed to do. I am bothered that the film distorts the meaning of the events, turning them into a conflict between native and Irish and reducing the problem of race to a footnote. Typical is the reviewer who noted that, "along the way, the mob kills the blacks it encounters." Neither the *New York Times* nor *America* pointed out that the story told in the film is false, every bit as false as the story Griffith told in his classic of white supremacy. To them, and to Scorsese, the white supremacy at the heart of the riots just happened "along the way."

Of the reviews I read, only two noted the film's problem with race. The first was by Ron Howell, writing in *Newsday.* Howell scored the film for "romanticiz[ing] the experience of Irish immigrants while slighting that of the city's blacks." The second was by David Denby, writing in the *New Yorker;* his review is worth quoting at length:

> Blacks are the repressed presence in this movie fantasy, and the omission makes nonsense of the sequences devoted to the horrific Draft Riots of 1863. There were populist elements in that rebellion (for three hundred dollars, a young man could buy his way out of conscription), and the filmmakers harp on them. Fair enough. But they also present the riot as an outgrowth of the Irish fight against the nativists. The tone of what we see is, at first, celebratory—it's a virtuous revolt, the Bolsheviks coming down the street—and then, as Union soldiers fire on the rioters, tragic. The actual rioters burned down a Negro orphanage and strung up black men on lampposts and set them on fire (the orphanage doesn't show up in the movie, the lynchings only in passing). It was blacks who suffered most in this tragedy. The filmmakers, hoping to memorialize the immigrant Irish as the soul of a new nation, went down the wrong path, then pulled back, only to end in confusion, halfway excusing an awful event.

With the two exceptions quoted above, the response of the reviews I have read is consistent with a long history of commentators seeking to apologize for or even glorify the rioters by saying that they were voicing working-class resentment, and that the riots were a progressive model of resistance to the military draft. (Sad to say, even Black 47, from whom we have come to expect better, took that line in their song "Five Points." And many have explained the 1974 reaction of South Boston Irish to school desegregation in the same way.) Yes, the rioters were spurred by poverty and anger at the inequities of the draft, but to call their actions an expression of working-class rebellion is to reduce class to a sociological category. It is also to spit on the memory of the black people, free and slave, who were even poorer than the Irish and who also were victimized by inequities in the draft and in the conditions of military service, but who acted with dignity and the assurance that the abolition of slavery was in the class interests of laborers everywhere.

In 1841, sixty thousand Irish, headed by the Liberator, Daniel O'Connell, issued an address to their countrymen in America, calling upon them to join with the abolitionists in the struggle against slavery. "Treat the colored people as your equals, as brethren," they declared, "and in America you will do honor to the name of Ireland." Six months later, William Lloyd Garrison, the abolitionist, reported that "not a single Irishman has come forward, either publicly or privately, to express his approval of the Address, or to avow his determination to abide by its sentiments."

Just a few months ago, I was on a radio show talking about white supremacy and the oppression of black people. A caller, identifying himself as of Irish descent, declared that the Irish had made it in America in spite of obstacles, and wondered why black people couldn't do likewise. What did he mean by "making it"? If he was like most ordinary "white" Americans, he meant a job he hated and at the same time feared losing, two weeks' vacation a year spent fixing up a house he would never own, constant worry at being left without health benefits, a spouse to whom he was yoked by bonds of mutual entrapment, children he did not understand who regarded him with mild contempt, and the loneliness of the suburban tract and shopping mall. I used to think that Garrison's words quoted above were the saddest yet written on the Irish Diaspora; now I wonder if they have been surpassed by celebrations of "success" in America.

There is a link between the refusal of Irish Americans of the last century to treat black people as their brethren and the willingness of their descendants to accept their present condition in place of freedom and dignity: How might the country be different today had the Irish, the unskilled labor force of the North, joined forces with the blacks, the unskilled labor force of the South? Those who dismiss the question as unrealistic, frivolous, or without contemporary significance do Irish Americans no service.

Re-Imagining the Gaeltacht

Maps, Stories, and Places in the Mind

ANGELA BOURKE

Almost since the foundation of the Irish state in the 1920s, "Gaeltacht" has been the official name for a number of areas, most of them along Ireland's Atlantic coast, where Irish[1] is believed to be the daily language of some 80 percent of the population. It is not entirely a coincidence that these are also areas of dramatic natural beauty, ranging from wild, boggy uplands to rocky, indented coasts with sandy beaches. In Scotland, similar regions of the Highlands and islands where Gaelic is spoken are called *Gàidhealtachd*—a different spelling of the same word. Both names originally referred, however, to something much more "virtual": Gaelic-speaking people as a language community and cultural polity, wherever they happened to be.

The idea that maps of Ireland can show a region or regions called "the Gaeltacht," where Irish has been spoken since time immemorial and English has yet to penetrate fully, is an invention of the early twentieth century, ripe for re-imagining a hundred years later. The only monoglot speakers of Irish now are the very young children of committed language activists, most of whom live outside the mapped Gaeltacht, while within the Gaeltacht, bilingualism and code-switching with English have long been the norm. Links among Gaeltacht areas, and between them and Gaelic-speaking Scotland, are more active than they have been for hundreds of years, however, and this is only part of a phenomenon whereby the Gaeltacht is becoming global.

Irish is one of Europe's lesser-used languages, surrounded by English wherever it is found, yet a number of lively Irish-language publishing houses regularly produce new works of poetry and prose, fiction and nonfiction. People speak Irish every day in homes, offices, schools, factories, farms, and fishing boats (71,000 people reported in the 1996 census that they did so); they listen to it on radio and television and read it in newspapers, magazines, and Web sites.[2] For perhaps 20,000 people, Irish is the language in which they are most themselves: the language of intimacy and creativity. When the internationally celebrated traditional singer Michael Mháire an Ghabha, of An Aird Thoir, Carna, Co. Galway, died, aged sixty-nine, on 7 March 2005, hundreds of people, young and old, gathered for his wake and funeral. No language was to be heard but Irish above a murmur in the dignified ceremonies of mourning and celebration. Irish was the language of Michael Mháire an Ghabha's most important relationships, as well as of his art; it would have been unthinkable to conduct his funeral in any other.

Curmudgeonly articles appear in print regularly, demanding that the pretense of an Irish-speaking Gaeltacht be abandoned, yet it remains true that there are significant areas of the island of Ireland where Irish is the normal and preferred means of communication. Most of them are in remote parts of the rural West and South, but one is in County Meath, within an hour's drive of Dublin, and another is a housing development in Belfast, where a group of parents built an Irish-speaking community in the 1970s around their children's primary school.

Recently, as immigrants set up new communities in Ireland's towns and cities, speaking and writing more languages than ever could have been imagined on this small island, language use has been changing, and so have the ideological parameters that first gave the Gaeltacht its identity. Economic circumstances have altered beyond recognition; electronic media have revised the significance of physical location for human communication, and the binary opposition of Irish against English is giving way to concerns about pluralism, regionalism, and globalization.

Today, the Gaeltacht seems under threat: fewer families in the designated areas speak Irish to their young children; more English is to be heard in school yards and shops; and statistics on language use suggest that the maps that delineate Gaeltacht areas should be redrawn. At the same time, however, more Irish than ever before can be heard on city streets, and in Ireland and around the world, Irish-language courses are heavily subscribed.[3] For many learners now, Irish is less about conservatism and more about cultural conservation: in 2003, when a class was set up in Galway specifically for asylum seekers, one participant remarked that her own native language, Kikuyu, was under threat, being spoken less and less by young people in urban areas.[4] Meanwhile, as people meeting face-to-face continue to speak Irish in the mapped Gaeltacht and elsewhere, people far apart are doing the same, invisibly, on telephones and on the Internet. Drivers stuck in traffic in Dublin or Belfast may well be listening to Raidió na Gaeltachta, all of whose broadcasts, on current affairs, music, history, or any of a surprising variety of specialized topics, are in Irish. Internet access delivers Irish-language radio and television programs all over the world, and radio listeners join e-mail discussions in Irish from some surprising locations. People born in the places marked on maps as Gaeltacht have always emigrated but now return more easily and more often, with cheap flights in and out of a number of new regional airports, and virtual visits even cheaper. For the first time, too, immigration is bringing people whose first language is neither Irish nor English to live in Gaeltacht areas.

The stories told in and about the Gaeltacht have changed, but they reach a wider audience now than ever before, and the networks of a new, virtual, global Gaeltacht are growing stronger. The identity and integrity of what Gaeltacht stands for have become less dependent than they used to be on fixed locations; more like those of a company whose workers "hot-desk," visiting the office only at intervals. To understand how the meaning of Gaeltacht is changing from the inside out, it is worth exploring how the original notion took shape and developed.

Throughout the nineteenth century, publications by scientists, churchmen, and social reformers drew attention to the chronic poverty and underdevelopment of much of the West of Ireland, where history conspired with geology to make dense populations dependent on poor, acidic land and precarious inshore fishing. People in the "congested districts," as these remote, inaccessible, Irish-speaking communities came to be called, paid grossly inflated rents. They worked tiny plots of stony land with hand tools and carried seaweed from the shore to manure them; they cut peat for fuel and salted fish for the winter. Although skilled in the techniques they needed for subsistence and possessing a highly developed tradition of oral history, literature, and music, they had few resources with which to meet the literate, industrialized, English-speaking world. Government policies drawn up in London made no provision for dealing with Irish speakers in their own language, and even education was available only through English. Life was hard, and many emi-

ANGELA BOURKE ๑๑

grated, to England and to North America, where they were easily classified as illiterate and unskilled.

In 1891, Arthur Balfour, then in his fourth and final year as chief secretary for Ireland, set up the Congested Districts Board (CDB) to develop industry and agriculture. Then, as now, "infrastructure" was a fundamental problem, but the CDB spent lavishly. It promoted cottage industries and employed local workers to construct roads, bridges, and harbors. Balfour's Light Railways (Ireland) Act of 1889 already provided government funding to allow railway companies to extend their services westward. In the years that followed, lines were carried into the remoter parts of counties Kerry, Clare, Galway, Mayo, and Donegal. One of the first was the Midland and Great Western Railway's 48-mile track from Galway to Clifden, where work began in 1891, with women toiling alongside men, carrying stones to build a railbed across the bog.[5] Charles Stewart Parnell died that same year, leaving the Home Rule movement in disarray. In the political vacuum that followed, cultural movements flourished. The Galway to Clifden railway and the other Balfour lines became carriers of ideas as well as of people and goods, for the West of Ireland soon assumed a new significance for Nationalists.

The notion that only through a national language could the soul of a people be adequately expressed was central to the imagining of nations in the nineteenth century, as Benedict Anderson demonstrated twenty years ago.[6] It became an article of faith for many, if not most, of those who fought for and achieved Irish independence in the early twentieth century, but most of them had grown up without hearing the Irish language spoken. From gradual beginnings, the movement to revive Irish gathered momentum, especially after November 1892, when Douglas Hyde delivered a resounding lecture in Dublin to the National Literary Society, titled "The Necessity for De-Anglicizing Ireland." He pointed out how recently Irish had been spoken in the vicinity of the east coast's major cities and towns, exhorting his listeners not to let it die everywhere else.

The following year, Hyde became president of a new organization, the Gaelic League, dedicated to the revival of Irish as a spoken and literary language through evening classes and weekend social activities. The League's appeal to a new generation of literate but often deracinated urban workers was immediate: it offered a distinctive identity and a youthful alternative to the complacencies of established parliamentary nationalism, at the same time as trains and bicycles began to give young people new mobility. In the smallest towns and villages as well as in cities, men and women could walk or cycle to the League's language classes, where they studied side by side in a heady atmosphere of equality. In the years before 1916, the classes would provide cover for military training, too. Born in 1879, Patrick Pearse was an early recruit to the League; later executed for his part in the Easter Rising, he would have a huge influence on the imagining of what was later called the Gaeltacht.

The opening of the Galway to Clifden line in 1895 came just two years after the founding of the Gaelic League in Dublin. Railways allowed ordinary people to travel for recreation for the first time, and cultural nationalists in Ireland were now able to combine summer vacations by the sea with opportunities to hear Irish spoken fluently and to improve their own grasp of the language and its oral culture. Miss Molly Ivors, in James Joyce's "The Dead," is one such person. She and her friends have planned a month in the Aran Islands, no doubt traveling by train to Galway, and then by steamship to Kilronan. She embarrasses Gabriel Conroy by calling him a West Briton, teasing him about his summers spent cycling in France, Belgium, or Germany instead of in the Irish-speaking West. Part of Gabriel's unease as the story ends is his sense that a greater authenticity may, after all, belong to the West than to his own life in Dublin: Michael Furey, who died at seventeen for love of Gabriel's wife, Gretta, was from Oughterard, in Irish-speaking Connemara, where the snow now falls on his grave.

In 1903, the Midland and Great Western Railway instituted a Tourist Express service to Clifden.[7] The train left Dublin at midday in summer, arriving in Clifden at 5:00 PM. At Oughterard, a majestic landscape of granite, peat bog, streams, and lakes began, where habitations were few, and gentry came to shoot and fish at a number of hunting lodges. The bare peaks of the Twelve Bens lay to the north and west, but some ten miles south of the line were the inlets and rocky headlands of the thickly populated, Irish-speaking coast. The train made a stop at Maam Cross, where horse-drawn cars were available for hire. One road ran south to Screebe, then west to the peninsula of Rosmuc, before continuing along the coast. Patrick Pearse had made his first visit to Rosmuc earlier that year. He was twenty-four. Brought up in the center of Dublin, son of an English ecclesiastical sculptor and an Irish mother, he had been fired with enthusiasm for the Gaelic Revival since his teens. Learning Irish at Gaelic League classes, he had taken up the editorship of the League's weekly newspaper, *An Claidheamh Soluis* (The Sword of Light), on 10 March that year.[8] At nineteen, he had visited the Aran Islands for a month and in the intervening years had made several more trips west, but Rosmuc was the very heart of the Irish-speaking West.

ANGELA BOURKE ⟲

Pearse was captivated by the landscape, the people, and the way of life he found in Rosmuc. He visited every summer; his fluency in the Irish of Rosmuc improved, and in February 1905, in *An Claidheamh Soluis,* he published the first of his own short stories in Irish, idealizing the simplicity and piety of the barefoot Irish-speaking children he met there. That same year, he purchased a plot of land overlooking Loch Oiriúlach for his romantic nationalism left space for a strong streak of practicality. With university degrees in arts and law (contemporaries mocked the "BA, BL" after his name), he was an enlightened educationalist, strongly opposed to the regimented "murder machine" of Victorian schooling. He saw an alternative model of education, compatible with the European models he admired, in the ways the people of Rosmuc used oral traditions as keys to living in an intricately patterned landscape. His plan was to found a school in Dublin that would educate boys bilingually, developing qualities of body, mind, and spirit, as the medieval sagas he read suggested had been the custom in ancient Ireland. He wanted to bring his pupils to Rosmuc during the summer for immersion in the natural environment and cultural milieu that he thought ideal. In 1908, he opened St. Enda's school in Cullenswood House, Ranelagh, two miles south of Dublin city center. The following year saw the completion of a small thatched house in vernacular style, above the lake in Rosmuc; over the following summers, Pearse brought several groups of boys from St. Enda's to stay there. His educational experiment was successful though short-lived. A number of the young men who fought alongside him in 1916 or went on to hold leading positions in government and administration were his former pupils.[9]

Learners of Irish needed things to read, but most of what was written, even in fiction, stayed close to the forms of oral tradition. In 1904, an tAthair Peadar Ó Laoghaire (the Rev. Peter O'Leary), published *Séadna,* a version of the Faust story based on the oral tradition of his native County Cork, and it became for many years the most widely read book in Irish. Pádraig Ó Siochfradha, writing as "An Seabhac" (the hawk), wrote books for children, drawing on the Kerry folklore with which he had grown up. Pearse, a learner of Irish rather than a native speaker, went further. In the ten short stories he wrote and published between 1905 and 1915, as well as in poetry, plays and essays, he set out his sense of what Ireland could learn from its marginalized Irish-speaking communities and hammered home a cultural propaganda designed to combat the attractions of emigration for Irish-speaking children. Despite plots that were often mawkish, thinly disguised versions of Victorian or Edwardian popular literature, the stories were vigorously written, powerfully evocative of both the Connemara landscape in summer and the rhythms of the Irish spoken there. Revivalists read them eagerly. Although the people of Rosmuc were still notoriously poor in material resources, Pearse portrayed them as rich in knowledge of their history and environment and capable of expressing their sense of identity with grace and eloquence. His adoption and invention of Rosmuc as a repository of the values of the Irish nation—rural, frugally self-sufficient, and Catholic—offered a less-than-adequate representation of the area's morale, but to the converted and the impressionable, it had the ring of a utopian grand plan.

The Congested Districts Board failed to deliver the improved economy and living standards that had been hoped for. Instead, Balfour's trains continued to carry young emigrants away from Irish-speaking districts. (Pearse's contemporary Pádraic Ó Conaire wrote about one of them in his celebrated short story "Nóra Mharcais Bhig" [1906].) But then Pearse was executed in 1916, and public opinion swung strongly in his favor and that of his comrades. His stories began to be more widely read, as did his articles, where the term "Gaeltacht" occurs often. Used by some native speakers to distinguish places where Irish was spoken from "Galltacht," where it was not, it now became familiar to English-speakers. With the foundation of the Irish Free State in 1922, "Gaeltacht" replaced "congested districts" as the preferred name for areas now felt even by middle-class outsiders to be distinct in terms of culture as well as of economic need. Pearse's sense of the West found a visual echo in the paintings of Paul Henry. Henry had been painting the West of Ireland since his first visit (by train) to Achill Island, County Mayo, in 1910, and gradually his landscapes had taken on an elemental form. Human figures became smaller or disappeared, while dramatic skies towered over thatched cottages and dark stacks of peat, in stony settings of gray, brown, and green. In 1925, the London Midland and Scottish Railway issued a travel poster for distribution to tourist offices in Europe and the United States. Featuring a reproduction of *Connemara*, by Paul Henry, it was called "Ireland This Year." In 1925 and 1926, the "Connemara" poster was widely displayed in Ireland and Britain. Members of the public bought more than nine hundred copies of it, and as Henry's biographer, S. B. Kennedy, puts it, the picture "became something of an icon, fixing what was to become the quintessential image of the West of Ireland in the public mind."[10]

In 1925 also, the new Dublin government, led by William Cosgrave, set up a Gaeltacht Commission to inquire into language use, education, and eco-

ANGELA BOURKE ඥ

nomic conditions in Gaeltacht areas.[11] The government and the commission recognized that the problems identified by the Congested Districts Board remained, and that the Irish language was most reliably to be found in the areas of greatest rural poverty. This time, however, the distinctiveness of the regions in question was to be celebrated, not deplored, with official recognition given to the Gaeltacht's importance in the cultural life of the state; a priority, therefore, was to establish its exact location and extent. The commission set conscientiously about its work. In 1926, after taking depositions from schoolteachers, priests, managers of co-operative societies, and other interested or knowledgeable parties and deliberating in detail, it produced a substantial report. John Walsh's recent *Díchoimisiúnú Teanga* describes the work and its consequences, with vivid quotations from evidence included in the commission's report. The picture that emerged was one of grinding poverty, rampant emigration, and a language in decline. Despite the best efforts of teachers, priests, and officials committed to the revival of Irish, many native speakers were ashamed, rather than proud, of their fluency. Irish-speaking parents often resented the fact that their children were now being taught through Irish, arguing that their sons and daughters would need English when they emigrated, as they surely would as soon as they reached adulthood. Walsh quotes the report's conclusion that

> in prestige, the position of the language in the Gaeltacht is low. The influence of a hostile government was thrown against it in the past; it was denied as a vehicle of education; it was ignored and repressed in administration. Generally, public representatives, businessmen, Church authorities, ignored it. The educated were ignorant of it, and . . . protected their position by affecting to despise it, or often despising it with conviction. Those who spoke it traditionally saw no avenue of advancement open to them or their children without English. Thus it came to be accepted that the language was destined to pass.[12]

The picture was very different from the one Pearse had painted of Rosmuc.

The commission's report was accompanied by a new map showing the boundaries of areas in counties Donegal, Mayo, Galway, Kerry, Cork, Waterford, and Meath, whose populations had been established to be at least 80 percent Irish-speaking; they would officially be deemed Gaeltacht or *Fíor-Ghaeltacht* (truly Irish-speaking districts). Additional, adjacent areas, where a lower proportion of people spoke Irish, were designated as *Breac-Ghaeltacht* (partly Irish-speaking districts). Perhaps inevitably, this act of decolonization followed the methods of empire in expressing political aspirations and achievements as colored areas on maps. Fíor-Ghaeltacht was colored pink, Breac-Ghaeltacht yellow. Fíor-Ghaeltacht areas as delimited in 1926 had 150,000 native speakers of Irish, while a further 100,000 lived in areas designated Breac-Ghaeltacht.

Government policy in the years that followed was committed to the maintenance of traditional life in Gaeltacht areas and to the revival of Irish as a spoken language throughout Ireland by means of schooling. Although it seems hopelessly naïve today, that ambition was not much out of step with policies pursued in many contemporary European states. Almost by definition, areas not designated Gaeltacht were deemed empty of native speakers of Irish. Moreover, when Article 8 of the 1937 Constitution made Irish "the national language," relegating English to recognition as "a second official language," most Irish people found themselves in the paradoxical position of being unable to speak their "native" tongue. Meanwhile Gaeltacht areas were assigned a privileged, if potentially ghettoizing, status, with grants given to families for each child brought up speaking Irish, and extra grants for the building and repair of houses. The Unemployment Assistance Act of 1933 provided a weekly subsidy—the "small farmers' dole"—to many smallholders who had formerly relied on seasonal migration to Scotland or elsewhere to support themselves and their families. Other grants were available to subsidize the lodging costs of students who lived for periods of weeks with Gaeltacht families in order to learn Irish, while a variety of schemes, from early attempts at vegetable growing in glasshouses, to factories in the 1960s, and fish farming in the 1970s, was instituted to subsidize the incomes of small-farm and fishing families and stem the tide of emigration among native speakers of Irish.

Despite the commission's recommendations about education and development, however, little was done to extend opportunity to Gaeltacht people or to allow them control of their own affairs. In most parts of Ireland, secondary schooling was provided in fee-paying schools by religious orders, which had expanded rapidly in the nineteenth century. Most Gaeltacht areas had been too poor to support convents or monasteries, however, so for forty years after the Gaeltacht Commission reported, only a small minority of children whose mother tongue was Irish received a high school education, and a large proportion of those who did were destined to become primary-school teachers. What economic development did take place was paternalistic and remote: Gaeltarra Éireann, set up in 1957 to coordinate Gaeltacht industries and develop exports, especially of woolen goods, was largely run from Dublin and staffed by managers whose knowledge of Irish was rudimentary. Dialects of Irish vary considerably from North to South in any case, and the fact that Gaeltacht regions were separated by English-speaking areas and had little contact with one another meant that once removed from their own home districts, even fluent Irish speakers were soon in difficulty and had to resort to English. It seemed that jobs could be provided only at the cost of destroying the language they had been intended to save.

Successive generations have loaded the Gaeltacht with stereotype: From being the ultimate real Ireland and a source of poetic wisdom and spiritual integrity, it had become by the 1960s a sort of subsidized summer camp for teenagers, where they could get away from their parents, learn a little Irish, and fall in love. Alternatively, the Gaeltacht was an enclave of cunning opportunism and special pleading, where the hard-earned tax money of English-speaking citizens was handed out to able-bodied people unwilling to work. For many of those who lived there, however, it was uncomfortably like a museum or a theme park, where they were expected to forego access to modernity and a share in Ireland's new prosperity in order to keep a myth intact for people far away. One aspect of government policy had worked, however: the Gaeltacht by now had a distinct identity, even if it was assigned from outside and fitted badly.

Change came in the 1960s, as T. K. Whitaker and Seán Lemass's new national economic policies began to take effect. Free secondary education became government policy, with new, lay-run coeducational community schools set up in Gaeltacht areas, as elsewhere, to prepare students for university as well as providing vocational training. Rising levels of education coincided with the civil rights movement led by Martin Luther King Jr. in the United States, and the adoption of its ideals in Northern Ireland. By 1970, a Gaeltacht civil rights movement, Cearta Sibhialta na Gaeltachta, was under way. One of its earliest campaigns addressed the control big landowners still exercised over fishing rights on rivers and lakes. Another led to the setting up of an unlicensed radio station in Connemara to broadcast in Irish (on the model of Radio Luxembourg and the "pirate" stations that broadcast pop music from ships moored off the coast of Britain, in defiance of the BBC). That initiative resulted in the opening of a new, licensed radio station, sponsored by the national broadcaster RTÉ, specifically for the Gaeltacht. Raidió na Gaeltachta began broadcasting at 3:00 PM on Easter Sunday, 2 April 1972. Eight years later, following sustained campaigning for more representative institutions to manage Gaeltacht affairs, Gaeltarra Éireann was replaced by Údarás na Gaeltachta. It would be based in the Gaeltacht, with a number of its members selected by direct elections. Raidió na Gaeltachta steadily increased its broadcasting hours, building a cohort of skilled workers in all aspects of radio production and presentation. From its small local stations in Gaeltacht areas of Donegal, Galway, and Kerry, and in Dublin, it kept people informed, breaking the mesmeric grip of centralized, increasingly standardized media and allowing the development of new, quirkily creative points of view. Significantly, many of the native speakers of Irish who staffed it had escaped the effects of religious-run schooling, with its emphasis on a tightly controlled "respectability": what James Joyce called "paralysis" and sociologist Tom Inglis terms "moral monopoly."[13] The fact that RnaG broadcast in all the dialects meant also that for the first time, Irish speakers from different parts of the country learned to understand each other. One long-running weekly program, *Sruth na Maoile,* even broadcasts jointly with BBC Raidio nan Gaidheal in Scotland, the Scottish presenter speaking Scottish Gaelic, and the Irish presenter Irish.

A century ago, when the concept of the Gaeltacht began to take shape, Irish-speaking people in a number of remote rural areas learned with pride, bemusement, indifference, or irritation that they were the true custodians of the Irish soul. As an identity, it was probably preferable in most ways to the one on offer from the Congested Districts Board, which a few years earlier had cast the same people as Ireland's indigent huddled masses, to be rescued from their primitive and pathetic condition by enlightened government. Both identities were assigned from outside, however, rather than projected from within: Their prefabricated components arrived by train or automobile from Dublin or some other city, ready for assembly, with little regard for the concerns and aspirations of the people who were expected to inhabit them. As a structure, however, despite its shortcomings, the idea of the Gaeltacht has proved remarkably durable, as the people who live there have inhabited, refurbished, and adapted it to changing times.

In 1990, a new controversy arose about the identity of the Gaeltacht, when geographer Reg Hindley's *The Death of the Irish Language: A Qualified Obituary* argued that attempts to revive the Irish language had failed, since most of the Gaeltacht areas shown on maps no longer had a critical mass of native speakers.[14] Scholars from other disciplines were quick to answer him, unwilling to agree that the shadings on a map offered an authoritative, or even a

ANGELA BOURKE ᏝᎧ

useful, measure of such a complex human activity as the use of language in a bilingual environment. Éamonn Ó Ciosáin's response was a pamphlet called *Buried Alive,* while Trinity College Dublin sociologist Hilary Tovey wrote a comprehensive review for the *Irish Journal of Sociology.* "If Irish is used at all, why not celebrate that?" she wrote; "But if we want to investigate it, let us proceed as we would with any other interesting form of life, through careful documentation of its situated appearance without preconceptions as to the criteria it must fulfill to be allowed to be 'living.'"[15] Irish, as we have seen, maintains a lively, organic existence in many spheres, but as a function of human communication, it does not always present itself for scrutiny.

In the years that followed independence, the sense that the Gaeltacht embodied the soul of Ireland informed broad areas of policy. In the twenty-first century, however, global corporations dwarf most nation states; almost everyone on earth speaks one of a handful of major languages (perhaps along with one, two, or three others), and religious metaphors for lesser-used languages have given way to ecological ones. The news that half of the world's 6,800 distinguishable languages face extinction in the near future because they are not being taught to children provokes the same sort of consternation as the threat the logging industry poses to the snowy owl. Linguistics professor James McCloskey of the University of California, Santa Cruz, writes about Irish as a world language. He notes that "every language that succumbs to the economic, political, and cultural pressures being applied all over the globe today, takes to the grave with it an encyclopedia of histories, mythologies, jokes, songs, philosophies, riddles, superstitions, games, sciences, hagiographies—the whole cumulative effort of a people over centuries to understand the circumstances of its own existence."[16]

The establishment of Raidió na Gaeltachta and Údarás na Gaeltachta marked the coming of age of a new, self-determined identity for the Gaeltacht, and a new awareness of the circumstances of its existence. They were joined in 1996 by Teilifís na Gaeilge, now TG4. Based in the Connemara Gaeltacht, but insisting that its mandate is to provide television programming for the language community and not for a particular area of the map, TG4 has one of the youngest television station staffs in Europe. The stories it tells have transformed the image of the Irish language and sent the Gaeltacht global.

The Gaeltacht has been celebrated as a source of stories and poetry since the early years of the revival. *Sheasfá sa sneachta ag éisteacht* (you would stand in

snow to listen) was a common way of praising singers in the so-called congested districts, as it is wherever Irish is spoken today. Beginning in 1897,
storytellers and singers from Waterford and Cork to Donegal performed in
competitions sponsored by *An tOireachtas*, the annual cultural festival held
by the Gaelic League in Dublin. Transcriptions of tales, legends, and songs
featured prominently in Irish-language publications. Traditional performers retained keen local audiences, too. At the same time as Pearse was imagining an Irish-speaking utopia, storytellers like Peig Sayers in Kerry, Éamon
a Búrc in Connemara, and Máire Mhic Fhionnlaoich in Donegal were trans-
mitting memories preserved for generations and imagining worlds of mystery and wonder for the entertainment and enlightenment of their neighbors. Music groups Clannad and Altan, and the singer Enya, all from the
Donegal Gaeltacht, are modern bearers of musical and singing styles handed
down through generations.

In 1935, the state supported the founding of the Irish Folklore Commission
to collect and catalogue oral traditions throughout Ireland, with a heavy emphasis on Gaeltacht areas. This was in line with the Gaeltacht Commission's
recognition that "in the memories, stories, folklore, songs and traditions of
the Gaeltacht there is preserved an uninterrupted Gaelic culture which constitutes the very soul of the Irish language."[17] Its report continues:

> The Commission recognizes that The Native Irish Speaker has a command of
> the beauties of language which is inculcated amongst English speakers only
> by the labored teaching of the classics. There is no parallel in English for this
> refined popular culture, which is the highly wrought product of generations
> of Gaelic civilization. This popular culture is in grave danger of being lost,
> and the Commission feels that the revival of the language, without the preser-
> vation of this culture, would rob Ireland of one of its richest and most digni-
> fied inheritances. A proper utilization of this material, especially in connec-
> tion with vocational training would, the Commission believes, serve to raise
> the whole mental and economic standard of the Gaeltacht to a level that could
> not otherwise be achieved.

Only in the 1970s, however, through an increasingly sophisticated engagement with various mass media, did the oral culture of the mapped Gaeltacht
begin to be integrated with vocational training. Since then, though, its people
have been empowered to enhance the quality of their lives at every level. Improved access to higher education, to decision making, and especially to the
technologies of broadcasting and filmmaking, has allowed the relationship

ANGELA BOURKE ᠙᠙

between Irish speakers in the mapped Gaeltacht and revivalists outside it to be renegotiated, as the Gaeltacht takes control of its own narrative.

In 1973, Bob Quinn, Seosamh Ó Cuaig, and Tony Cristofides founded the film company Cinegael in the Connemara Gaeltacht. They have been producing innovative and evocative work on low budgets since then. In 1996, their film *Graceville* offered a challenge to received migration history when it traced the journey and subsequent fate of twenty-four Irish-speaking families who traveled from Galway and Mayo to Graceville, Minnesota, in 1880. It prompted one Graceville native, Berkeley professor Bridget Connelly, to embark on a study of her own family's lost Irish connections, replacing the story of the migration "as it had always been written" with a more nuanced one gleaned largely from oral sources on both sides of the Atlantic. Her book, *Forgetting Ireland,* appeared in 2003.[18]

Since the early 1990s, and especially in response to the setting up of TG4, which commissions much of its work from independent filmmakers, Cinegael has been joined by a number of younger companies. A search with the word "Gaeilge" of the Screen Producers Ireland Web site produced twenty-two hits, many of them young film companies based in Gaeltacht areas. Daniel O'Hara's beautiful, witty, short film *Yu-Ming Is Ainm Dom/My Name Is Yu Ming* (2003) won many awards. Critics who don't speak Irish have read it as a scathing satire on the pathetic state of the Irish language revival; critics who do are more likely to celebrate it as a subtle take on the complexities of bilingualism and multilingualism in Ireland today. The barman may think Yu Ming is speaking Chinese, but this audience knows he's speaking Irish so the joke is on the barman. And Yu Ming does find his niche: working in a bar in the Gaeltacht, which does, after all, exist.

In the last ten years, as poets like Cathal Ó Searcaigh, Nuala Ní Dhomhnaill, and Biddy Jenkinson, writing out of the poetic imagination and emotional intelligence encoded in the Irish language, have been finding committed readers at home as well as far afield, both in Irish and in translation, newspapers and Web sites are going from strength to strength.[19] The first issue of *Foinse* (www.foinse.ie) appeared in October 1996. Published each Saturday from offices in the Connemara Gaeltacht, using the most modern computer and printing technology, it now has forty pages per issue, of which sixteen are in color; according to the UK-based Audit Bureau of Circulations, its average weekly sales for 2004 were 7,324. The first Irish-language daily newspaper, *Lá* (www.nuacht.com), launched in April 2003 and published in Belfast, now sells 5,000 copies each day throughout Ireland. "BEO!"

(www.beo.ie), which describes itself as an "Internet magazine for Irish speakers in Ireland and worldwide," caters for learners of Irish as well as fluent speakers, with links to translations of less common words. It has been appearing monthly since 2001. A counter on the site shows the number of people currently reading it; as I type, late on a Saturday afternoon in 2005, that number is 156.

But perhaps the most significant development is in the area of Irish-medium schooling. The Shaw's Road Gaeltacht in Belfast, which grew up around an Irish-medium school, is now in its second generation, and the *Irish News* reported on 12 August 2004 that a similar development, starting with twelve houses, is planned for County Tyrone. Gaelscoileanna (www .gaelscoileanna.ie) is a voluntary national organization of schools outside the mapped Gaeltacht where Irish is the language of instruction and of communication among teachers, children, and management. In 1972, there were fewer than twenty such schools; by 2004, there were almost two hundred, with more opening, or receiving full accreditation, every September. Teachers in Gaelscoileanna are both native speakers of Irish and learners, and the children who attend some of them are fluent speakers of new, creolized dialects of Irish—evidence, if evidence is needed, that this language is anything but dead.[20] Irish-medium schools are found on both sides of the border, and demand for places in them is intense, even among parents who do not themselves speak Irish.

The Gaeltacht of the early twenty-first century reflects the fact that one-way, lifelong migrations of Irish speakers out of the Gaeltacht and out of Ireland have given way to a much more complex pattern of comings and goings, both real and virtual. In the nineteenth century, some of the regions hit hardest by poverty, famine, and, inevitably, by emigration were those in the mountains and on the Atlantic seaboard, where the first, and for many, the only, language was Irish. These emigrants may have known a few words of English—about as much as tourists pick up from phrase books—but they had to learn to speak it when they went to America.[21] Not many people manage to express their wit and insight—much less all the nuances of their emotion—in a language learned in adulthood. As Garrison Keillor puts it, "You are never so smart again in a language learned in middle age, nor so romantic or brave or kind. All the best of you is in the old tongue, but when you speak your best in America you become a yokel, a dumb [foreigner], and when you speak

English, an idiot."[22] The special difficulty Irish-speaking people experienced on migrating to America in the nineteenth century was all but invisible to others, just as their language, stigmatized by history and drowned out by English, was inaudible.[23] But modern migrants from Ireland are totally at home in English. If they are from the Gaeltacht, mapped or virtual, they speak Irish too, and instead of poverty and backwardness, the image they carry with them is of multicultural cool: hybrid, creative, adaptable.

The Gaeltacht is still a series of places on a map, and a different language on road signs; it still suffers inequalities and disadvantages, notably in the quality of its roads, but travel, technology, and a new sense of empowerment have changed it. Now in the undisputed possession of people who speak Irish, it is both a place in the mind and a fertile antidote to the bland and paralyzing uniformity of globalization.

NOTES

1. The Gaelic language spoken in Ireland, commonly so-called to distinguish it from (Scottish) Gaelic, to which it is closely related. For the development of the idea of the Gaeltacht, see especially Nuala C. Johnson, "Making Space: Gaeltacht Policy and the Politics of Identity," in *In Search of Ireland: A Cultural Geography*, ed. Brian Graham, 174–91 (London and New York: Routledge, 1997), and Caitríona Ó Torna, "Cruthú Constráide agus an Turas Siar: An Ghaeltacht i dTús an Fichiú hAois," in *Aimsir Óg, Cuid a Dó, 51–64* (BÁC: Coiscéim, 2000).

2. In Ciarán Mac Murchaidh, *"Who Needs Irish?" Reflections on the Importance of the Irish Language Today* (Dublin: Veritas, 2004), thirteen mostly urban Irish speakers write about their varying experiences and emotions in ways that resist stereotyping and simplification. See also the Web site of Foras na Gaeilge, the body set up in 1999 to promote the Irish language throughout the island of Ireland under the terms of the Good Friday Agreement, especially http://www.forasnagaeilge.ie/language/default.asp?catid=16.

3. In 2003–4, for instance, more than 120 undergraduate and graduate students at the University of Notre Dame, Indiana, took Irish-language classes. By comparison, during the same period, 95 took Russian and 135 took Japanese (Source: http://www.nd.edu/~irishstu/new_department.html).

4. Anna Heussaff, "More Irish Than the Irish Themselves?" *Irish Times* (Dublin), 26 November 2003.

5. Thanks to Caitríona Ó Ceoinín, Carna, for this information.

6. Benedict Anderson, *Imagined Communities: Reflections on the Origin and Spread of Nationalism* (London: Verso, 1983).

7. Kevin O'Connor, *Ironing the Land: The Coming of the Railways to Ireland* (Dublin: Gill and Macmillan, 1999), 87–90. For Joyce, see Friedhelm Rathjen, "James Joyce as a Cyclist," *Joyce Studies Annual* 14 (Summer 2003): 175–82.

8. See Ruth Dudley Edwards, *Patrick Pearse: The Triumph of Failure* (Dublin: Poolbeg, 1990, 26–69, and Regina Uí Chollatáin, *An Claidheamh Soluis agus Fáinne an Lae, 1899–1932* (Baile Átha Cliath: Cois Life, 2004), 54–55, 90.

9. Elaine Sisson, *Pearse's Patriots: St. Enda's and the Cult of Boyhood* (Cork: Cork University Press, 2004).

10. S. B. Kennedy, *Paul Henry* (New Haven and London: Yale University Press, 2000).

11. See John Walsh, *Díchoimisiúnú Teanga: Coimisiún na Gaeltachta 1926* (Baile Átha Cliath: Cois Life, 2002).

12. Walsh, *Díchoimisiúnú Teanga*, 116.

13. Tom Inglis, *Moral Monopoly: The Rise and Fall of the Catholic Church in Modern Ireland* (Dublin: UCD Press, 1998).

14. Reg Hindley, *The Death of the Irish Language: A Qualified Obituary* (London: Routledge, 1990).

15. Hilary Tovey, "Review of Reg Hindley, *The Death of the Irish Language: A Qualified Obituary*," *Irish Journal of Sociology* 1 (1991): 165–68.

16. James McCloskey, *Guthanna in Éag: An Mairfidh an Ghaeilge Beo?/Voices Silenced: Has Irish a Future?* (Baile Átha Cliath: Cois Life, 2001), 36.

17. Walsh, *Díchoimisiúnú Teanga*, 69.

18. Bridget Connelly, *Forgetting Ireland: Uncovering a Family's Secret History* (St. Paul, Minn.: Borealis Books, 2003).

19. Ní Dhomhnaill and Ó Searcaigh are translated into many languages, including Japanese, and are widely read in English; significantly, Jenkinson enjoys considerable critical acclaim, although, as "a small rude gesture" of defiance against the ubiquity of English, she refuses to allow her work to be published in English translation in Ireland.

20. McCloskey, *Guthanna in Éag*, 48.

21. References in Kerby A. Miller, *Emigrants and Exiles: Ireland and the Irish Exodus to North America* (New York: Oxford University Press, 1985) to, for example, "Irish-speaking peasants' ingrained fatalism and apocalyptic tendencies" (476) have been roundly rejected by other scholars, but his study is one of the few to take any account of language diversity among immigrants from Ireland.

22. Garrison Keillor, *Lake Wobegon Days* (London and Boston: Faber and Faber, 1985), 65.

23. Angela Bourke, "Legless in London: Pádraic Ó Conaire and Éamon a Búrc," *Éire-Ireland* 37, nos. 3–4 (Fall/Winter 2003): 54–67.

The Universe of the Gaeltacht

AODÁN MAC PÓILIN

I address myself here to the half-forgotten and fragile culture of the Irish language—not, I may add, the anemic, sanitized version that was visited on generations of schoolchildren but the living culture hanging on by its socio-linguistic fingernails.

Matthew Arnold once wrote that the Celts have difficulty in accepting the despotism of fact. I've always taken that as a compliment. If you're faced with a despotic fact—an unpalatable actuality—you have two choices. You can lie down, wave your legs in the air, and let actuality trundle over you. Or you can imagine a new and better actuality—and then will it into being.

I belong to a community that has taken the second route, that has created a bubble of alternative actuality—a neo-Gaeltacht, an urban Irish-speaking community—in Belfast, a town that was set up exactly four hundred years ago by Sir Arthur Chichester, whose agenda was "first to plough and break up those barbarous people and then to sow them with seeds of civility." In other words, to destroy the language, civilization, and society of the recently conquered Irish-speaking locals.

Before I give a brief account of this linguistic bubble, I'd like to establish a couple of first principles:

A language communicates at a level far beyond the utilitarian—it is more than another way of asking someone to pass the salt. A living language is the expression of an evolving civilization which is itself diverse. It is a complex of ways of interpreting the world—or the universe.

The Donegal writer Seosamh Mac Grianna once wrote, "The whole world is beyond the little shadow of words we put on it." In other words, language simplifies and distorts the real world. But—importantly—every language has a different pattern for simplifying and distorting reality, every language provides a unique lens, a unique window—a unique partial view—of the world. The sum total of these distortions is the sum total of that part of human wisdom that can be put into words. And we need all those distortions.

You may have guessed by now that I am making an argument for cultural and linguistic ecology. The Irish language is, I believe, the cultural and linguistic equivalent of a small to medium-sized rain forest. And it's our very own rain forest. It is Ireland's privilege to have the sole care of a unique bit of humanity's heritage, and it is Ireland's duty to ensure that this irretrievable civilization does not go down the toilet.

It seems to me that the cultural ecology argument is irrefutable. Who could possibly be in favor of the death of a language and its attendant culture? Some people are; I've met them. They all belong to that class which knows the price of everything and the value of nothing, but they can be broken down into subcategories: gradgrind philistines, vulgarians, pseudo-cosmopolitans who embrace every kind of diversity but the one on their own doorstep, cultural cringers, lumpen-utilitarians, and begrudgers.

Some of our friends are almost as bad—one early revivalist organization miscalled itself the Society for the Preservation of the Irish Language. There isn't a single linguistic eco-warrior in the world who wants to preserve a language. A language is not jam, conserve, or marmalade. It cannot be put into a deep-freeze, salted, pickled, tinned, smoked, or dehydrated. Languages and their cultures are not static; they do not live in libraries and archives and theme parks. They live in communities, in a constant dynamic between a complex past and a complex present.

How do you create a new Gaeltacht community, a willed bubble of linguistic reality, a spit in the face of the tyranny of fact? It must be said from the outset that this is a significantly different process to that of maintaining the organic linguistic communities of the historic Gaeltacht. It is essentially an act of repossession—of learning the language that your ancestors had to abandon, bringing your children up in your second language, and creating a new linguistic community. It should be noted that what is repossessed does not have the rich resources of what has survived in the historic Gaeltacht. Like English, it is a kind of creole, but one that is now developing its own creativity.

Given that 20 percent of the population in the English-speaking part of the island of Ireland can speak Irish, it is surprising that there have been so few new Gaeltacht communities. Not that it hasn't been attempted. A government-funded neo-Gaeltacht scheme was proposed for Dublin as early as 1927, but

Irish speakers appear to have an in-built reluctance to sharing the same physical space with other Irish speakers. When the father of that great scholar Colmán Ó hUallacháin was asked to join this new community, he responded that it was bad enough to have to meet other Gaels at festivals and meetings of the Gaelic League without having to live next door to them. To be fair to the elder Ó hUallacháin, endangered minority languages tend to attract nutcases, and the Irish language movement is infested with a disproportionate number of tunnel-visionaries, impossiblists, messiahs carrying their cross for Ireland, linguo-masochists who are attracted solely to lost causes, grammarians, grant-pimps, soft-core Celtic spiritualists, and hard-core Catholic fascists.

One neo-Gaeltacht set up in Cork in the 1960s never grew beyond three or four families. Another was to be established in Dublin around the same period, but apparently the prospect of a certain well-known language fanatic joining the community put everybody else off. I know of two other clusters, one of three families and one of four, but they kept their existence a secret, largely for fear of who might join them. For some reason, only in Belfast is there a significant urban neo-Gaeltacht, a geographically coherent community of Irish-speaking families.

This developed in the Catholic Falls Road district—the largest ghetto in Western Europe—from a working-class social club, Cumann Chluain Ard, which in 1951 established itself as an English-free zone. Not only did it act as a magnet for radical language activists, it also functioned indirectly as a kind of dating agency, offering young couples a way of continuing their language activism in the married state. It appears to have been the first organization in Ireland to have created a critical mass of urban Irish-speaking families who were prepared to live alongside each other.

The first meeting to establish the community took place in 1961, when nineteen Irish-speaking couples began to plan the development of a small housing estate. It was 1969 before the first group of five houses was built on the Shaws Road in Andersonstown.

Even if you wanted to, you cannot protect a minority language behind a wall of brass three hundred cubits high. What the community tried to achieve reflects another theme which emerged during the conference—a strategy for maintaining minority identities in a global and globalizing context. Children, thankfully, tend not to be ideologues, but language use, fortunately, is largely a matter of habit. The challenge facing the community was to create a pattern of language use among the children in which it was natural for them to use Irish among themselves and with other Irish speakers while at the same time preparing them for a largely English-speaking world.

To our surprise, this actually worked. The next generation, now mostly in their twenties and thirties, has adopted a form of code-switching in which Irish is used instinctively except when the presence of English speakers makes English necessary. A surprisingly high proportion of them use Irish as their language of preference, and many of them are bringing their own children up as Irish speakers. The community now consists of sixteen families, and there are plans to build six new homes. All the new houses are being built by children from the community, and a third generation of Irish speakers is being created. My daughter is building one of these houses, and I asked her why. She had two answers. One was that she could avail of a free babysitting service. The second was that her upbringing had made her secure in her own linguistic identity, and she wanted to pass this gift on to her own children.

This community has also had an extraordinary influence on its wider environment. Within my own lifetime, the number of active Irish speakers in Belfast has exploded; we have a range of interlinking networks of Irish speakers, several social venues, a significant increase in the number of Irish-speaking families, two thousand children receiving their education through the medium of the language, and the beginnings of a self-sustaining social infrastructure.

However, while our linguistic bubble is remarkably vibrant, it has not yet attained the critical mass that would ensure its long-tem viability. To secure the future of the language, we still need new generations to rebel against the despotism of fact.

The Protestant Gael

A Scottish Perspective on Ireland

MALCOLM MACLEAN

My view of both Ireland and Britain is different from the Anglocentric perspective that usually dominates this discourse. It is not a conventionally "British" perspective but a Scottish and, more specifically, a Gaelic view. It is a view of Gaelic Ireland from its parallel universe in Gaelic Scotland, the Scottish Gàidhealtachd.

Over the past five years the devolution process and the new Scottish Parliament have thrown up new challenges and new opportunities. Like the Irish, the Scots are coming to develop a new sense of what Scotland, and Scottish identity, actually means in the twenty-first century. Unlike Ireland, we have no widely recognized colonial or postcolonial analysis of who we are. Scotland had a different relationship with the British Empire and has yet to make up its mind if it was more colonized or colonizer.

The Scottish Gàidhealtachd—which can mean either 1 percent of the population or 50 percent of the landmass—is acquiring a new significance in Scotland, redeveloping the ancient connection with Ireland and opening up new possibilities and perhaps some fresh perspectives on issues of Irish and Scottish identity. One of the promised outcomes of the 2003 Scottish Parliament election, for example, is the introduction of a Gaelic Act granting secure status to the Gaelic language in Scotland. This is a major development that will underpin and reinforce the recent dramatic growth in the Gaelic cultural economy.

The past ten to twenty years have seen a rapid expansion of both Gaelic playgroups (from zero to more than two hundred) and Gaelic-medium schools (from zero to sixty-five). Skye's Gaelic college, Sabhal Mòr Ostaig, has emerged as a cornerstone of the University of the Highlands and Islands, and Gaelic radio and television broadcasting have significantly expanded to broadcast throughout Scotland. The long-running Gaelic TV series, *Eorpa,* is the only European current affairs series on UK television. Numerous Gaelic-led community initiatives have emerged across the heritage, environmental, and social and economic development sectors. The Gaelic arts infrastructure has developed a network of thirty arts tuition festivals for young people, a theater company, summer schools, arts centers, arts and media training programs, new publishing initiatives and a wealth of emerging musical talent. Scottish Arts Council investment in the Gaelic arts has increased from approximately £50,000 per year in the late 1980s to more than £1 million in the coming year.

There are only 650 words of difference between Irish and Scottish Gaelic, but the historical context of the language in Scotland is very different from that in Ireland, North and South.

First, there is the issue of state recognition. The new Scottish Gaelic Act is the first formal political recognition of Gaelic in Scotland in more than 250 years.[1] In the sixteenth century, Gaelic was spoken by 50 percent of the population of Scotland. At the turn of the twentieth century, Gaelic was still the first language of the northwestern half of the Scottish landmass, known as the Highlands and Islands—our Gàidhealtachd. In the course of the twentieth century, however, the number of speakers diminished from 250,000 to 60,000 at the 2001 census.

The key reason for this decline was the blanket hostility of the British state to Gaelic. My parents' generation, in the overwhelmingly Gaelic-speaking Western Isles, was punished by their teachers for speaking Gaelic in the school playground. In Ireland, you were more likely to be punished for speaking English.

A second difference is the fact that, according to census figures, there are now more "native" speakers (as opposed to "learners") of the Gaelic language in Scotland than there are in Ireland. While Scotland has a growing learners culture, the majority of Scots Gaelic speakers come from communities where Gaelic is still the first language. This is largely attributable to Scotland's island geography, which has rendered full assimilation into monolingual English-speaking Scotland problematic, despite the best efforts of the state.

The third difference is the fact that the language issue in Scotland is not politicized as it is in Ireland, where it is seen by many—in Northern Ireland in particular—as a badge of Catholic Republicanism. No Scottish political party has taken up the banner of Gaelic promotion, with the result that Scottish Gaelic speakers vote for all parties and none. Over recent years we have endeavored to turn this negative into a positive, and the language is being successfully promoted in Scotland on a cross-party basis.

Finally, the widespread Northern Irish association of Gaelic with the Catholic Church is contradicted by the fact that the vast majority of Scotland's Gaels are not only Protestant, but seriously Presbyterian. The Reverend Ian Paisley's church is modeled on the Free Church of Scotland, for example, which is overwhelmingly Gaelic-speaking. My personal background is typical of many Scots Gaels. My family was devoutly Protestant, Gaels who had migrated from the Western Isles to Glasgow, where I was brought up with Gaelic as the first language of the home. In the homes of my closest childhood friends, I heard Polish, Italian, and Irish Gaelic spoken and initially assumed that every family had their own private language and that English was the language of the street. My primary school was literally across the road from the Rangers soccer stadium in Ibrox. The Rangers were viewed as a "Protestant" team, but Ibrox, the name of their base, is derived from the Gaelic, "Atha Bhroc," meaning Badger's Crossing, producing a submerged ironic contrast—given the Loyalist Rangers fans' negative view of Gaelic and "hallowed ground" view of Ibrox. By the time we were ten, though, my schoolmates and I had an extensive repertoire of Orange Order songs. We had no comprehension of what these songs were about, but we liked the tunes. We thought that "Ireland" was somewhere in the east end of Glasgow—home to Rangers' great rivals, Celtic, who were seen as an "Irish Catholic" team. Rangers and Celtic still function as a shorthand for "Protestant/Catholic" or "Scotland/Ireland" for many Scots.

It was as an adult that I discovered that Ireland's real relationship to Scotland was more complex, more significant, and much more interesting than Rangers and Celtic. This more informed understanding of Ireland has been slowly surfacing in the Scottish schools' curriculum since the arrival of Scottish Gaelic-medium education in the late 1980s. This view of Ireland from Gaelic Scotland is what you could call the Greater Gàidhealtachd perspective, in which Scotland is Ireland's Great Lost Colony. In a cartoon chronology, this Greater Gàidhealtachd history might be summarized as a process of convergence, divergence, and potential reconvergence:

First there was a thousand years of convergence and common culture, between the sixth and sixteenth centuries. Such Irish Gaels as Colmcille, known as the Scoti, migrated into the West of Scotland from the sixth century onward. After three or four hundred years of colonization, they united the country and created a Gaelic-speaking court. They also gave this new country its—their—name. Historians can find no meaningful difference between Scottish and Irish Gaelic culture throughout this period.

Then came four hundred years of Gaelic divergence following the Reformation and a policy of divide-and-rule by the British state. This division of the Gaels was compounded in the twentieth century by the insularity of the newly independent state in the south of Ireland and its imperative to define itself as different from Britain. The view that Ireland was Gaelic and Britain was not may have been important to Ireland's self-definition and a political reality, but it further obscured the linguistic and cultural reality of the Greater Gàidhealtachd. Thirty years of Troubles in Northern Ireland, British military policy, and people's reluctance to travel the short distance through the North from either direction have further distorted this ancient equation.

Over the past ten years the unexpected possibility of potential reconvergence has been evidenced by a renewal of links between Gaelic Scotland and the North and South of Ireland. This increasingly energetic process has been given significant momentum by the Good Friday Agreement. Should this Gaelic reconnection continue to gather momentum, it could make a significant contribution to the normalization of relationships across these islands.

The Celtic scholar and professor at Aberdeen Colm Ó Baoill has this to say about the first period, of convergence:

> It cannot be emphasized too strongly that the early Gaelic literary, linguistic, and cultural world was a single unit. The modern division into three distinct Gaelic languages (if that is what they are) is not visible much before the sixteenth century. And so the early poetry, unless we really know where it was composed, should not be labelled Irish or Scottish or Manx but simply Gaelic.[2]

Historians can find no material distinction between Gaelic culture in Ireland and Scotland for a thousand years. The most famous artifact from Ireland's "Golden Age," *The Book of Kells,* originated on the Scottish Island of Iona. It was the Gaels who united the tribes of Scotland in the ninth century and made Gaelic the language of the medieval court. Four kings of Ireland are buried in Scotland (on Iona), and the Scottish Hebrides used to be mapped as the Irish Isles. The music traditions of both countries are full of songs and music that cannot be definitively attributed as originating in one country or the other because of the high degree of commonality and musical interaction. The "Irish" Gaelic culture of the Scottish Highlands and Islands even survived that of Ireland itself by a century and a half.

Professor Duncan MacMillan, author of the definitive *Scottish Art 1460–1990,* has described the second period, of divergence, as

> nearly five centuries of religious and political division imposed by forces of history far beyond the control of the people of either country. The peace process in Northern Ireland is the fading of the last aftershock of the Reformation. The fault-line from that cataclysm . . . is not unique in Europe, but uniquely, it has remained tragically active until now and it is this that has split Ireland from Scotland . . . Once united by language they were divided by faith.[3]

These religious and political divisions have dominated Ireland and Scotland's relationships for centuries, and the Scots have often been a source of great strife in Ireland. The plantation of Scots into Northern Ireland, 1916, the War of Independence, Irish neutrality during World War II, and the recent Troubles have all served to reinforce division. All of this is well documented, but it is only a part of the picture.

Despite the Reformation there remained continuing connections between Ireland and Scotland. A surprising proportion of those in the leadership of the United Irishmen in 1798 were educated in Scotland, and there was particularly close collaboration between the Irish and the Highland Land Leagues in opposition to nineteenth-century "landlordism." Michael Davitt, an Irish Catholic, was asked to stand as MP for the Presbyterian Isle of Skye. Hundreds of thousands of Irish workers migrated into rapidly expanding nineteenth-century industrial Scotland. The twentieth-century Irish patriot James Connolly was born in Edinburgh, and Irish poet Cathal O Searcagh has spoken about his father's agricultural work in Scotland. The Irish, together with the Gaelic-speaking Highlanders, have generated well over 50 percent of the current population of the city of Glasgow and made a huge contribution to that city's identity. Eminent Scottish historian Tom Devine estimates that 40 percent of Scots have Irish ancestry. For most people, however, this deeply rooted Scottish/Irish connection has been totally overshadowed by more confrontational images of sectarianism and a British army, with Scottish regiments, at war with the IRA.

The seeds of potential reconvergence were sown through numerous tenuous but highly significant connections that, paradoxically, built up during the Troubles. Within the Scottish Gaelic community this period coincided with a recognition of impending language crisis and a whole new approach being taken to Gaelic development. The Scottish Gaelic community had a cultural and linguistic imperative to maintain the links with Gaelic Ireland at a time when the rest of Britain, and indeed the Republic, were avoiding the North as a war zone.

This process of reconnection has progressively intensified over the past twenty years through contact between academics, festivals, summer schools, musicians, artists, poets such as Sorley Maclean and Iain Crichton Smith, and, crucially, the annual Gaelic poets and musicians exchange, Turas na bhFilí. The fact that Scottish Gaelic was not officially recognized by the British state was significant as it meant that these vital cultural reconnections remained apolitical and detached from, and unsullied by, the conflict in the North.

When the Peace Process came, it meant that there was an emergent network of Irish/Scottish Gaelic contacts. This left the Gaels unexpectedly ahead of the game when the Irish and British governments suddenly became the best of friends, and, over the past few years, these new connections between Irish and Scottish Gaels have been significantly strengthened.

The potential for reconvergence is perhaps best illustrated by Iomairt Cholm Cille—the Columba Initiative—which was established in 1997 specifically to renew and reforge the Gaelic links. The Iomairt is supported by the Scottish Parliament, the Northern Irish Assembly, and the Republic and has made remarkable progress in a relatively brief time.

There are now an annual Scottish/Irish Gaelic youth parliament, an annual youth theater summer school, two annual *seann nos* festivals exploring our shared song tradition, radio and television coproductions, community exchanges between the West of Ireland and the Hebrides, and joint research projects between the University of the Highlands and Islands and Irish universities.

Perhaps the most visible achievement is *An Leabhar Mòr/The Great Book of Gaelic.* This major collaboration between more than two hundred Irish and Scottish poets, visual artists, and calligraphers has created a book for the twenty-first century with roots in the *Book of Kells.* The Leabhar Mòr exhibition, Canongate book publication, BBC/RTÉ TV documentary, radio series, education pack, Web site, and events program offer a fresh re-imagining of Ireland, and Scotland, from a Gaelic perspective. The project has enjoyed a remarkable degree of popular and critical success since it was launched in Glasgow's Gallery of Modern Art six months ago. In abbreviated form, *The Great Book of Gaelic* had its North American premiere at the "Re-Imagining Ireland" conference in 2003.

I have obviously aimed to highlight our affinities. It is equally important, however, to recognize our differences because there is a great deal to be learned from them. The Gaelic experience in the Republic, Northern Ireland, and Scotland has been particular to each location, and this has left us, each and all, with singular forms of historical baggage. In the Republic, the Gaelic language has been a symbol of the state. In Northern Ireland, it has been a symbol of opposition to the state. In Scotland, it was neither but occupied a kind of Celtic Twilight Zone that until recently rendered it officially invisible. The language itself is innocent in all of this.

Current experience implies that our linguistic and cultural connections may run deeper under the skin than political or religious divisions suggest. President Mary Robinson observed that "there were no two countries in Europe with more in common than Ireland and Scotland," and this is especially true of Gaelic Scotland. These commonalities have been deliberately obscured, to the detriment of both our countries. The extent to which a re-imagined Ireland (or Scotland) can transcend the straitjacket of aging national identities to embrace a "Greater Gàidhealtachd" cultural identity remains to be seen. Irish exposure to Scotland's Protestant Gaelic tradition, however, is already having a healthy effect on some of the fixed positions that have built up around outdated notions of Gaelic identity in both countries.

NOTES

1. The Scottish Gaelic Language Act was finally passed by the Scottish Parliament on 21 April 2005.
2. "Early Irish and Scottish Gaelic Poetry," in *An Leabhar Mòr/The Great Book of Gaelic*, ed. M. Maclean and T. Dorgan (Edinburgh: Canongate Books, 2002), 17.
3. Duncan MacMillan, "Scottish and Irish Visual Art," in *An Leabhar Mòr/The Great Book of Gaelic*, ed. M. Maclean and T. Dorgan, 7.

From *An Leabhar Mòr*

Two Poems

Dubbed a twenty-first-century *Book of Kells, An Leabhar Mòr na Gaeilge/The Great Book of Gaelic* is an extraordinary collaborative project developed by Proiseact nan Ealan—the Gaelic Arts Agency. Edited by Malcolm Maclean and Theo Dorgan, *An Leabhar Mòr* combines the work of contemporary Scottish and Irish artists, poets, calligraphers, and typographers, bringing together fifteen centuries of Scottish and Irish culture, celebrating mythologies, traditions, and a language that binds them together. Twenty of the one hundred framed folio (42 × 25 in.) pages were presented at the "Re-Imagining Ireland" conference. A powerful testament to the enduring creativity of Gaelic culture in Scotland and Ireland, *An Leabhar Mòr* recalls and represents deeply rooted connections between the cultures of both islands, virtually challenging myths of disconnection and difference that have infiltrated public consciousness at home and abroad. Two poems from *The Great Book of Gaelic* follow—in the original Gaelic, with English translations. The illuminated versions of those poems, featuring the art of Alan Davie and Scott Kilgour, are reproduced on the last page of the gallery of color images. All of the original exhibition pages, with accompanying verse and extensive commentaries, are represented in *An Leabhar Mòr/The Great Book of Gaelic* (Edinburgh: Canongate Books, 2002).

GAN AINM
(anonymous)
c. 900–1000

Scél Lem Dúib

Scél lem dúib:
    dordaid dam;
snigid gaim;
    ro-fáith sam;

Gáeth ard úar;
    ísel grían;
gair a rrith;
    ruirthech rían;

Rorúad rath;
    ro cleth cruth;
ro gab gnáth
    giugrann guth.

Ro gab úacht
    etti én;
aigre ré —
    é mo scél.

Brief Account

Brief account:
    Stag's complaint.
Cold front.
    Summer's spent.

High cold blow.
    Sun holds low.
Short the day.
    Sea just spray.

Bracken brown,
    Broken down.
Geese all mouth,
    Heading south.

Chilled each quill.
    Feathers' flurry.
Weather's hoary.
    End of story!

Translator: Fearghas
MacFhionnlaigh

Máirtín
Ó Direáin
1910–1988

Bí i do Chrann

Coigil do bhrí,
A fhir an dáin,
Coigil faoi thrí,
Bí i do chrann.

Coigil gach ní,
A fhir an dáin,
Ná bog ná lúb
Roimh anfa an cháis.

Fan socair,
Fan teann,
Is fair an uain
Go dtaga do lá.

Corraíodh an ghaoth,
A fhir na laoithe,
Gach duille ort thuas;
Do stoc bíodh buan.

Uaigneach crann
I lár na coille,
Uaigneach file
Thar gach duine.

Daingean crann
I dtalamh suite,
Cosa i dtaca
Cuir, a fhile!

Coigil do chlí,
Coigil d' aird,
Coigil gach slí
I gcomhair an dáin.

Tá do leath baineann,
A fhir an dáin,
Bí fireann, bí slán,
Bí i do chrann.

Be as a Tree

Man who makes poems,
Keep back their true import,
Conceal by three,
Be as a tree.

Gather in all that's known,
Man who makes poems,
Don't stir, don't bend
Before this present tempest.

Stay steady,
Unswaying,
Watching the weather
Until the right day.

Let the wind disarray,
Maker of lays,
All your outer foliage;
Your trunk don't budge.

A tree is alone
In the wood's midst,
Among people a poet
Above all is loneliest.

A tree is steadfast
In its portion of land,
Poet, set yourself, man,
Take a stand!

Save your frame,
Gather your knowing,
Focus in every way
Prepared for the poem.

Maker of poems,
You are half womanly,
Be male, be whole,
Be as a tree.

Translator: Colm Breathnach

Myths and Mind-sets, or How Can We Be Real?

DECLAN McGONAGLE

Irish people at the beginning of a new century have a challenging task: to try to construct a real identity in an unreal world—a world being globalized on a base of narrow ideological values which are disempowering for a majority of people on the planet. This requires an intentional cultural practice and a cultural consciousness parallel to those enlisted in the service of the nation's economic and social development. I refer to a deliberate re-imagining of what we Irish have inherited and to a self-conscious construction of identity based on what we can now make and do to add value to the quality of our lives. A culture that merely absorbs global norms is a culture at risk, because the commonality of global consumerism—and that is what is on offer—leads to a commonality of passive consumption, rather than active participation and creative development.

The norms of global commerce do not really entail a vision of a global community, functioning in a real democratic space, but ratify a thin version of democracy, a one-dimensional version of human experience. Global marketers see community as a worldwide field of exchange in which we are allowed the right to make choices, but only from a consumerist menu. The pressing question, therefore, is, How do we construct and sustain viable, local identities—how can we be real, or authentic, not just nostalgic? How can we be culturally present, in the face of commercial imperatives that work to confirm the alienating "surreality" of a culture of global consumerism? And what role can the arts play in that process? Because of rapid economic development in Ireland since the mid-1990s, these are crucial questions.

A generation of artists in Ireland is attempting, in their work, to articulate points of interaction between local identity in an Irish context and a transnational perspective. (Photos of the artworks mentioned here are included in the volume's color gallery.) Of interest as an early effort is the video installation *Greetings* (1996), in which the young Irish artist Caroline McCarthy presents, on two video monitors, archetypal images of the Irish landscape—wet, green, and misty—into which, at the bottom of each screen, the head of the artist appears momentarily and then disappears from view. As a young Irish woman, McCarthy is saying she has no purchase on this landscape and its received meanings. She and her generation simply do not inhabit the inherited pastoral myth. Instead, she and they have set out to renegotiate projections of innocence, of a natural state that is the globally recognized "Ireland brand," a brand that has functioned externally but also defined a sense of self internally for many Irish people in the twentieth century.

One of the themes of this book is the socioeconomic implications of Ireland's position as the most globalized economy in the world. And in any thoroughgoing consideration of this issue, the arts must be positioned as a process crucial to the weave of Irish society today.

Historically, the dominant conditioning model for art in relation to nonartists, to people in general, has been the passive, consumer model. This model is an aspect of what I would call "signature" culture, in which the artist is defined as genius and artistic engagement as necessarily hierarchical. This model holds all but artists, a cultural elite, outside the circle of artistic value—standing mute, mere noncreative onlookers. But a new model of active cultural participation is possible and necessary. It can and has to be articulated and put in place alongside, functioning in tandem with, but not as a replacement for, existing models of signature culture.

The great illusion of signature culture is that it adheres to values and standards that are somehow objective, independent, and unconditioned by social circumstances. Thus, a complex and powerful framework that actually holds signature value in place, by giving it context and meaning, is effectively denied. The fiction is that art stands and speaks for itself and that quality is naturally determined, or that art emerges spontaneously, as though from a state of elemental nature.

In the West, dominant concepts of the production and distribution of art are tacitly governed by this view. Many practitioners will argue that natural, if trained, creative genius ensures artistic quality and excellence, thus unselfconsciously affirming their special status in terms of their individual signature as artists. The position has an internal consistency and validity, but, as I have suggested, it is based on a problematic, exclusivist claim to truth. The assumption is that the artist alone, somehow located beyond society, occupying a "scouting," avant-garde position, gives art its value. Such frontier thinking implicitly relies on what I think of as a particularly white Anglo-Saxon perspective on history. The idea is that culture unfolds in a way that serves the interests of a meritocracy that is somehow preferred by God and is given the authority to control an end in sight.

I remember Protestant protestors in Northern Ireland shouting, "We are the people" in the face of the emerging civil rights campaign of the late 1960s. The meaning, whether those individuals who were shouting knew it or not, was, "We are the people in charge of history." And for a period in Northern Ireland they were, indeed, the people who exercised non-negotiable power. That power could not be altered by electoral process because the sectarian fault line guaranteed a gerrymandered majority/minority situation which, at root, was cultural, as well as political and religious. The battle cry, in other words, represented a fundamental mind-set, a self-validating sense that was based on a myth of the way that things naturally and elementally are and must always be.

Foundation myths of this kind have served to fix cultural identities on each side of the sectarian fault line. This is clearly suggested by two text murals in Derry City in Northern Ireland. One, at the entrance to the Catholic Bogside area, famously states, "You Are Now Entering Free Derry," marking the point beyond which the area was a "no-go" for security forces in the early 1970s. The other, which is much less well known but is equally significant, stands at the entrance to a small Protestant area, known as the Fountain, on the fringe of Derry city center, and states, "No Surrender. Londonderry Loyalists. Still Under Siege." Each statement articulates a foundation myth for the originating community. The Protestant "myth," revolving around being in power, controlling the castle, and not giving it up, is expressed in other slogans and graffiti. Among these are "Not an Inch" and the poetic "We Will Never Forsake the Blue Skies of Ulster for the Grey Skies of An Irish Republic," a slogan which Derry-based artist Willie Doherty used in an early black-and-white photo-text work. Such sentiments contrast with the more aspirational expressions of the Catholic "myth" of not having power: "Tiocfaid Ar La" (Our Day Will Come) and, borrowed from the American civil rights movement of the 1960s, "We Shall Overcome," among others.

The political fault line articulated in the language of local cultural identities, myths, and mind-sets is "Continental" in the sense that it dates from the issues of Royal succession that played out on the European stage in the seventeenth century. Until very recently, we in Ireland inhabited a conceptual topography that had been mapped, in socio-political-cultural terms, in that era. Whereas in other parts of Western Europe many issues of contested identity seemed to have been resolved, or, if not resolved, then outgrown and no longer the cause of conflict and violence, the clash of inherited mind-sets festered for centuries in Ireland, extending right up to the present.

My point is that, in the particular context of Ireland, the root of conflicting identities and contested power is fundamentally cultural and will only be transformed or outgrown when it is fully addressed, culturally. I am also suggesting that the particular context of Ireland and its recent model of negotiation in political space, if connected to a new model of arts and cultural space as similarly negotiable rather than fixed, can also transform the nature and role of art.

In this framework, art is to be understood as lateral rather than linear, that is, as synchronically generated across the breadth of a changing culture, rather than as a line of exclusivist, modernist activity, traced out over time, within it. Art in this context serves to re-imagine Ireland in forms that have something of enormous value to say to the world, without self-regard or parody. Such an outlook accords with a wider, powerful redefinition of artist and the arts process. Such a model moves beyond time-honored notions of the artist as signature producer to the idea of artist as "negotiator." The artist now stands in negotiation with tradition and history, with the present, with context and social processes, and with lived experience.

In his color photowork *Longing/Lamenting* (1987), Willie Doherty addresses the issue of duality—with emblematic images of land (green grass) and sky (bright blue and virtually cloudless)—with the words "LAMENTING" and "LONGING" superimposed in white text. Doherty has developed as a leading artist of his generation, internationally as well as nationally, and is unambiguous in his statement that landscape is ideological, that meanings are projected onto nature, through which it is re-presented as subject. Doherty's important complementary works *Incident* and *Border Incident,* a matched pair of aluminum-based, Cibachrome photographs of two burnt-out cars on two different country roads, take this concept further. Doherty is playing with the expectations and knowledge that a viewer generally brings to the work in a gallery: namely that, however seductive, these are images depicting the jarring results of political violence.

The use of the word "border" in one title does take the viewer in this direction. But, in fact, one of the cars had merely been burnt-out in the process of dumping it, for domestic rather than political reasons. The other had, indeed, been burnt-out after an "incident" close to the border between the Republic of Ireland and Northern Ireland, close to Derry City, where the artist still lives. The issue thus becomes the construction of meaning in viewers' minds and the issue of how re-presentations are negotiated in general. There can be no fixed meanings, least of all in photographic media and mass media, which Doherty's works attempt to disrupt.

Northern Ireland, in particular, has been re-presented constantly, internally and externally, over the thirty-year drama of the Troubles, but the representation of "truth" depends on the relative positions of the reporter and the reader. There are at least two sides to every story, and Doherty regularly uses double imagery and/or dual projection in his more recent work, to generate a dialectic into which the viewer/reader can enter and participate in the making of meaning.

A commitment by artists to creating works that serve as media of negotiation, encouraging the general public to view art as one aspect of participatory culture, can have profound consequences. Such intentional developments can create a vital, contemporary framework of support and value for participatory practice in the arts (lateral, inclusive, collaborative, negotiable, and outside modernism). But this framework can also co-exist and interweave with a framework that supports the idea of signature culture (linear, exclusive, individual, and within modernism).

Ezra Pound once said that the role of the modern artist—though he should have more precisely said the modernist artist—was "to make it new." This statement concisely reflects the arrogance of modernism and its relegation of Ireland and places like it to the margins. What I am arguing for is not an Ireland or Irish art as "novel"—the next new thing, in a linear chronology—but as a context with its own dynamic, where the shift to a new paradigm of practice overcomes aesthetic abstraction, prompting artists to take responsibility for their work as vehicles for participatory understanding and mutual appreciation in the world at large.

Paul Seawright, for example, is an artist who uses photography, and the properties of photography, to create images that are specific by-products of the Troubles—like the aftermath of bonfires and the unsentimental interiors of police stations and other security installations—but have the banality of everyday experience and actually reveal something more universal. Policemen and soldiers spend their working lives in such dramatized environments; Seawright presents these environments as brutal and brutalizing and mostly unseen by the public.

Caged Belfast pub entrances, in his 1997 works *Cage I* and *Cage II* (C-type photos on aluminum), are images of structures that were created as protective airlocks, so that people could be seen on security cameras at a distance from actual doors. They are expressions of the visible dislocation and alienation of civil society in both the Protestant and Catholic communities in Belfast, where abnormal architecture and behavior became normal. These images, while resonating specifically to Northern circumstances are also reminiscent of all urban environments in extremis. Seawright's art recalls places where the civil society has lost its cement and people have been brutalized by socioeconomic, or political, or religious factors and by historical divisions. His work thus suggests a sort of parity or universality of disempowerment and the ordinariness and commonality of despair on the basis of class.

Without a commitment to a participatory culture, a truly civil culture, it will finally not be possible to sustain democracy. By civil culture, I mean a culture belonging to and shaped by its citizens, one within which art is produced, distributed, and understood as an act of participation and expressive emancipation. A civil culture is culture conceived of as a relation of negotiation in the process of creative production, rather than merely as products received in the act of consumption.

The idea of participatory emancipation and resulting empowerment has, I would argue, been intrinsic to artistic production for millennia. This fact has, however, been obscured and devalued in the nineteenth- and twentieth-century modernist mind-set. Passive consumption is the way that most people now gain purchase on value and status in society. And the psyche of passive consumption yields a mind-set that tends to commodify all human experience—the arts and cultural processes in particular. The logic of passive consumption and commodification is implicit in the modernist promise or offer, and this, suggests the English literary critic John Carey, is the revenge of the bourgeoisie for the emancipation of the working classes in the nineteenth century.

Whether that is the case or not, the fact is that the consumer model of citizenship, which is now being bedded down as the defining model in Ireland, inevitably represents a disabling model for most people. In the Irish context, individual experience is losing its communal dimension, becoming isolated in a culture defined by consumption, a "me-centered" culture that leads to a retreat from the idea of a common civil space. Personal reality is now more and more defined by how many goods one consumes and gathers. Sharing, contact, and mutual participation run counter to the consumer ideal.

Art and artists, and arts programmers have a responsibility to engage social space, to intervene creatively and interactively, to foster forms of negotiation that implicitly affirm commonality and promote community. And in a sense, this is nothing new, just something forgotten, or marginalized. The arts have historically provided a primary means of articulating and communicating what we as humans have in common and how we define and celebrate value in life.

I am not arguing for the replacement of what I have called signature culture, or for burning down the Temples of Culture, or even the temples of shopping. None of this is possible anyway. But the consumerist model of citizenship always means working to someone else's impersonal script, and I am arguing for writing a new cultural script and suggesting that artists are essential to this process on a societal scale. Art can contribute to the telling of another story or stories, not as a postcolonial footnote to a larger narrative in the Irish context, but by establishing a new armature of values more generally, coexistent and in confident negotiation with the existing frameworks of power. The resulting dialectic will be porous and accessible, which is not to say easy.

We should be thinking about and making art "politically," that is, without innocence. This implies an immersion in and renegotiation of the given, of what we inherit, in Ireland and elsewhere, in whatever sphere of human experience. Precedents for this in the Irish context include the *Crane Bag Magazine* from the 1970s and the Field Day Theatre Company's "fifth province" of the 1980s, where the artistic and social dialectic was challenging but nonthreatening.

DECLAN McGONAGLE 〰

The dialectic I am describing is emergent in Ireland, though not yet wholly visible or coherent across artistic practice. But the culture as a whole has been awakened to the possibilities of negotiating communal and social realities by way of the political process in Northern Ireland, and by the Peace Process in general. The renegotiation of inherited narratives has led to the beginnings of a new civil society in Northern Ireland and a new constitutional position in the Republic. In effect there has emerged a new common myth of inclusive values which offers and validates the broadest possible participation in our political power structures. The resulting Agreement is still imperfect and still under construction. But the success of the model of negotiation, which includes the offer of full cultural participation for all parties and entails the granting of a universal parity of esteem, will finally depend on our "cultural" capacities. Our participatory democracy, constructed in a process that allows for the renegotiation of old myths and the divisions they support, will rely especially on the fundamental capacities of language, image making, and the articulation of meaning.

A re-imagined Ireland provides a context of engagement in which artists and writers can articulate and generate new and necessary forms of participatory cultural production and distribution. The conditions are not unique to Ireland, but perhaps uniquely among highly industrialized and commercialized cultures, we Irish find ourselves forced to come to terms with radical conflicts between our "long story" and our "short story," between tradition, community, and a new individualism.

Sociologists talk about our contemporary "collision culture," referring to a clash between ancient and mythical ideas of the nation and a new sense of national self based on very recent economic growth and social change. As a society we are positioned in the middle of this dynamic, trying to negotiate a productive future and to construct a civil reality that supports an armature of multidimensional, multicultural values. In a re-imagined space, we are being called to develop further the capacity to bridge to new positions, to generate and hold in play more than one way of being Irish in the world.

My point is that we can neither abrogate these challenges and rely on the anesthetizing comforts of life in a consumer culture, nor revert to some idealized and also incapacitating myth of our traditional culture—which nowadays is often commercially bound up. When we do either, we show ourselves, as do some Northern parties to the Peace Process, more comfortable with an "unreal" life in a sort of virtual, suspended political space than with the task of constructing a "real" identity in the present. Our call is to take political, economic, social, and cultural responsibility for our condition in the world, in the present tense, from here on.

Of course, this argument also has specific force for Irish artists who have absorbed the stories of Nationalism and conceive their work within a signature model of practice that is disconnected and therefore, supposedly, not responsible. The call is to be engaged, and to be engaged is to take on the social and moral responsibilities of art as well as its aesthetic responsibilities. It is to do more than seek to ride an aesthetic wave, being rewarded for providing one more distracting opportunity for consumption.

There are increasing numbers of artists who do take responsibility for their work in the world, who make art politically, without innocence, and address the power processes, whether their art "moments" are realized within or without the white or black box. The issue, after all, is not about changing the location of the art experience, but about changing the ideology of the experience. To take such responsibility in the Irish context is to acknowledge the dualities which define our experience, Irish/English, North/South, local/global but also rural/urban, male/female, and currently, in the larger urban centers in Ireland, black/white.

The fault lines of power amplified by political violence in Northern Ireland during the last thirty years have, in the same period in the Republic, been localized, first, in issues of gender and, latterly, in issues of economic and social relations. Artists, mostly based in the Republic, have extensively explored, alongside practitioners in other disciplines, the issue of female/male relations.

The idea that the female is feral—automatically, somehow—is both a pagan and a Christian concept and is present, in particular, in the work of Alice Maher, an artist who has made sculptures, paintings, and striking large-scale charcoal drawings of hair. Her regular use of real hair and equivalent materials, like flax, reflect the idea that women's hair, particularly in abundance, is associated not just with beauty, but with wildness and witchery. Her highly seductive *Berry Dress* (1994) is at one level just a reminiscence about a type of seasonal pantheist activity in premodern communities. But this small-scale, pretty work—a child's dress cased in luscious red paint with hundreds of berries attached to the lower part of the dress—reveals how beauty may coexist with aggression and pain. When installed for viewing on a glass shelf, positioned slightly above eye level, the inside of the work is seen as a forest of pins that are actually holding each individual berry in place.

From this perspective the work looks, at best, like an apparatus of penance and, at worst, like an instrument of torture. As with her *Staircase of Thorns* (1997), *Berry Dress* deals with ideas of pleasure and pain, the pious and the profane, by insisting on the availability, indeed the presence, of duality.

One of the defining shifts unique to the twentieth century, and one that challenged modernism, was the naming of the unconscious. Dorothy Cross's work often combines this idea with an emphasis on sexuality, using startling combinations of materials—for example, cowhides with udders and dressmaker's mannequins—in her sculptures and installations, which express a surreal sense of the properties of objects in relation to the female image.

Cross's *Teacup* (1997), a video work which is shown on an editing monitor, uses a nostalgic, stereotypical folk image from the West of Ireland—fisherman rowing a *curragh* (a fragile, wooden-framed, tarred-hide boat) in a rough sea. The moving image, which is a clip from Robert Flaherty's film *Man of Aran* (1934), is digitally superimposed on the surface of the tea in a china cup that is filmed complete, on a saucer with a willow pattern, underneath it a lace tablecloth. The fault line being exposed and explored is that between nature and culture, trapped in a struggle as never-ending as the fisherman's battle with the sea—especially when acted out, mythically, in the West of Ireland, now less a place than an idea. The overall effect—touching on memory, history, man, and nature—is a kind of shorthand for arguments about the meaning of Ireland and the nature of the Irish mind as contested and contesting sites. The piece alludes to fault lines that, as the clouds of the Northern "Troubles" seem to evaporate, are increasingly visible in Ireland.

Throughout his career, Shane Cullen has taken the ordinary apparatus of official bureaucracies, like train timetables (in the case of an early work, the timetable to Auschwitz), to create revelatory effects that evoke "the banality of evil." Juxtaposing the ordinary and the monstrous in social space, he explores the much-discussed distinction between a fixed "official" Ireland and an "unofficial" Ireland that must be lived day to day, an Ireland in which one has to negotiate multiple realities.

Cullen's work may often be monumental, but the message he conveys is not the information of official monuments. His *Fragmens sur les Institutions Républicaines IV* (1993–97), 16 feet tall and running 192 feet, is intended to be installed to surround the viewer. The artist selected excerpts from highly unofficial, secret messages—the "comms," or communications, written on cigarette papers and smuggled in and out of the Long Kesh/Maze Prison by the IRA, up to and during the Hunger Strikes of 1981. He painstakingly stenciled and hand-painted the texts on this monumental scale. The work has been exhibited in museums and alternative art spaces, galleries and centers in Ireland, England, Europe, and the United States. Far from denying fault lines, this installation holds in tension the personal and the official—echoing the voices of those imprisoned, evoking the form of the very structure in which they found themselves contained.

Art and culture are contested processes, not consensual, and therefore negotiable. And it could be said that the negotiable space of the Irish mind is the ideal zone in which to explore, construct, and test new possibilities for understanding and artistic expression in what for many of us has become a secular, post-faith era.

Brian Friel has described the Irish condition as "speaking English, thinking Irish." Of course, he did not mean literally thinking in the Irish language. He was describing the coexistence in one "body" of competing mind-sets. A collision of cultural, therefore political, continental plates has been manifest in Ireland and metaphorically describes a condition of the Irish mind that has prevailed for some time. But the same collision of competing mind-sets is now also visible in the wider world, dramatized but not explained by the catastrophic cultural-political intersections of September 11, 2001, and its aftermath.

Ireland cannot call for cultural coexistence or the validation of multidimensional human experience on the basis of its economic or political weight in the world. But our artists and writers have been taking steps to advance that argument culturally. In re-imagining Ireland—a cultural act—it may also be possible, and it is certainly necessary, also to create a model for re-imagining the world.

A number of contemporary Ireland's artistic "voices"—mentioned in Declan McGonagle's essay—are represented in this gallery of color images. The works included are from the Irish Museum of Modern Art and were featured in the Irish Art Today exhibition at the University of Virginia Art Museum, as part of the "Re-Imagining Ireland" program. Also included in the gallery are two images by Scottish artists featured in the *Leabhar Mòr na Gaeilge*, which in abbreviated form had its North American debut during the conference, in the Dome Room of the University of Virginia Rotunda.

Dorothy Cross, *Teacup*, 1997, single-channel video. (Courtesy of Kerlin Gallery, Dublin)

Comrade, What a day - a real super effort!! Don't know whether to laugh shout or cry. The news was greeted here in silent jubilation (we are very security conscious you see!!) Now I wonder will the opposition be just as quick to declare that the IRA have that popular support they were claiming would be seen if we won this seat. Good old Austin [Currie] was quick to say we hadn't and it wasn't a vote for the RA [Republican Army]. Up yours too, Austin my boy. Just looking at the figures; it would appear that our honourable opponent, farmer West, received an amount of nationalist votes - fair play to the dear sensible bastard. Up theirs too!! Onward to victory. Hope you have sobered up sunshine I'm sitting here picturing the heap of you swilling down loads of black brew and making right idiots of yourselves and boy am I jealous??... I'm away here to relax for a wee while. The strain of this last week has been too much man!! Congrats to one and all you wonderful people. We really showed them. Take care and God Bless... Up the good old RA and other such outrageous outbursts. Nite, nite and God Speed. Bik.

Liam Óg 10.4.81 from Tony H5

...Fr. Murphy was in his (Ray's) cell tonight and told him he was talking to Bobby this evening after the election result. Bobby was having a bath and was overjoyed. Fr. Murphy was saying that he thought that there was a good chance that the British Government will act on the issue now seeing as we got 30,000 people to stand behind us. He added that he was also talking to Frank and he was very happy with the result...Comrade I find words hard to describe the jubilation felt here this evening. With the result of the election there is a feeling here tonight which has not been here in a long time. The screws are visibly shattered already - just great.

Brownie [Gerry Adams] 29.4.81 from Bik

Comrade Mór, got your very welcome comm, today. Good to hear from you. This is really some situation isn't it? A terrific thought struck me two days ago and that was that there was every possibility the Brits will not say anything at all or make any attempt at dipping in attractive offers, but just stand back and let things run their course. I think your analysis of the Brit mentality is about as close as anyone can come i.e. their stupidity is unbelievable. I still don't think they have learned that oppression breeds resistance and further oppression - further resistance!! As for their arrogance - I never saw the likes of it (of course I'm not a much travelled individual but I reckon I'd have to go a long way to meet persons of a similar 'superior' nature). However, as you said, they will regret their stupidity. How I wish I were out - just to light the blue touch paper and retire if you know what I mean!! Old habits die hard though some of mine had to be re-directed as you well know. Anyway, one day I'll make a few noises in the right sectors. Now, where was I? Yes, Brit arrogance. I mind Tom McKearney quoted me a bit of Rudyard Kipling (I think that's the guy who makes exceedingly good cakes!) According to old Rudy the British are immune to logic - a sensible enough assertion I would say. They're the only people I know who are perfectly correct when they are entirely wrong. I was over there a couple of years and found that this attitude was prevalent among all classes. Though I suppose it's wrong of me to generalize in such a manner. Oh balls to the British - why waste skibs and ink? As you know I saw Bob on Saturday - it was quite an experience and in all honesty I haven't felt the same since. I just had a short yarn with him and when I was preparing to leave he said quietly: 'I'm dying Bik.' Don't think I can describe how I felt just then. I couldn't say anything except God Bless. I told him I'd see him again very soon and he just gave me a quiet laugh. Man, what a feeling!!...

To Liam Óg 29.4.81 12.30 A.M. (of 30th)

Shane Cullen, panel from *Fragmens sur les Institutions Républicaines IV,* 1993–97, text on Styrofoam panels, 12 blocks, 98⅞ × 189 × 2½ in. each. (Collection of The Irish Museum of Modern Art; purchased 2000)

Willie Doherty, *Incident*, 1993, Cibachrome on aluminum, 49½ × 73½ in. (Collection of The Irish Museum of Modern Art; purchased 1994)

Willie Doherty, *Border Incident*, 1994, Cibachrome on aluminum, 49½ × 73½ in. (Collection of The Irish Museum of Modern Art; purchased 1994)

Willie Doherty, *Longing/Lamenting,* 1987, color photographs with text (2 panels), 30 × 40 in. each. (Collection of The Irish Museum of Modern Art; donated by Dorothy Walker)

Alice Maher, *Berry Dress*, 1994, rosehips, cotton, paint, sewing pins, 12 × 10 × 6 in. (Collection of The Irish Museum of Modern Art; purchase from the Foley Fund)

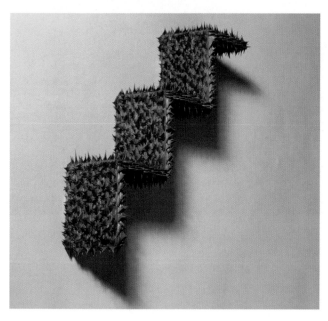

Alice Maher, *Staircase of Thorns*, 1997, rose thorns and wood, 15 × 15 × 4 in. (Private collection, Dublin)

Caroline McCarthy, *Greetings,* 1996, video installation. (Collection of The Irish Museum of Modern Art; purchased 1996)

Paul Seawright, *Cage I,*
1997, C-type photograph
on aluminum, 80 × 64 in.
(Collection of The Irish
Museum of Modern Art;
purchased 1997)

Paul Seawright, *Gate,*
1997, C-type photograph
on aluminum, 64 × 64 in.
(Collection of The Irish
Museum of Modern Art;
purchased 1997)

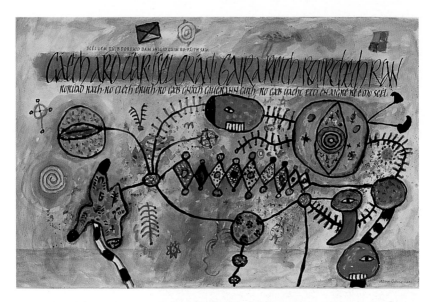

Alan Davie, *Scél Lem Dúib*, 2001, from *An Leabhar Mòr na Gaeilge;* Louise Donaldson, calligrapher.

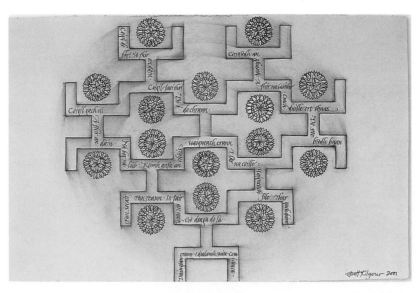

Scott Kilgour, *Bí i do Chrann*, 2001, from *An Leabhar Mòr na Gaeilge;* David McGrail, calligrapher.

Re-Imagining
Irish Music and Dance

MICK MOLONEY

Irish music and dance traditions are among the most visible global symbols of Irishness in the world today, defining and articulating a cultural center at a time of unprecedented social change at home and abroad. Most performing artists, enthusiasts, and cultural commentators would probably agree that Irish music and dance are enjoying the best of times in an extraordinary cultural renaissance.

There are, of course, multiple genres of Irish music. They range from older traditional styles of playing and singing to classical Irish music in the European tradition; the fifes, drums, flutes, and lambegs of the Northern Unionists; the modern rock sounds of world-famous groups like U2, the Cranberries, and the Corrs; the musical fusions created by composers such as Bill Whelan; and the magisterial collaborations between traditional and classical musicians, spearheaded by innovators like Micheal Ó Súilleabháin and Shaun Davey.

Then there is the vast trove of musical expressions associated with the Irish Diaspora around the world: songs of the Irish transported to the British colonies, songs of the Irish laborer in England, songs of the Irish fishermen and loggers in the Canadian Maritime Provinces, and the many traditions of popular music and song associated with the Irish in America.

Over the past two centuries, Irish and Irish American traditional, classical, popular, and various hybrid musical forms have emerged, coalesced, and sometimes vanished at different times and under different conditions. Minstrelsy, Irish American Tin Pan Alley songs, vaudeville routines; the pub-singing genre pioneered by the Clancy Brothers and Tommy Makem, Sean O'Riada, and Ceoltóirí Cualann; the Chieftains, Horslips, and Irish folk rock; Planxty and the Bothy Band in the 1970s; and, of course, *Riverdance* are just a few examples of innovative Irish or Irish American musical hybrids. And then there are Irish artists such as U2, the Cranberries, the Corrs, and Van Morrison who have gained an international reputation playing music that derives its primary inspiration from British and American rock genres.

Millions of people are purchasing recordings and videos of Irish music and dance in stores, by mail order, and online all over the world. Outlets for the music have increased dramatically; one can hear Irish music today inter-nationally at concerts and festivals, in bars and clubs, on radio and TV, and in films. Irish musicians and dancers in large numbers are making a full-time living. Thousands more have become accomplished performing artists, mak-ing a part-time living from their art. And more men and women than ever before from within and outside the ancestral culture are learning to perform Irish music and dance.

What is really Irish about the disparate approaches to Irish music that are emerging in Ireland and in the Diaspora? What is Irish, for example, about music in the western classical style that is written in Ireland by Irish-born composers? What does it owe to Ireland and what does it owe to European high-art traditions? What is Irish about the music of U2, for example, beyond the obvious fact that the band members are Irish-born? Have jazz or experi-mental music played in Ireland any real claim to being "Irish"?

These are all questions that are being posed in contemporary Irish musi-cological studies, amid perceptions that certain forms of musical discourse have been privileged over other forms by popular acclaim and also by aca-demic institutions and cultural organizations. Such privileging is often cri-tiqued as motivated by a barely concealed agenda of cultural nationalism which has its roots in the romantic nation-building movements of the nine-teenth century.[1] The debate is often intense.

Against this backdrop is the simple fact that Irish people have chosen to express many of their deepest cultural concerns through certain genres of music and song, doing so during centuries of political and social strife and resistance to colonial rule. Over the past two hundred years, major themes in Irish history and social life have also been addressed through music, and

MICK MOLONEY

music in its various forms remains one of the most powerful connections that the Irish have to their cultural identity—and indeed to multiple cultural identities.

One of those identities is said to be "Celtic." And the question, "What is Celtic?" is about as tricky as the issue of what "Irish" may mean. The "Re-Imagining Ireland" conference was held in the southern United States, a region with a large population that can lay claim to both Irish and Scottish ancestry. Clearly there are historic and cultural connections between the peoples of Ireland, Scotland, Wales, Brittany, Galicia, and other European regions. But is "Celtic" today simply a term that denotes ancestral connections? Or does use of the term imply that there are contemporary cultural connections, and are those connections informed by historical commonalities? Is the whole concept of a Pan Celtic identity largely amplified if not entirely invented by cultural nationalists like the great Breton musician Alan Stivell? Is it a notion that stresses cultural commonalities, primordial ancestral connections, and a unified history marked by marginalization and oppression, by which identity is deliberately suppressed as part of colonial policy? And inevitably then the next question is: even if this is so, then how are these connections constructed or articulated? Which voices are heard in public on this subject? Usually they are not the voices of the performing artists, most of whom quickly tire of this backdrop of ideological fulminations and simply want to get on with their art.

It seems clear that the term "Celtic" has widely different meanings to different people. It may mean little to many in the "Celtic" countries themselves. Does it mean more perhaps in the United States, where the word "Celtic" has become synonymous with the mass marketing of cultural symbols, particularly Celtic music, as commodities to be bought and sold?

Of course, all musics created in Ireland or by Irish composers in the Diaspora can validly claim a measure of Irishness. I would like to look at one of these forms, the music generally known as traditional Irish instrumental music, and the ability to sustain itself that it has shown over time. This music has preserved a core identity while accommodating a variety of outside influences—an experience that indeed encapsulates the general cultural history of the island itself.

While there are seemingly never-ending discussions about its precise parameters, the art form known as traditional Irish instrumental music both within and outside Ireland is the music played in a distinctive style on instruments such as the fiddle, uilleann pipes, flute, concertina, accordion, tenor banjo, and tin whistle with a variety of accompanying instruments such as the bodhrán, piano, guitar, bouzouki, and keyboards. There is also the tradition of the Irish harp, once an elite instrument, which since the late eighteenth century has been emblematic of the country of Ireland itself.

In any historical discussion of Irish traditional music, the first point that should be made is that innovation and modernization have always been the cornerstones of this music rather than a rigid conformity to artistic norms—which is an idea more often than not associated with antiquarian notions of tradition.

There are many pervasive myths about Irish traditional music—the biggest of all being that it is very old. There are some mediaeval strains in the music, particularly in the nondance forms, and some traditions such as the music of the harpers can be traced back to the seventeenth century. But the form, structure, and style of the traditional music played today in fact come from the late nineteenth and early twentieth centuries. Most of the repertoire is in fact post-Famine.[2] It is a music based on a strophic eight-bar system in which two, or sometimes more, eight-bar strains are repeated a limited number of times. This is a structure shared by the whole Anglo Celtic Diaspora in the instrumental dance music of Ireland, Scotland, and the Maritime Provinces of Eastern Canada, New England, and Appalachia.

Even the now-dominant social context for informal traditional music making is new. For every serious Irish traditional musician, the group musical "session" is a home base—a kind of regenerating chamber to which one returns for grounding and inspiration. If polled informally, most musicians would probably say that gathering for a session is an age-old custom. In fact, the pub session is of very recent origin, dating back probably no earlier than the early 1950s, beginning in London and New York.

It's nice to be involved in something that is rooted in ancient mystery rather than contemporary history. Thus many of us thrive on myths that cite an invented antiquity for our music. We do so partly because of an inherited ideology of cultural nationalism, but maybe also because the notion of antiquity in times of rapid change somehow helps to ground us. This in fact may be the key to the enduring contemporary appeal of the term "Celtic" as a mass-marketing tool.

Again, the fact is that most Irish dance tune genres such as jigs, reels, and hornpipes are imported forms, probably some derived from England and others like the polka, schottische, waltz, and mazurka from Continental Europe.[3] Most of the instruments on which Irish traditional music is typically played came from England or Continental Europe into the musical culture in the eighteenth and nineteenth centuries. The fiddle arrived in the early eighteenth century, the flute a few decades later. The concertina, melodeon, and accordion enter at various points in the nineteenth and early twentieth centuries. Their accommodation was often contested vigorously. The *Gaelic American* newspaper, for example, issued a call to arms against the increasingly popular accordion:

> The strains of the violin, the pipes or the flute are not heard as frequently or as generally in the land as of old, and in their stead the ears are tormented with the racking, discordant screech of the concertina and accordion. What prompted Irish boys and girls to adopt these instruments of torture and discard the violin, the pipes and the flute, it is hard to find out . . . The man or woman, boy or girl, in sympathy with the revival of things Irish—the music as well as the language of the race—should make a firm resolution and to act up to it, wherever and whenever he or she gets the opportunity, destroy every concertina and accordion that can be reached. The most ear-splitting one of these instruments ever made in Germany is not proof against a scissors or a knife—a hole in the bellows silences it forever. Every concertina or accordion destroyed in Ireland is a blow struck for the restoration of Irish national musical taste . . . Nature loves harmony and will bless you for the act.[4]

The piano begins its journey into Irish music in the immigrant dance halls of Irish America and in the early 78-rpm phonograph recordings made in the United States in the early decades of the twentieth century. The guitar was used sporadically in some of the early 78-rpm recordings but did not enter the music in earnest until the 1960s. It was also in the 1960s that the bouzouki, a Greek instrument, was introduced by genial Johnny Moynihan in the group Sweeney's Men. Only the uilleann pipes, harp, and bodhrán can be considered truly native Irish instruments, and even those did not evolve independently of European influences.

But it's what players of these instruments have to do to be appropriate within the canons of the tradition that ends up being more relevant in determining membership than where the instruments came from and when. It's not necessarily an easy accommodation—as a tenor banjo player I have learned firsthand that the process of acquiring membership in the musical community is not an easy journey.

The tale of how the banjo ended up as an instrument used in traditional Irish music is remarkable, spanning several centuries and involving a great movement of music and musicians across and between three continents. The story of its incorporation in Irish musical culture is a fascinating example of the way a living, dynamic tradition revitalizes itself and accommodates innovation and change in the complex process of its evolution. It is worth telling this story in some detail to underscore the complexity of cultural accommodation and cross-fertilization.

The early origins of the banjo are obscure, but that its precursors came from West Africa to America, probably via the West Indies, is by now well established. The banjo did not arrive from Africa in any literal sense; slaves brought no possessions with them. But they brought the idea with them of an instrument left behind in their tribal culture. The multitude of African peoples, languages, and musics makes it very difficult to associate the banjo with any specific African prototype. From various historical references, however, it can be deduced that the banjar, or bangie, or banjer, or banza, or banjo was played in early seventeenth-century America by Africans in slavery who constructed their instruments from gourds, wood, and tanned skins, using hemp or gut for strings. This prototype was eventually to lead to the evolution of the modern banjo in the late eighteenth and early nineteenth centuries. Until about 1800, the banjo remained essentially an African American instrument. What brought the instrument to the attention of the nation, however, was the grotesque representation of African American culture by white performers in minstrel shows. A great number of the performers in minstrelsy were Irish immigrants—a marginal population performing on a marginal instrument, presenting stereotypical misrepresentations of a group even more stigmatized than themselves.[5]

Though banjos of various kinds were likely brought to Ireland in the early nineteenth century by visitors and returning emigrants, it wasn't until 1843 that the banjo was formally introduced to Ireland in public performance, when the Virginia Minstrels toured in England, Ireland, and France in 1843, 1844, and 1845. Two members of the Virginia Minstrels were Irish Americans. Both of them—Dan Emmett, one of the most prolific songwriters in minstrelsy, and Joel Walker Sweeney, whose antecedents came from County Mayo—were virtuoso banjo players.

The earliest Irish banjos were fretless. Up to the turn of the twentieth century, banjos were generally plucked and strummed by the fingers or a thimble. So originally the banjo was used in Ireland for rudimentary accompaniment of songs and tunes with perhaps some of the simpler melodies being plucked out by the fingers. From the beginning, it was on the fringes of the musical culture adopted primarily by Travellers, who continue to occupy

MICK MOLONEY ๏๏

a marginal role in Irish culture to this day. The instrument was very effective in attracting attention in the kind of outdoor setting where Travellers sold their wares and particularly useful in hawking the broadsheets and song-books that they sold at fairs, horse races, and other public gatherings.

The kind of banjo favored in the music was to change at the turn of the twentieth century. Frets had been added to the instrument in the 1880s, and then steel strings were invented. Influenced by the use of the plectrum in mandolin playing, Irish banjo players in America started to experiment with different plectral playing styles. The idea of tuning the banjo in fifths, just like the fiddle or mandolin, caught on around this time as well. Many players began to remove the short fifth string from the banjo, and, before long, banjo makers started manufacturing four-string banjos, originally called plectrum banjos, which were full-sized twenty-two-fret banjos, just like the five-string banjo. Then, around 1915, the tango, or tenor, banjo was invented, coinciding with the popularity in America of the new exotic dance form imported from Latin America, which was sweeping the nation at the time. The tenor banjo had seventeen or nineteen frets, a shorter neck tuned in fifths just like the mandolin or fiddle, though not at the same pitch, and was played with a plectrum. It was perfect for Irish music, where the majority of the instrumental pieces had been composed by fiddlers. The journey into the Irish musical culture was now complete. Today there are more than five thousand tenor banjo players in Ireland, representing a remarkable transition from the fringes to the center of the tradition in less than a hundred years.[6]

There is of course a central conservative core to the creative process in Irish traditional music, otherwise it could hardly continue to exist as a recognizable art form. What is involved in this core is the preservation of the eight-bar strophic structure and the phenomenon of micro-ornamentation and embellishment on a restricted central theme. This kind of micro-elaboration is a unifying aesthetic in most forms of Irish artistic expression, ranging from Celtic calligraphy to music and dance, and also, I would suggest, in the kind of social interaction one finds everywhere in Ireland, rural and urban.

I remember the first time I visited the town of Duleek in County Meath in the mid-1960s. Duleek was and still is a great place for gossip and yarns, much of it the acerbic variety, and I would sit in the Murray household on many a night and marvel at the litany of stories about local life. One of the most colorful characters in Duleek was a man named Tony Murray who now lives in San Francisco. At some point in the evening, Tony was sure to come in the door with a royal sense of occasion and tell what he'd been up to that night and with whom.

One night he "arrived in" when things were a bit quiet. "You'd never guess what happened to me tonight," says he. And I remember May Murray, who was sitting on the couch, piping up, saying, "Tell us, Tony, and be sure to put a stretch on it."

The memory of that phrase stayed with me because it seemed to sum up something very important and very enduring about an Irish style of artistic expression. In a way, "putting a stretch on it"—an elaboration beyond the functional necessity of conveying mere information—is the cornerstone of what makes for a distinctive Irish style. Such elaboration elevates the prosaic to the artistic and is central to Irish traditional musical expression. Even in conditions of extreme flux, something remains identifiably Irish, and it's always a matter more of style than substance.

What is involved in all excellent performances of traditional music is a highly innovative spinning out of an infinite set of possibilities within an essentially limited structure. Because of the limited structure, the process of creativity in the art of Irish traditional music is a journey that can take two directions. One is to embellish the outer form—that is, add textures, tone colors, and harmonies or indeed new instruments to arrangements of tunes or tune medleys. The other, more fundamental, journey is into the interior landscape of the music, exploring endless melodic and rhythmic possibilities for micro-ornamentation and variation on recurring eight-bar motifs. It's this penchant for variation and ornamentation that makes it easy for musicians to tell the difference between Irish music and other Anglo Celtic genres, even though particular tunes are shared by all these musical traditions.

On a fiddle tour of the United States, which took place in the early 1990s, Irish traditional, Appalachian old-time, bluegrass, and Texas swing styles were showcased. At the end of the tour, Kenny Baker, the great East Tennessee fiddler, was asked if he had ever had an interest in playing Irish music. "Hell, no," he said famously, "I ain't that nervous."

What Kenny was alluding to, of course, was the constant serpentine melodic and rhythmic ornamentation and variation that he heard in the Irish fiddling, a style of playing contrasting sharply with the kind of straight ahead, powerful swing and drive that form the core aesthetic values in his own musical tradition.

The possibilities of elaboration within the eight-bar strophic boundaries are literally endless, and this is in part why so many brilliant contemporary

Irish traditional musicians and composers are perfectly happy to work with this seemingly limited structure. Composers less "enculturated" in the norms of the musical tradition might consider this very constraining, but scores of tune creators in the traditional idiom clearly do not.

Again it must be stressed that these core identificational issues have little to do with the subject of where the instruments or musical forms originally came from. Issues of historical truth may be of considerable importance, however, to members of cultural nationalistic organizations such as the Gaelic League and Comhaltas Ceoltóirí Éireann (the Musicians Association of Ireland), just two of the organizations that at various times between the late nineteenth century and today have appointed themselves as custodians of aspects of the native culture—including sports, language, and music and dance traditions. The Gaelic League began its activities in America after the visit of Douglas Hyde in 1898, and members quickly began to make statements about the notion of purity in Irish culture.

> When the Gaelic League took up the revival of Irish National Dances, it found them, like the language, confined to the last strongholds of the Gael in the remotest sections of the island. In the towns, villages, and less isolated portions of Ireland, the ancient dance like everything else, became Anglicized; vulgarisms like the Lancashire clog, and what the League designates "barrack-room steps," gradually crept into it until the beautiful and time-honored forms of the "poetry of motion" degenerated into an unsightly, unedifying, floor-pounding trial of endurance. The Gaelic League, through a system of elimination, has now the old dance pretty well re-established throughout Ireland. The syllabuses issued by the League for the great dancing contests held under its auspices invariably contain the warning: "Lancashire clog, stage and barrack-room steps barred."

> Where is the land can boast a dance which equals that of Ireland?
> Tis pure in its conception like the music of our Sireland.
> Unlike the waltz and two-step whose morality we question,
> Tis characteristic of our race and free from all suggestion.[7]

These neo-Victorian, puritanical commentaries seem somewhat ridiculous to us today, but the position the Gaelic League took at that time raises a broader question of the value of strong affirmative action toward the traditional arts—the kind of patronage, in essence, that Western elite arts have enjoyed for centuries. Today we celebrate the renaissance of Irish traditional arts, but one could also reflect on the question of whether the art forms could have developed so magnificently if they had not been in effect ghettoized for so long.

Fusion, or syncretism, or hybridization is often defined as the coming together of two or more discrete cultural elements to create a new form. But, paradoxically, all the fusions that have taken place in Irish music and dance recently might not have happened at all had not the core styles and repertoires enjoyed or endured a kind of protectionism determined by a strange combination of circumstance and design. There cannot by definition be a fusion unless the disparate elements that come together exist discretely in the first place. As celebrated an example as *Riverdance* might not have happened at all had there not been an element of institutional protectionism overseen by cultural activists such as the members of the Irish Dancing Commission, an organizational outgrowth of the Gaelic League.

It has become fashionable these days to label leaders of organizations such as the Gaelic League, the Irish Dancing Commission, and Comhaltas Ceoltóirí Éireann as cultural reactionaries, but whatever the internecine organizational politics that play out from time to time internally or on the national stage, these activists are men and women whose primary motivations have always been governed by the highest regard for those aspects of Irish traditional culture that they view as endangered.

Much of the energy of these organizations has been spent in countering the forces of cultural commodification in the global marketplace. In truth, on any occasion when a performance takes place for some kind of financial compensation, then, in a sense, the art performed becomes a commodity. But it is worth making a distinction between the artist's exploitation of his or her own art directly and the packaging and marketing of that art for gain and profit by others. We are now in an era where both happen at a level unknown in the past.

Essentially what we are looking at in the global marketplace, where there are generally no readily identifiable shared cultural norms, is decontextualized art—art as commodity. In the marketplace, the original social functions of art—in other words, the multiple roles it plays or has played in the culture of the traditional society—are irrelevant. Some lament the dislocation of traditional arts from a community matrix, while others see this as a liberation from inherited social, economic, and political constraints—and this freedom, of course, is the very foundation of the Western notion of individual liberty.

MICK MOLONEY ⟨⟩

In Ireland there have been very definite landmarks in the processes that led to the commodification of traditional music over the last half century. These landmarks were all part of the business of creating musical genres that could be presented on stage as acceptable and palatable public performance for nonparticipating, listening general audiences. Those audiences were possessed of disposable income in a new Ireland where the power of a generation of wage earners (unleashed by the economic growth of the 1960s and 1970s) was becoming a decisive social force in determining the shape of market forces—a far cry from the days when the woebegone figure of Blind Raftery played for empty pockets.

Between the late 1950s and the mid-1970s, artists such as Sean O'Riada, Ceoltóirí Cualann, the Chieftains, Planxty, and the Bothy Band became the central figures in a paradigm shift, creating new possibilities in the way that Irish traditional music could be arranged or performed for general audiences, who sought to passively enjoy and then purchase recordings of the music they had heard. During this period, the Irish in growing numbers began to affirm their heritage of traditional music, as the movement to present such music gathered momentum. Such consolidation heralded the beginning of the reversal of negative, some would say postcolonial, attitudes toward the native culture. A tendency which had begun in the 1960s, with the radio broadcasts of Sean O'Riada and Ceoltoiri Cualann and the burgeoning success of Fleadh Cheoil na hÉireann under the stewardship of Comhaltas Ceoltóirí Éireann, would enter a triumphant phase with the dazzling emergence of *Riverdance* on the world stage in the mid-1990s.

It is important to note that cultural symbols and forms of expression can mean one thing in the home country and something quite different in the Diaspora. Shortly after arriving in the United States in 1973, for example, I discovered that Irish traditional music was just one part of an arsenal of potent ethnic symbols that were used to represent Irish ethnic identity in a multicultural society. Paradoxically, the very symbols treated with affection and respect in America—including the shamrock, shillelagh, and leprechaun—were already considered old-fashioned (even embarrassing) back in the home country.

I remember well the first St. Patrick's Day parade that I attended in the United States. It was in Savannah, Georgia, where, along with other Irish musicians, I was hired by a local Irish cultural organization to perform in a 16 March concert and then invited to attend the parade the following day. My fellow Irish-born musicians and I were mortified to find that we seemed to be the only people attending the parade who were not wearing green! It didn't take me long to learn, through people's life stories, that to be Irish in America was very different from being Irish in Ireland. We here were part of a general story in which we were distinguished from others by cultural symbols that have become more potent for the ethnic population than for those left behind in the homeland—a story very familiar to refugee and immigrant populations all over the world.

In all the visits I have made back home over the past thirty years, I have found that Ireland takes its traditional music and musicians far more for granted than do Irish Americans of any generation and, in particular, first-generation immigrant Irish. This is partly because, in the Diasporic context, the "pure drop," however that might be defined, often has more resonance with an immigrant or ethnic audience—confirming a sense of security in familiarity—than do more acculturated musical forms.

There are, of course, major generational differences in audiences that support different kinds of Irish musical events in America as well as differences in class, education, and general musical taste. But I have been involved in programming concerts and festivals in the United States for over thirty years and have learned, often the hard way, that there is an ongoing process of complex negotiation between inherited or acquired musical tastes and the willingness or openness to embrace change.

Audiences in Ireland today seem, however, to have little trouble embracing change. In fact, almost paradoxically, most innovations in Irish music are now far more likely to come from Ireland than from America, a society and culture founded on the willingness to change rather than accept conformity.

Certain varieties of commodified art inevitably end up being more privileged than others in the marketplace. Irish music that is highly arranged, acculturated, and modified has a clear edge in the global market; mass audiences are generally not interested in supporting or consuming less acculturated forms. But the core of traditional Irish musical culture is so strong that there seems little possibility that market forces will lead to the kind of displacement that often happens with art forms that have a weaker foundation. The strength of Irish traditional music can be seen most of all in the remarkable ubiquity of public "sessions" now taking place in bars all around the world.[8] In such settings—thoroughly modern social contexts for music imbued with the behavioral norms of a pre-industrial pastoral culture—the old and the new are found in a state of creative and finely balanced dynamic interplay.

What it comes down to is that in Irish traditional music—and also, I should say, in Irish step dance traditions—the artistic core is so strong and powerful that surface changes or collaborations with nontraditional artists pose little threat to the essence of the tradition. Such collaborations, in fact, have helped to enliven and showcase the music's fundamental power, its adaptive potential, and, most important of all, its *beauty*. Indeed, exposure to Irish-based, highly accessible works produced by popular artists such as Paul Brady, Christy Moore, Moving Hearts, and the Afro Celt Fusion has for many listeners over the years become the first step in a transformative journey into the interior landscape of the deep core of the tradition.

Measured by the level of affirmation at home and abroad, the sheer aesthetic value of Irish music and dance forms has turned out to be as enduring and important as their cultural meaning. Together the power of their appeal has proved irresistible. The art is valid strictly on its own terms. But Irish traditional music and dance also retain their power for every generation because they continue to be imaginatively relevant in periods of dramatic social and cultural change. Without this primary appeal, they would just become museum pieces, admired at a distance, remnants of a once-great tradition. Extreme cultural nationalists might favor this kind of pristine preservation over a more acculturated living variety. But the music and dance would then exist in a vacuum, having lost their connection to a living tradition. Instead, in a time of unparalleled global transformation, the traditional music and dance emphatically ground Irish culture. They have demonstrated that they can have enduring parallel half-lives as both abstracted art objects and cultural icons and have become in the process a roaring success in the global marketplace—one that defines and validates Irishness across the world.

NOTES

1. A series of issues of the *Journal of Music in Ireland* in 2002 and 2003 featured an ongoing lively debate on this topic. Much of the debate was focused on Irish classical composition, which, in the view of regular contributors, has been relegated to the perimeter of Irish music by cultural biases. The same argument is presented forcibly by Harry White in *The Keeper's Recital: Music and Cultural History in Ireland, 1770–1970*, in *Critical Conditions: Field Day Essays and Monographs 6* (South Bend and Dublin: University of Notre Dame Press, 1998).

2. Reg Hall offers a good discussion of the post-Famine social and cultural context of the traditional music. See Reginald Hall, *The Crossroads Conference 1996* (Dublin: Ossian Publications, 2000), 77–82.

3. See Breandán Breathnach, *Folk Music and Dances of Ireland* (Dublin: Talbot Press, 1971) and Fintan Vallely, ed., *Companion to Irish Music* (Cork: University College Cork and New York: New York University Press, 2000). Both contain extensive general historical information on the evolution of Irish traditional music forms, individual and regional style, and the incorporation of instruments into the musical tradition.

4. *Gaelic American* (New York), 16 December 1905, 4.

5. For a good general history of the banjo in nineteenth-century America, see Karen Linn, "That Half Barbaric Twang," in *The Banjo in American Popular Culture* (Chicago: University of Illinois Press, 1994) and Philip F. Gura and James F. Bollman, "America's Instrument," in *The Banjo in the Nineteenth Century* (Chapel Hill: University of North Carolina Press, 1999).

6. Ireland's primary banjo maker and repair expert, Tom Cussen from Clarinbridge, Co. Galway, has informally come up with this total from his extensive database.

7. *Gaelic American* (New York), 14 July 1907.

8. The traditional Irish music session is a complex, rule-ordered, uniquely open event located in public space where good manners and neighborliness are expected and, indeed, demanded. Even the least-accomplished aspiring musician, drunk or sober, should he or she interfere with the dynamics of a session, would rarely be confronted publicly but dealt with indirectly, in a manner least designed to ruffle sensibilities.

MICK MOLONEY ೧౨

Re-Imagining Irish Traditional Music

NICHOLAS CAROLAN

Irish traditional music is a large subject. There has been human settlement on the island of Ireland now for over nine thousand years, so there has been traditional song in Ireland for over nine thousand years—and in many languages, not just in the most recent Irish and English and their many dialects. There has been traditional dance in Ireland for over nine thousand years because dance, like song, is universal in the human species. Instrumental music isn't, but for various reasons, including our knowledge of ancient European music, it is highly probable that musical instruments have been played in Ireland for over nine thousand years.

As I say, it's a large subject. And yet it can have a simplicity.

When I was trying to imagine what "re-imagining Irish traditional music" might mean, it seemed to me at first that imagination would be most called for in relation to the future of this music. That seemed obvious. But the future of Irish traditional music is not, in fact, too hard to imagine because we are already in that future and have been entering it warily and with many misgivings for more than a hundred years now. We are now in what I would call the Second Age of Irish traditional music.

What does that mean? Why is it the Second Age? What was the First Age?

The First Age of Irish traditional music began when the first settlers came to Ireland from Britain in the Mesolithic or Middle Stone Age, and it began to end in December 1877. All performances of Irish song, instrumental music, and dance in those first nine and more millennia—no matter what the language of the song, or the technology of the musical instrument, or the grouping of the dance—all performances had one thing in common: they were all actual real live performances happening in real time. In hut or in hall, a living person had to sing, play, or dance for or with other living people who were actually there, who were actually looking at him or her in the same space, who were forming with him or her an actual living breathing musical community.

And all the consequences that flowed from that un-notated reality defined Irish traditional music in the past, defined its age-old processes of creation, performance, transmission, preservation, and survival in a highly varied patchwork of myriad versions and local traditions. The composer made the music in his or her head or on his or her fingers. The composition was held in memory. Its nature was partly governed in mnemonic structures and devices by the human need for repetition, and partly in original motifs and phrases by the human need for change and novelty. Sooner or later a new composition was performed live, probably to an audience. The audience learned it by ear, or forgot it, or changed it. The pupil learned from the master. Everything was personal, face-to-face. It was the old oral/aural world of tradition. What happened in December 1877 to change that essential unity? What began to usher in the Second Age? Something profound. In that month and year, in the United States, Thomas Edison invented sound recording.

Now the necessary link between performance and the old lived reality was broken. Now it became possible to put a musician in a box, to listen to the dead, to make the piper on the record play the tune over and over and over, quickly or slowly—and now he played it exactly the same every time. Space had been abolished along with death, time, and human interaction.

You might never have been to Donegal, but now in some way you could know the music of Donegal. Now the visual dimension was gone: listening to a recording you couldn't necessarily tell whether the musician was young or old, male or female. Since the recorded performance was unchanging, the need for novelty had to be satisfied now by more and more recorded performances by more and more performers—far, far more than could ever have been experienced in the old world. The communality of the old lived occasion was gone. You didn't know the musician, and he or she didn't know you. You could now listen to this music as you drove by yourself from Dublin to Cork, or New York to Los Angeles, or Tashkent to Beijing. Sound recording enabled the exportation of Irish traditional music in boxes, and transformed it from national forms of music to global forms. The beginning fiddler sits in Tokyo and receives personal tutorials by Internet from Ireland. Soon the position will be reversed. We in Ireland, and we in the Irish Diaspora, no longer own Irish traditional music—we only own its past. Sound recording has created an international metacommunity of performers and listeners for this

VOICES ∞ NICHOLAS CAROLAN

music, anchored in Ireland but linked by technology rather than by intimate shared experience, by aesthetic preference and not necessarily by blood.

For over a hundred years now, Irish traditional music has been colonized by sound recording and the other forms of telecommunication, of virtual reality, of surrogacy, made possible by sound recording. We now have thousands of thousands of unique recordings; we have radio and television, the tape recorder and the video, the silicon chip, the satellite dish, the Internet, the CD-ROM, and the DVD. We lack only the hologram. Here we are in uneasy possession of a body of music created in another age, in another world. We have many of the songs, the tunes, and the dances that were created in the last, recent centuries of the First Age, but the world that made them, the world that shaped them, has fallen away, has almost disappeared. Live performance *of course* continues, but now it's relatively invisible. We go to a concert now and then; we play in a pub session now and then. We *know* that live performance is at the heart of everything; we *know* that it is the vital source.

But life is more manageable with the CD player. We are swept along in a world of music that is outside our control, distracted from minute to minute by the calls of each new release. Our only certainty is that this music continues to have a power, continues to attract, continues to be of value.

Will there be a Third Age for Irish traditional music? I don't think so. I think that the semi-actual but mostly virtual reality in which this music now exists will become even more of a norm. Instrumental music will continue to flourish in different ways in small actual communities of players, or at least certain kinds of it will: dance will continue to flourish in different, rather larger actual communities of solo and group dancers, or at least certain kinds of it will. Song will continue to decline. We will cease to pine for the irrecoverable world of the cottage and farmhouse, the village and the city ghetto, and will finally and fully accept semi-virtual reality as true reality. At least, so I imagine.

And imagination was needed, it seems, not so much to see the future of Irish traditional music, but far more to see its past. Imagination to project ourselves back into a foreshortened, dimly grasped, barely recorded, and hardly knowable musical past, imagining as we go the meanings and functions that the music may once have had—fitting together ambiguous hints from archaeology with passing references in historical and literary writings, and matching a knowledge of earlier society and of human nature with our musical suppositions.

Re-Imagining Irish Dance

JEAN BUTLER

For those of you who don't know what happened before *Riverdance,* Irish dance existed in a very small *world* called competition. The competition rounds were very similar to those in the Olympics. Dancers went through several qualifying heats, or *feiseanna,* to get to the world championships, to compete among their peers from different countries. When I began dancing, the Americans were not winning at the World Championships. The Irish and the English were the top winners, and the level of dance in America would have seemed to be quite low. When I was about fourteen years old, the Americans started breaking through and winning competitions. Why and how this happened can be attributed to the growing number of Americans who traveled to the World Championships, therefore allowing influences from the Irish and English style to be integrated into the dance as it was taught in America.

Soon afterward, the Americans started performing more like the Irish and the English, in order to win at the World Championships. The Australians unfortunately were still very far behind. So the first shift in the form can be characterized by a homogenization of style across three different countries. A new breed of Irish and English teachers, who would travel to the States to teach workshops, further incorporating the "winning style," enhanced this homogenization.

Once all the countries were on a similar footing (excuse the pun), another shift took place. The shift toward individualism was now the emphasis, in a competitive world where styles were becoming increasingly similar. As styles converged, new material was needed for dancers to stand out in the crowd. Colin Dunne was among a handful of dancers that changed and shaped the form. He was, I believe, the most significant of dancers during that time, as his rhythmic and innovative virtuosity was envied and copied by all. Many modern steps, such as the triple-click, fast trebles, and syncopated rhythms can be traced back to Colin. He was the one dancer everyone from America looked to for future trends in style and content.

So the second phase in contemporary Irish dance was more about the dancer and his or her innovative style. As with any new shift in form, costumes were also altered to keep up with the modern era. Slowly but surely, the extremely heavy and inappropriate use of velvet as the main fabric for costumes was changed to lighter cotton, allowing for the greater elevation that was required for new steps. Hard shoes were altered to provide a split sole for point work, which was also on the rise.

And then something interesting happened that would change the face of Irish dance forever. That something was *Riverdance*. To put *Riverdance* into context, I have to remind you that, at that time, the only professional outlet for dancers after their competitive careers were over was teaching. There were a chosen few, myself among them, who had the wonderful opportunity to perform with the likes of the Chieftains, Mick Moloney's Green Fields of America, and Joannie Madden's Cherish the Ladies. But other than the odd St. Patrick's Day parade or dance, most Irish dancing continued behind the closed doors of the competitive world. What happened with *Riverdance* was critical to the confidence of the art form. Irish dancers were suddenly proud to be dancers.

When I was growing up, like many dancers, I never admitted to being an Irish dancer. I didn't because the stereotype of what Irish dance was, was stronger than the reality of what I knew it as. Therefore it was easier not to have to try to explain what it was I did, because until *Riverdance* nothing existed to support that explanation. For dancers, *Riverdance* not only now provided another professional outlet, it instilled a professional pride never known before.

I like to think of *Riverdance* as an accident, a brilliant accident conceived by its producer, Moya Doherty, who had the nerve to fly in the face of opposition and tradition. I have dissected the tape from the Eurovision contest over and over again, in an attempt to understand the impact it had. The dancing is traditional. That music is not solely traditional but derived from tradition while incorporating eastern European time signatures. The costumes were adapted from tradition for stage. So what was it? It was precisely what Irish dance had never had before—stage, set, lights, and most important, an audience. And that's when the Irish dance stereotype changed forever. It became new and modern for people who had never seen it before, and also for those who had preconceived notions of what it was all about. But other than the necessary trappings of "stage," the dance was the same for the dancers who were doing it.

You have to remember that most of the dancers on Eurovision night had not performed publicly before. So although there was this amazing excitement about doing something different, the dancers had to be focused on this spot at this time, doing this step, or else the piece would not work. It did work though, as we all know, and thanks to *Riverdance* the next phase of Irish dance began.

If I dare say that *Riverdance* did more for the country than it did for Irish dance, I need to bring you up to speed with where dance is presently, nearly ten years on from Eurovision night. Once the show took off and several other copy-cat shows followed, the dance was almost left behind in the flurry of excitement that comes with global success and acceptance. It was a natural progression and initially a very exciting time. The commercialization of Irish dance was sweeping the planet, young dancers were given the opportunity to perform, and dancing schools were inundated by new students wanting to ride the wave of *Riverdance.*

The competitive world was now open to the larger world that had seen *Riverdance.* Ironically, the competitive world was now also "on show." At the World Championships held in Killarney a month ago, an estimated fourteen thousand people "paid-in" during the ten-day competition. I was one of them, and I was somewhat shocked by what I found. What I saw was a very narrow view of what used to be a living, breathing, moving, growing tradition. The dance seemed "stuck" in a somewhat confused state. In trying to keep up with the now-established commercialization of dance, there seems to be an incredible lack of individuality, both in dance and appearance. Styles have converged so much that a man next to me who had never been to a championships before thought that all the dancers were doing the exact same steps. The introduction of wigs confounded the issue, as all the dancers also looked exactly the same. To illustrate my point further, if you imagine the corps dancers in any show, they all dance uniformly in a line wearing the exact same costume and the exact same hairstyle. It is only the principals who get to dance as they might in a competition, showing off the difficult moves and steps that they have worked so hard to accomplish. The corps dancers are dancing far easier traditional reel and jig steps. The reason for this is that it is easier to create lines of dancers doing these steps, and it is this line of dancers doing these steps that makes for the show-stopping, hairs-on-the-back-of-your-neck numbers that continue to bring the house down. But where does that leave the dance and competition?

Because of the uniformity of the "company numbers" in most shows, and because of the strict inherent trends of competition, the art of dance is marginalized, in the absence of any creative, free-form arena. Unlike Olympic ice skating, which has a "freestyle" competition in which skaters, after their formal competition, have the chance to interpret music, interpret their skating, and choreograph for themselves, Irish dance does not have such an outlet. And if the outlet were to suddenly exist in Irish dance, I would be afraid that dancers would not have the tools to think originally. I would be afraid that they would simply copy the "moves" of some better-known personalities that are on the professional scene. Because what you have to remember is that, since Irish dance comes from a competitive environment, the dancers need to know only what they have to in order to win. Or now with the commercialization of Irish dance, they need to know only what they have to in order to dance in line. It is a dilemma.

A dilemma that Colin Dunne and I foresaw. And that is why we mounted *Dancing on Dangerous Ground*—out of a reaction to where dancing was and to the spectacular shows that were already on the market. We thought there would be room for something else. We wanted to do a different kind of show—a show that concentrated on the *dance* and how *dance* could move forward—not on the set, costumes, or fireworks around it, but on the *dance*. And that was a very unique and rewarding experience. I felt for the first time that the dancers I worked with understood what it was like to be a dancer, to be a dancer inside, to be a dancer who understood the mechanics of the body, a dancer who was not afraid to interpret original moves, a dancer who was more than simply a dancer "on show," and a dancer who was not there to be "adjudicated."

Although the dancers appreciated the experience, we didn't get much support from the competitive society. We also had mixed reactions from the public. I can understand this entirely because *Riverdance* (I cite *Riverdance* again because it was the first and best executed of all the shows) branded Irish dance to the point where it was very difficult to penetrate the stereotype with any other sense of the form. The show was so popular, so successful, that it came to seem that this was all audiences wanted to see—and it was all they understood at that time. So, although it was quite frustrating, *Dangerous Ground* was a very important step in the evolution of Irish dance. It was an attempt to bring it all back to the *dance,* to nurture the dance and move the dancers into the next era.

A friend of mine has a great analogy about the current state of Irish dance. He likens it to teaching people how to paint, but only how to paint an apple and an orange. With those skills alone, they would never be able to paint a bowl of fruit or anything else for that matter.

The next era in Irish dance is waiting to happen. I would love to turn it all on its head, to create an outlet for dance that is not strictly competitive. I want to push for a national company in which classical training and new choreography are on the agenda. Only if something like that happens will we foster a continuing art form that will enable dancers to cross boundaries into different fields. Only then will we create more jobs for Irish dancers—jobs that are not limited to the shows that are out there, jobs that will continue to test the professional boundaries that *Riverdance* pioneered.

Moving Images

Cinema and the Re-Imagining of Ireland

MARTIN McLOONE

The most remarkable Irish film of the last decade is Neil Jordan's *The Butcher Boy* (1997), an adaptation of Pat McCabe's highly regarded 1992 novel. Like the book, the film is a complex and unsettling examination of the Irish psyche, filtered through the imagination, fantasies, and thought processes of an ultimately very disturbed twelve-year-old boy, Francie Brady. The novel is narrated by Francie in the first person, full of the wit and idioms of his rural speech and detailing a heart-breaking tale of neglect, abuse, rejection, and loss that propels his final descent into madness. Jordan translates this first-person narrative into film by visualizing the boy's fantasies in surreal terms, considerably reconfiguring the visual landscape of cinematic Ireland in the process.

One striking fantasy sequence, really Francie's drug-induced hallucination, is set against a panoramic view of Ireland's natural beauty—green hills in the background, and below, a verdant valley and azure-blue lake. This sequence was filmed in Glendalough in County Wicklow, one of Ireland's most famous beauty spots and an important destination on the tourist trail. It is a familiar image, in other words, of a romanticized and stylized rural Ireland, a picture-postcard Ireland of a kind that has dominated cinematic representations for decades. The shot is held for a second as Francie's best friend,

Joe, appears in the frame. "Is that the lake?" the confused Francie asks him, drawing the audience's attention to the blue lake in the background. Then, behind Joe's smiling face, the lake suddenly erupts in the mushroom cloud of a nuclear explosion, literally blowing away beauty, shattering the natural landscape.

In the scene that follows, Jordan re-creates Francie's small rural hometown in the aftermath of the nuclear explosion, devastated and barren, scattered with the charred heads of pigs and populated now by mutant humans with the heads of insects. These are images that literally shatter audience expectations of rural Ireland and offer the most subversive representations of Ireland that the cinema has yet produced. The film is a complex exploration of a changing society in which old certainties of religion and family are blown away and anxiety and doubt replace them. The explosion and the abused child become extended metaphors for Ireland itself, traumatized by its colonial past and its religious/Nationalist present and considerably shaken up by the cataclysmic influences of contemporary culture.

By contrast with this vision, most of the imagery that dominated the representation of Ireland and the Irish in the twentieth century was established in Ireland during an extraordinary period of cultural ferment that lasted from the 1890s to the early 1920s. This great era of Irish cultural Nationalism encompassed a remarkable revival in Irish literature and theater, providing the cultural underpinnings for Ireland's Nationalist aspirations. The Irish undertook what could be described as the first "modern" imagining of Irish identity, one predicated on a perceived need to distinguish Irish culture from that of imperial Britain. Thus, "Irishness" and the imagined community of Ireland took on a particular set of romanticized characteristics in the popular mind. The country saw itself as an essentially rural society, distinguished by its Gaelic culture and Irish language, its strong commitment to the Catholic religion, and its dogged determination to be self-sufficient in economic, political, and cultural terms.

The society and the culture that emerged with the successful conclusion of the War of Independence in 1922 was a mirror image of this cultural imagining. For most of the twentieth century, Ireland was a self-contained, conservative, and Catholic society. Its culture reflected the "frugal self-sufficiency" of the original imagining, dominated by largely romantic images of rural life. A remarkable degree of national consensus was established around the shared vision of Church and State with the family (and the family farm)

MARTIN McLOONE ∽

located at the center of society. In this conservative and rather traditional culture, it is hardly surprising that the cinema, the art form of twentieth-century modernity and urban life, was slow to develop. In the absence of a native film industry, most cinematic images of Ireland were the product of either Hollywood or the British film industry. American cinema tended to glamorize romantic rural Ireland, an image already sunk deep in the nostalgic imagination of the Irish American Diaspora and perhaps best exemplified in John Ford's 1952 romantic comedy *The Quiet Man*. British cinema, on the other hand, reflecting the antagonistic political relationship between the two islands, tended to see Ireland as an inherently violent society populated by a particularly fractious people and best exemplified in Carol Reed's 1947 British classic *Odd Man Out*. Both films, in their different ways, reflected an Ireland out of step with the modern world, either an undeveloped rural utopia or a fractious political backwater caught in the grip of increasingly irrelevant obsessions.[1]

Since the early 1990s, however, two fundamental and interlinked factors— economic prosperity in the South, the Peace Process in the North—have transformed Ireland and set off a chain of rethinking and reappraisal. Ireland's people have fundamentally reimagined their national identity, reassessing and transforming their sense of nationhood, moving beyond the narrow limits of the traditionalist consensus. This process has influenced all the art forms in Ireland and has given rise to a second cultural revival that has embraced the traditional arts as well as the more popular forms of contemporary culture. Perhaps the most remarkable consequence of this new cultural ferment has been the emergence of a state-sponsored indigenous film industry.[2]

In April 1993, Ireland's most internationally renowned filmmaker, Neil Jordan, received the Best Original Screenplay Oscar for *The Crying Game* (1992). In Ireland, the recently appointed Minister for Arts, Culture, and the Gaelacht, Michael D. Higgins, used the occasion to reestablish the Irish Film Board, a film-funding body that had been set up originally in 1981, but that had lain dormant since the mid-1980s, a victim of government cuts at a time of deep recession. The reconstitution of the Film Board was indicative of the newfound cultural confidence that characterized the early 1990s and was made possible by the rapid improvement in government finances. This initiative marked a decisive turning point for indigenous filmmaking in Ireland. Film as an art form finally came in from the critical and institutional cold and entered the mainstream of Irish cultural life. This new cinema has played an important role in supporting the contemporary re-imagining of Ireland and the Irish, representing in a popular idiom many of the transformations, renegotiations, and aspirations that have characterized a rapidly changing society.

The success of Michael D. Higgins's initiative in the South was to become something of a model for film lobbyists in small countries elsewhere. It provided the stimulus for the relaunch in 1997 of the Northern Ireland Film Commission, securing similar state-support mechanisms for filmmaking in Northern Ireland. Ireland, North and South, finally had a vibrant film industry.

In the years of the Film Board's existence down to 2005, over 120 feature films and hundreds of short films have been made in Ireland. These films are both a reflection of and a contribution to the process of cultural re-imagining that has been informed by and served to energize recent economic and social change. The films have reenvisioned Ireland by offering alternative cinematic images to those stereotypes, Hollywood and British, which dominated the screens for most of the twentieth century. The short films and features which were made in Northern Ireland during this period provide an equally valuable artistic record of the mood in Northern Ireland as the cease-fires took hold and the Peace Process moved slowly forward. By looking closely at some of these films, from both the North and the South, we can glean something of the extraordinary cultural ferment and change that has characterized Ireland in the last fifteen years.

Landscape and Religion

As we have seen, Irish landscape, especially the West of Ireland, was deeply significant in cultural, ideological, and political terms for the original imagining of Nationalist Ireland. Rural Ireland was often portrayed as the residue of traditional Irish values—Catholic, Nationalist, and Gaelic. The elemental purity of this Ireland is still often posited as the antithesis of the alienation, decadence, and sullied national identity associated with urban Ireland (especially Dublin) and the wider urban world beyond (perhaps especially Britain). This debilitating contrast may have originated in the city itself, among the urban Nationalist intelligentsia, but it has had a wider currency throughout the twentieth century and lies at the heart of the traditional cinematic image of romantic Ireland.

In this tradition, Ireland is most often portrayed as a kind of rural idyll, with its feisty colleens; amiable, brawling drunks; and wise-owl priests living a life of modest but self-fulfilling coziness in the magnificent splendor of the western landscape. This vision of an organic, harmonious community is contrasted to the anxieties and tensions of urban modernity. It is a premodern utopia where life is lived at a slower pace and on a more human scale, offering the prospect of respite and recuperation to the weary city dweller. This is the premise behind the cinema's most enduring image of rural Ireland, *The Quiet Man*. Myth and the curative powers of the West of Ireland underlie *Into the West* (1992), Mike Newell's critique of urban modernity (which was written by one of Ireland's leading filmmakers, Jim Sheridan). Such, indeed, is the universal attraction of the image that it remains an underlying promise of much of Ireland's contemporary tourist literature.

Unfortunately, also, even today—and despite all the changes that have taken place in contemporary Ireland—it continues to turn up on cinema screens with alarming regularity (as the success of the irritatingly clichéd *Waking Ned Devine* exemplified in 1999). It is hardly surprising that in an era of flux and change, exploring and exploding the myths of rural Ireland should be a factor in the re-imagining process.

As is the case with Neil Jordan's powerfully allegorical *The Butcher Boy*, Thaddeus O'Sullivan's *December Bride* (1989) subverts traditional representations of the Irish landscape. Adapted from Sam Hanna Bell's influential novel of 1951, the film is set in turn-of-the-twentieth-century Ireland, beautifully filmed on location in and around Strangford Lough, near Belfast, and concerns the scandalous relationship between a young woman, Sarah, and the two unmarried brothers she keeps house for, Frank and Hamilton Echlin. This unconventional ménage à trois takes place within a close-knit Presbyterian community, shown as extremely hard working and God fearing but deeply conservative and conventional in social and sexual matters.

By thus peopling an otherwise recognizable Irish rural community, O'Sullivan's film offers an extra layer of challenge to traditional representations. Indeed, the insertion of a devout Presbyterian community (replete with its Orange drums and July Twelfth rituals) into the Irish landscape is a reminder that the industrial workers of Belfast are only part of the Protestant story and that the romantic Nationalism of Catholic Ireland is only part of the story of Irish landscape.[3]

While *December Bride* is one of the first attempts in Irish cinema to represent Protestant and Unionist culture in sympathetic terms, the depiction of

Protestant communities in Irish film has been the exception rather than the rule and the source of interesting and sometimes controversial debate. Most reappraisals of rural Ireland are concerned with the stifling influence of Catholic teaching and Nationalist dogma on communities already wracked by poverty and disintegrating as a result of emigration and enforced isolation. These films are mostly set in the 1950s and 1960s and explore the hypocrisies and oppressiveness of then-president Eamon de Valera's vision of an Ireland of "frugal self-sufficiency."

Jordan's and O'Sullivan's films are the two major reengagements with rural Ireland in modern Irish cinema, but they reflect a much broader impulse to explore the legacy of Ireland's rural past and its devotion to the Catholic Church. One of the earliest films to explore the misery of rural life in 1950s Ireland was Pat O'Connor's breakthrough production *The Ballroom of Romance* (1982). The West-of-Ireland settings are beautifully photographed, but this ineffably sad and moving film also captures the lives of quiet desperation lived out in this visual splendor. The eponymous ballroom is cruelly and ironically named. There can be no romance or glamour in such a dying rural culture. This is a society populated by an assortment of aging men and women, the sons and daughters left behind (or abandoned) like so much human jetsam by successive waves of emigration. They grope blindly toward each other, desperately seeking marriage partners and enduring their social and sexual repression with a mixture of philosophical resignation and childish immaturity. The suffocating emptiness and sterility of such rural communities is a factor in many revisionist portrayals of rural Ireland. In Kevin Liddy's short film *Horse* (1992) and his feature film *Country* (2000), rural Ireland is represented as an emotionally stunted and cold world, devoid of love, sympathy, and basic human communication. A palpable sense of cruelty hangs over these films and a sense of suppressed male violence, fueled by frustration and lack of opportunity, inhabits their bleak landscapes.

Often the films explore more directly the influence of the Catholic Church and especially the violent abuse that religious orders in schools or orphanages visited on their charges. The most harrowing of such films is Scottish filmmaker Peter Mullan's *The Magdalene Sisters* (2002), an Irish Film Board–supported production which looks at the infamous Magdalene laundries run by the Sisters of Mercy. In these repressive and exploitative institutions, unmarried mothers or young women who were deemed by family or Church to be otherwise morally suspect were incarcerated under a strict regime and labored for long hours in the laundries. This feature is set in the 1960s, as

Ireland began its first period of industrializing change. Part of the pathos of the film comes from the witness it gives of the repressive regime visited on young women in contrast to the more liberal optimism of the world beyond the convent walls. Mullan based his script on the testimonies of women who went through the laundries in the 1960s, and the film has all the harrowing realism of firsthand accounts.

One of the finest of the films set in the 1950s is Syd Macartney's *A Love Divided* (1999), based on real events that occurred in the Co. Wexford village of Fethard-on-Sea. The action takes place in 1957 and depicts the Catholic Church at its most militant, most powerful, and most authoritarian, and explores, unusually for Ireland, sectarian tensions and anti-Protestant prejudice in the South. The events themselves were hugely controversial at the time. The Church organized a boycott of the vulnerable Protestant community in Fethard, accusing them of complicity in the disappearance of Protestant Sheila Cloney and her two children. Sheila had married Catholic farmer Sean Cloney, and, in accord with the Vatican's "Ne Temere" decree, the couple had to promise to bring up their children as Catholics before the Church would agree to sanctify the "mixed marriage." When the time came for the oldest girl to go to the local Catholic school, the Protestant Sheila refused to comply. Under pressure from the local priest and her increasingly belligerent Catholic neighbors, she took her children into hiding.

The subsequent boycott was long and bitter and became an international news story (most famously, *Time* magazine ran a piece on it). The government of Eamon de Valera was severely embarrassed by the whole affair and eventually put pressure on the Vatican to have the boycott ended.

Macartney's film approaches these events obliquely, recasting them as a romantic melodrama of thwarted love—a kind of mature Romeo and Juliet story that works by playing the love story off against a climate of tribal loyalties and communal conflict. Nonetheless, it remains an effective and hard-hitting attack on the authoritarian nature of Irish Catholicism, and its depiction of rural Ireland, wracked by blind prejudice and overbearing authority, is politically powerful. The early romantic scenes, set in the beauty of rural Ireland, are familiar and cinematically impressive as they establish the environs of Sheila and Sean's impossibly idyllic love story. However, these same fields and hedgerows will later assume a more sinister and malevolent character as the campaign against Sheila's Protestant family turns violent. The idyllic becomes a nightmare, and the effect is to raise fundamental questions about the whole myth of rural Ireland as an Edenic, organic community.

All these films about rural Ireland are set in the past, but it is important to note that they are quite contemporary documents nonetheless—films from an era of constantly rising expectations and from a time of considerable and conspicuous affluence. These are, in other words, "Celtic Tiger" films. In some of them, there is also an attempt to come to terms with the sectarianism in Catholic culture and to understand the anxieties that come with being Protestant in Ireland. This tentative rapprochement with Protestant culture and tradition no doubt reflects changing attitudes in Ireland in the wake of the Peace Process in the North. However, it is also a reflection of the diminished status and declining influence of the Catholic Church in Ireland following the abuse and sex scandals of the 1990s and the greater secularization that has accompanied economic success and affluence. In many ways, the films reflect the passions and obsessions of a young, vibrant culture coming to terms with what it sees as a disabling past—and maybe settling old scores with the repressive institutions of this past. Interestingly as well, both *A Love Divided* and *The Magdalene Sisters* are concerned with events that the contemporary Catholic Church felt compelled to apologize for in very recent years. Nothing better sums up the changed and diminished role of the Church in Ireland today than the artistic representation and dramatization of events that led up to such retrospective apologies.

Imagining and Re-Imagining the City

In a culture that has been so dominated by images of the rural, it is hardly surprising that Irish urban life, until relatively recently, was largely absent from the screen. However, with the growth of indigenous filmmaking, Irish urban experience has become a recurring theme in the emerging new cinema. In the 1990s, as the economy boomed and society became more affluent, films that probed violence and organized crime in Dublin became especially popular. There were, for example, three film versions of the life and death of real-life Dublin gangster Martin Cahill—John Boorman's *The General* in 1997, Thaddeus O'Sullivan's *Ordinary Decent Criminal* in 2000, and a BBC Northern Ireland television film, *Vicious Circle*, in 1999. All these films contrasted the violence of organized crime in Dublin with the paramilitary violence more typically associated with Ireland. There is an ironic reference to this in the title of O'Sullivan's film (*Ordinary Decent Criminal*), and in *Vicious Circle* it is clearly articulated by one of the investigating police officers. "Dublin is turning into Dodge City," he says to a suitably sleazy politician, "and the IRA have nothing to do with it." There have also been two versions of the story of Veronica Guerin, the investigative crime reporter shot dead in 1996 by the Dublin gangsters she tenaciously pursued through her newspaper columns. John MacKenzie's *When the Sky Falls* (1999) and the big-budget Hollywood version, *Veronica Guerin* (2003), directed by Joel Schumacher, use Guerin's story to probe Dublin's organized crime culture and to valorize the kind of self-help determination that Guerin represented.

This concern with the Cahill and Guerin stories was part of a process of reclaiming the city from representational neglect. Dublin is presented as a contemporary urban environment much like anywhere else. The films emphasize the contrast between "ordinary" gangsterism and paramilitary violence—in some of these films, Cahill becomes a kind of Robin Hood or Jesse James character—and this effort is part of the reclamation process. It is an attempt to "normalize" the cinematic image of Ireland—Ireland is not backward and rural, it is not run by the IRA—even if this means showing that urban Ireland suffers from much the same kinds of problems that cities in other developed countries do (especially the problem of drug-related organized crime).

These were all relatively high-profile films. Throughout the 1990s, a continuing number of low-budget indigenous films also probed crime in contemporary urban life, again drawing attention to the drug culture that is now indelibly associated with city life. Thus in Paul Tickell's *Crushproof* (1996), a raw and edgy Dublin of endless suburbs and grim housing projects is populated by dysfunctional teenagers and alcoholic and drug-addicted adults. The "Dodge City" element of this bleak cityscape is suggested by the incongruous horses that the teenage boys look after and ride around on. In Joe O'Byrnes's *Pete's Meteor* (1999), the horrific devastation caused by drugs and drug-related AIDS provides a realistic contrast to the fantasy world that twelve-year-old Mickey constructs around the meteor that lands in his back garden. Grim, earth-bound realities are juxtaposed to the heavenly promise of transcendence. Even in John Lynch's mature love story *Night Train* (1999), the romance between middle-aged Michael and Alice is threatened by his previous crimes that come back to haunt and threaten his present.

The status of such depictions could be regarded as problematic, for the attraction of the once-dominant myth and images of romantic, rural life is precisely that they provide an escape from this kind of urban alienation and disharmony. Films that explode the myth, though reflecting an otherwise understandable desire to represent the city and its problems, could prove counterproductive, reinforcing prejudices against city life, confirming rather than challenging rural romanticism. For most of the younger filmmakers who emerged in the 1990s, however, the city is a cause for celebration, not a source of anxiety.

This fact is reflected and perhaps explained by the preponderance in recent years of another kind of urban-based film, constituting a cinema of "hip hedonism." These films celebrate and even glorify a certain kind of urban lifestyle, one that revels in the signifiers of contemporary global youth culture and is populated by the "beautiful people" of Celtic Tiger Ireland. They are Irish, certainly, but they epitomize a kind of transglobal "cool." Though drugs and crime still form part of the imagined background, these are presented as lifestyle choices or get-rich-quick schemes removed from any social consequences.

Most important, such films are much lighter in tone than more political urban cinema and are driven by an infectious and deliberately irreverent humor. The Dublin they portray is a city of luxurious apartments and well-appointed offices, their beautifully decorated rooms looking out onto spectacular cityscapes. Dublin emerges as a city of conspicuous consumption where life revolves around contemporary art galleries, trendy restaurants, stylish coffee and wine bars, and modernist pubs. Above all, in representing Dublin as a city of promiscuous sexual abandon, these productions announce the new cinema's final assault on the values of the old Ireland. The films suggest that the vision of a Catholic, Nationalist Ireland passed down to Ireland's young population from their grandparents (or, ironically, gleaned from those Irish films that seem to be still obsessed by this dead past) is now merely a faded memory.

Though a wide variety of Dublin-based films display such characteristics, constituting a significant and identifiable trend in recent Irish cinema, three films in particular epitomize this new hip hedonism: Gerry Stembridge's *About Adam* (2001), Liz Gill's *Goldfish Memory* (2003), and John Crowley's *Intermission* (2003). Interestingly, all three films work through multiple story lines and circular plots; they are, it could be said, contemporary Irish versions of Arthur Schnitzler's nineteenth-century play *La Ronde* (and Max Ophuls's 1950 film of the same name). In these films, the multiple characters play games with one another in pursuit of love and sex (and the filmmakers play a game with the audience as the circular plots weave around coincidences and overlapping encounters).

In *Goldfish Memory,* all possible combinations of sexual coupling are explored—straight, gay, lesbian, and bisexual—played out against a highly

MARTIN McLOONE ᐁᕮ

stylized Dublin that was originally shot on digital video and then considerably "sweetened" through postproduction computer imaging. This postproduction process suffuses the final film with enhanced colors—oranges, soft blues, and warm greens—creating an almost subliminal sense of well-being, a visual "feel-good" factor that makes the city of Dublin appear uncharacteristically bright and attractive. Just as the film explores alternative love possibilities, so too the stylized cinematography re-imagines an alternative Dublin, providing an almost impossibly attractive contemporary milieu for the film's daring sexual politics.

The film is punctuated by a series of high-angle shots of the city taken from a variety of perspectives and at various times of the day or night. In this way the film becomes a celebration, not just of Dublin, but of urban life itself—its secret and exciting spaces of sexual freedom and exploration. The main characters are lesbian women and gay men, and their pursuit of uncluttered sexual encounters amounts to a reworking of the very notion of love and family. Indeed, there is an ironic conservatism in the film's message; the gay men become the fathers for the lesbian couple's children so that the family is reinstated in a radical and extended form.

In these urban lifestyle films, the camera seems to have become obsessed by good looks and designer clothes, lovingly dwelling on the beautiful and handsome faces and bodies that inhabit the reconfigured city. The cast of *Goldfish Memory* in particular is uniformly young and attractive, but the same is true of *About Adam*, dominated by charismatic performances from Stuart Townsend as the film's handsome serial seducer and Kate Hudson and Frances O'Connor as two of his attractive lovers. The centrality of designer good looks is also evident in Fintan Connolly's *Flick* (1999), another film that explores a lifestyle of hedonistic excess, even if this view of contemporary Dublin has more rough edges than *About Adam* and *Goldfish Memory*. The film is centered on middle-class drug dealer Jack Flinter, played by David Murray, and the camera seems at times to be mesmerized by Murray's presence. There are long sequences in the film that follow Jack through the clubs and pubs of contemporary Dublin as he buys, sells, and imbibes his drugs, and the camera seems to prowl along, eyeing him with almost voyeuristic zeal. A presumably largely young audience is invited to look and to empathize.

For all their imaginative and seductive style, such films partake of the self-obsessed narcissism of designer-label chic and could be accused of smug complacency. To some extent, of course, they are a true reflection of one aspect of Celtic Tiger Ireland—the rampant consumerism that comes from economic success and greater affluence. And yet social problems to which global consumerism contributes cannot be simply imagined out of existence. The ugliness of the real world cannot be digitally enhanced or removed like a postproduction video image. Not everyone is a winner in Celtic Tiger Ireland.

Peace, the North, and Protestant Culture

The hesitant but nonetheless successful Peace Process has profoundly transformed attitudes and culture in Northern Ireland. In the early 1990s, nightlife and city-center culture in general were reborn, especially in Belfast, and as the 1990s progressed, cinema manifested a new engagement with the politics and violence of the North. Although they deal with the worst aspects of the Troubles, the resulting films are essentially Peace Process films in that their concerns and their perspectives are informed by an improving political and social environment. It was almost as if the cinema needed the calmer atmosphere of relative peace before it could explore the legacy of violent communal conflict.

One surprising aspect of these films is that they have redressed an imbalance in the representation of Protestant and Unionist culture. Until relatively recently, there has been a paucity of cinematic portrayals of Unionist culture in general and Loyalist paramilitaries in particular, confirming for many Unionists the enduring truth that their case has been little understood and poorly represented by a hostile mass media. In one way, this is not surprising, given the number of films made since the 1980s that have (albeit equivocally or even negatively) portrayed the Nationalist community or have featured IRA activities as significant plot elements. In any event, such absence of cultural representation seems to offer an element of justification for the siege mentality within Loyalism.[4] That mentality was exemplified during the Loyalist picket of the Holy Cross Catholic School in the Ardoyne area of Belfast, when the world saw disturbing video footage of screaming Loyalists hurling abuse at primary-school children. The negative global reaction to these events merely reinforced Loyalist intransigence. "Nobody loves us and we don't care" became a favorite saying in Loyalist Belfast.

It should be noted that the absence of Loyalist representations in mainstream popular culture has also been a cause of great concern to Nationalists and Republicans. The result of this tendency, they would argue, has been to cement the impression abroad that Republicans alone are to blame for the

MARTIN McLOONE ໑໑

violence in Northern Ireland, effectively exonerating Unionism and Loyalism from any culpability. The Unionist sense of grievance, on the other hand, arises from a false assumption. It assumes that, cinematically at any rate, Republicans have been represented favorably—that their politics have been accorded some legitimacy by virtue of public display.

In truth, there have been no IRA propaganda films. At best, films like *Cal* (1984), *Michael Collins* (1996), or *The Boxer* (1997) have shown IRA violence as ultimately self-defeating and pointless, liable to initiate a cycle of events that spins out of control into mayhem, internecine conflict, and civil war. In this paradigm, romantic love is impossible and family relationships are inevitably destroyed. Here, tendencies to violence become a version of the workings of fate, reflecting a "tragic flaw" in the Irish themselves, one as much part of the environment as the changeable Irish weather or the awe-inspiring scenery.

At worst, such films and countless bigger-budget Hollywood productions, like *Patriot Games* (1992), *The Devil's Own* (1997), or *Blown Away* (1994), merely use the IRA as a convenient plot device, or to provide "backstory," as Hollywood scriptwriters would say. These films depict violence in Ireland as attributable to particular psychotic individuals working on their own, either acting out of blind fanaticism or from irrational urgings for revenge. In *Patriot Games* (1992), Sean Bean plays a renegade IRA man who loses all sense of political purpose, pursuing a mission of personal revenge against Harrison Ford's CIA man, Jack Ryan. Most outlandish of all is Tommy Lee Jones's Ryan Gaerity, in *Blown Away*, the cinema's ultimate IRA renegade psycho, whose expertise in bomb making allows him to exercise a personal grudge against a former colleague.

In those few films which have dealt with Loyalist paramilitaries, the portrayals are similarly formulaic. Thaddeus O'Sullivan's *Nothing Personal* (1995) and Marc Evans's *Resurrection Man* (1998), based on Belfast writer Eoin McNamee's novel of the same name, both deal with Loyalist violence in 1970s Belfast. The films demonstrate great visual flair in creating the bleak cityscape of these years. *Nothing Personal*, in particular, creates an impressive urban setting of streets, alleyways, and dingy clubs, shot mostly at night, using dominant blues and misty grays to create a real feeling of inner-city claustrophobia. The main plot is centered on a gang of Loyalist gunmen, barely under the control of their more politically motivated commander, Leonard (Michael Gambon). Leonard attempts to work out a cease-fire with his IRA counterpart, Cecil (Gerard McSorley), and to set "civilized" ground rules for conducting their conflict. The younger activists on either side are not impressed by these peace moves and seethe and posture in the background. On the Loyalist side, Leonard's main lieutenant is the attractive and charismatic Kenny (James Frain), whose own lieutenant is the clearly disturbed Ginger (Ian Hart). Ginger just hates Catholics and takes great pleasure in killing and mutilating them. As played by Hart, he is a twitchy, uncontrollable psychopath, and though he is allowed one speech in which to articulate a crude Loyalist politics, he is clearly of the same lineage as the many Republican psychopaths depicted down the years. The IRA does not have a monopoly on dangerous renegades.

In *Resurrection Man*, to chilling effect, Stuart Townsend virtually combines the characters of Ginger and Kenny in his portrayal of Victor Kelly, a "Shankill butcher" psychopath. Victor is as handsome and as charismatic as Kenny and likes to mutilate his Catholic victims with colder and more calculating pleasure than does Ginger. The only explanation offered for his almost vampiric love of Fenian blood is a "mammy's boy" Oedipal problem. Victor's father is an impotent, ineffectual Catholic. Ashamed of this Catholic taint, Victor must prove his Protestant credentials by ever more extreme acts of violence.

The most recent attempt at depicting Loyalism is the film version of Gary Mitchell's disturbing stage play *As the Beast Sleeps* (2001). Here Loyalism is presented as an ideology in crisis. On the one hand, violent Loyalism is being dragged by the Peace Process toward the brave new world of consumerism and entrepreneurial affluence. On the other hand, increasing uncertainty and a residual fear that the Republicans are winning the peace draws Loyalism back toward the security of its primitive and brutal sectarianism. Loyalist paramilitaries, the film argues, were trained and propagandized to carry out a limited number of tasks—basically to kill Republicans and Catholics and to rob and steal to support the needs of their own culture (symbolized by the UDA club at the center of the story). In the era of the Peace Process, the front-line "hard men" are like a demobbed, ill-trained, and uneducated army, flailing about without a sense of purpose and nostalgic for the simple verities of the sectarian conflict. What marks the film as different from *Nothing Personal* and *Resurrection Man* is its attitude to these hulking brutes. There is sympathy in the film for the dilemma that they face, an understanding and appreciation of the ideological cul-de-sac that they have got themselves into. But at the same time, these Loyalists are far removed from the romantic hero figures of their own myths or the idealized freedom fighters in murals that adorn the gable walls of their bleak housing estates and high-rise flats. Brutal and largely inarticulate, they are being left behind as the Peace Process proceeds, and their only future lies in arresting that process and returning to the conflict that made them. The continuing Peace Process and the "normalization" of society create real problems for the hard-line Loyalist.

As the Beast Sleeps is the first film that tries to understand Loyalism on its own terms and to show the enormous frictions and tensions that erupt periodically in internecine strife. In this regard, the film marks a considerable advance on previous productions and is to be welcomed for that. But its dull visual style, its disturbing theatrical language, and its air of claustrophobic nihilism also make it a truly bleak viewing experience.

Loyalist idealism is seemingly resistant to representation. Despite the greater insights of *As the Beast Sleeps,* all three of these films collapse story into visions of psychopathology in their exploration and depiction of violence. In many ways, the films confirm a dominant mode of representing Loyalism—as fascism prone to human depravity and deficient in even the pretense of political idealism. This might satisfy the expectations of Republican and Nationalist prejudices, but the enduring mood of these films is that of a whole society which has fallen below the civilized standards of rational behavior. Just as is the case with most of the IRA films, the message reflects understandable humanist frustration, but these representations are hardly likely to help the political process.

Peace Process Films and the Reconstruction of Belfast

In the same way that post–Celtic Tiger cinema in the South has developed a hip new image for the city of Dublin, Peace Process cinema in the North has been busy re-imagining the once pariah city of Belfast.[5] The two most interesting Peace Process films are Michael Winterbottom's "adult comedy" *With or Without You* (1999) and Declan Lowney's amiable romantic comedy *Wild about Harry* (2000). The sectarian geography of Belfast is here replaced by images of urban renewal. The iconography of both films is that of an affluent middle class with its culture of high-spend consumerism and metropolitan aspirations. One of the main urban locations in *With or Without You* is the Waterfront Hall in Belfast, an ultramodern concert, conference, and exhibition center that came to symbolize the new, aspiring, and increasingly affluent Belfast of the late 1990s, the Belfast of the Peace Process, as opposed to the Belfast of the 1970s.

The film's protagonist, Rosie Boyd, is approaching thirty and desperately, though unsuccessfully, trying to start a family with her husband, Vincent. Rosie works as a receptionist in the Waterfront Hall, so that much of the film is shot inside and outside the Hall, its art galleries and chic restaurants giving an unusually modern and cosmopolitan view of contemporary Belfast. Rosie's inability to get pregnant is beginning to strain her relationship with Vincent, and when an old French pen pal, Benoit, turns up unexpectedly in Belfast, the pressures increase. The light romantic comedy of the film lies in Rosie's attempt to work through these tensions to a final reconciliation with Vincent. Compared to the hedonistic sexuality of the Dublin films, *With or Without You* ultimately offers a conservative message about the nature of true love and the sanctity of marriage.

However, it is hard not to read Rosie's eventual pregnancy and reconciliation with Vincent as an upbeat metaphor for the affluent, middle-class, and consumerist Northern Ireland that is itself struggling to be born in the wake of the Peace Process. The fact that Rosie and Vincent are Protestants is also deeply significant. The film clearly implies that Unionists in general, perhaps the Protestant middle class in particular, have most to gain from the reconstruction that is implicit in the Peace Process. Just as the traditional images of conflict have been evacuated, so too have the problematic, working-class, Loyalist ethics of previous films. The Unionist middle class is being offered a new dispensation that promises them an affluent future if only they will embrace the new order. Benoit's role in the film is merely to secure Vincent and Rosie's relationship, maybe representing in the process a kind of European, metropolitan influence from which their community in general can benefit. In fact, there is a strong sense throughout the film that a European bourgeois society is struggling to be born out of the Peace Process, and hence the great emphasis on classical music, wine and cuisine, consumption and culture. This bourgeois Unionism is a long way from the psychotic Loyalists of *Resurrection Man* or the aimless foot soldiers of *As the Beast Sleeps*.

The main premise of *Wild About Harry* is that, after a random mugging in which he is severely beaten about the head, minor television celebrity Harry suffers a form of amnesia that wipes out all memory of the last twenty-five years of his life. This includes not only the memory of his local fame as a celebrity chef but also the memory of his philandering, his drunken escapades that are followed salaciously by the local tabloids, and the hurt and suffering he has visited on his alienated wife and children. The amnesia is timely, in other words, giving him a second chance to repair his broken marriage before final divorce proceedings are concluded and to find again the excitement, idealism, and optimism of his eighteen-year-old self.

The film's setting and its Belfast locations are crucial to its meaning. In fact, the conceit of the film is that peace may call for a kind of political amnesia in which twenty-five years of political strife and urban violence are excised magically. The film creates a Belfast that is, strangely, both beyond and before the Troubles. Like Harry's life, it is a Belfast of reconstruction and rebuilding, a second chance to re-imagine the once pariah city. There is, as in *With or Without You,* an emphasis on affluent, corporate, professional Belfast—luxuriously appointed offices, comfortable, even wealthy homes with well-stocked liquor cabinets.

The crucial reconciliation scene in the film between Harry and his estranged wife, Ruth, is shot at night on location in Royal Avenue in Belfast, with the illuminated dome of the City Hall framed in the background. Harry apologizes to Ruth: "I know what I was," he says, "what I became. I hate what I did to you." It is hard not to read this scene metaphorically, to see it as being as much about the rehabilitation of Belfast as it is of Harry, as though the dome itself were speaking on behalf of the pariah city. Beautifully framed and lit in romantic light, this dome is the civic, historical Belfast reaching out for a new beginning. Ulster has decided to say "Yes."

Cinema as a Mediator of Change

Indigenous Irish cinema, through a set of alternative and at times confrontational themes and motifs, provides an invaluable artistic record of a changing society rapidly re-imagining its cultural identity and its relationship to its own past. Indigenous cinema grew out of those larger social, political, and cultural processes which have transformed Ireland over the last fifteen years, but it has also become a key site through which these processes have been mediated. Thus the films have mapped out the renegotiations and reappraisals that have accompanied profound social and cultural change. They have illustrated positive aspects of the new global Ireland that is now emerging and visualized the aspirations of a uniquely young population. The films also illustrate the negative aspects of the new Ireland; a close reading of recurring motifs and predominant themes illustrates well that not everyone is a winner in the Ireland of the Celtic Tiger or the Northern Ireland of the Peace Process.

Traditional cinematic representations of the Irish fall into two broad categories. The Irish are either romantically cute or pathologically violent. The problem, of course, is that neither of these generalizations is adequate to the complexities of contemporary Ireland, and both massively misrepresent the country in all its diversity and changing configurations. Most important, then, new Irish cinema represents a belated but dramatic response to once-dominant cinematic images of the culture of Ireland and of the Irish themselves, to characterizations that have circulated unchallenged for too long.

NOTES

1. The early history of the cinema in Ireland and the first academic study of Irish film representations was Kevin Rockett, Luke Gibbons, and John Hill, *Cinema and Ireland* (London: Croom Helm, 1987).
2. Another consequence of the emergence of a cinema industry in Ireland has been the growth in academic film studies. See, for example, Martin McLoone, *Irish Film: The Emergence of a Contemporary Cinema* (London: bfi publishing, 2000); Lance Pettitt, *Screening Ireland* (Manchester: Manchester University Press, 2000); and Ruth Barton, *Irish National Cinema* (London: Routledge, 2004).
3. For more detailed discussion of this important film, see Martin McLoone, "December Bride: A Landscape Peopled Differently" in *Contemporary Irish Cinema: From "The Quiet Man" to "Dancing at Lughnasa,"* ed. J. MacKillop (Syracuse: Syracuse University Press, 1998), and Lance Pettitt, *December Bride* (Cork: Cork University Press, 2001).
4. For more detailed discussion of media representations of Protestant culture and Unionist politics, see Brian McIlroy, *Shooting to Kill: Filmmaking and the "Troubles" in Northern Ireland* (Trowbridge: Flicks Books, 1998) and Alan F. Parkinson, *Ulster Loyalism and the British Media* (Dublin: Four Courts Press, 1998).
5. A more detailed analysis of cinematic Belfast can be found in Martin McLoone, "Topographies of Terror and Taste: The Re-imagining of Belfast in Recent Cinema," *Keeping it Real: Irish Film and Television,* ed. R. Barton and H. O'Brien (London: Wallflower Press, 2003).

Hollywood and Ireland

TRISH McADAM

Hollywood may be based in America, but it is a global, industrialized, billion-dollar industry made up of a number of media conglomerates controlled by global shareholders, not just Americans. It manages the output of the studios and broadcasters in order to satisfy its shareholders and the distribution networks which it often owns.

While the big-budget, mass-audience potential of the Hollywood system attracts filmmakers from across the world, there is growing concern about the extent to which it dominates the global marketplace. The corporate, profit-orientated Hollywood machine threatens the creative and cultural diversity that characterizes national cinemas, including the American independents.

It is impossible for cinema owners to resist facilitating their biggest supplier, and so impossible for smaller films to get cinema releases. It is, in other words, difficult for creative directors to work in the Hollywood system and difficult for their smaller films to get distribution. This is bad for the filmmaker, bad for national cultures, and it limits the kinds of films available to audiences.

We have little choice but to live with corporate Hollywood. However, we should also respect the need to protect film practitioners and local film cultures from the worst excesses of the bullying tactics of this global industry. For example, it was reported in *Screen International* (February 2003), that "MPAA [Motion Picture Association of America] president Jack Valente wrote to President Fox of Mexico warning retaliation measures against the Mexican Film industry for applying a one peso levy to all cinema admissions to help boost the local film industry."

There is growing resistance to this kind of interference in national cultures. In Australia, filmmakers are part of a cultural coalition created to argue against the inclusion of film in world free-trade agreements (this free trade opens up local markets to the dominant Hollywood system, with predictable consequences). The Australians argue that their government should "retain comprehensive rights to devise and implement policies to sustain and develop a diversity of cultural expressions in Australia." They quote Article 15 of the UN "International Convention on Economic, Social, and Cultural Rights": "Each culture has a dignity and value which must be respected and preserved."

On its own, Ireland can neither protect its film industry nor change international trends, but an affiliation of advocates from different cultures worldwide can successfully defend the right to freedom of expression as well as campaign for a system of fair practice.

The European Media Program, whose aim is to promote European film, has tried to take on Hollywood. However, instead of promoting our own strengths—the diversity, experimentation, vision, and style of European directors—they decided that European film should assume the industrial model, that European filmmakers should look to Hollywood for inspiration and lessons on how to be successful.

Evidence of this can be found in the focus of the training programs of the European Media Program. Many Hollywood screenwriters and producers are involved in training courses, and there is an active promotion of the producer as the dominant force in film culture. Few courses can be found to encourage creative individuality, directing skills, or directors' rights.

The Hollywood "philosophy" has now infiltrated the whole of the filmmaking process in Ireland. From conception, through script development, production, and critical analysis, the box office potential has become the measure of success.

Across Europe, we need to reestablish the belief in our right to make films that focus on creativity, self-expression, witness, observation, experimentation, and the desire to communicate honestly with an intelligent audience. We need to look at new ways of developing audiences, to challenge the film critics who, reneging on their role as intelligent mediators of new cinema, have bought into the dominant system. We need to reestablish the writer/director team as pivotal to the development and production process and to strengthen their copyright position so that they can benefit from the success of their own films.

We must re-imagine an Ireland in which commerce and culture are balanced, and put the "art" back into the film "industry." Film directors from

Ireland, America, and across the globe want to be able to reach their audiences without going through the creative "mincer" that the corporate Hollywood system has become. Like the bully in the playground, Hollywood needs to be controlled for its own sake, for the sake of others, and, most important, for the sake of the medium of film itself.

The War of the Flea and Other Tales

ROD STONEMAN

Before

In March 1994, I was invited to speak at the Filmbase AGM, an access organization in Dublin. I began by saying that "There isn't and never will be a film industry in Ireland." This comment was met with a somewhat stunned and disconcerted response from the filmmakers present—perhaps understandable as I was a Brit who had just blown in from Channel Four television in London to help set up a national film agency in Ireland. I tried to go on to explain that, in my view, there wasn't a film industry in Italy or Britain or France either, and to formulate a distinction between the industrial mode of production which could be found in the bottom left-hand corner of the United States (with minor variants in Hong Kong, Bombay, and Cairo) and the artisanal modes of production which existed everywhere else.[1]

I tried to propose that the most strategic response to the hegemony of industrial cinema was the "war of the flea"—the production of a wide range of diverse films, made with vision, integrity, authenticity, and something to say. We should work to enhance radical pluralism and risk-taking within and between national cinemas, to build alliances, to play to our cultural strengths, to accept and celebrate the scale and diversity of the world's cultural production.

It was also necessary to avoid generalized condemnation and dismissal of Hollywood as "a bad thing," somehow intentionally wicked and malevolent—let's be clear, one of the reasons it has achieved dominance is as a result of the strength and precision of its narrative effects. Much Hollywood film is well made and pleasurable; it is indeed its pervasive hegemony that poses a problem for the rest of the world.

During

In the succeeding ten years I was busy enough: the Irish Film Board's budget went from €1 million in 1993 to €12 million in 2003. We supported more than one hundred feature films, television series, and many hundreds of documentaries, animations, and shorts. The staff of the organization increased from three to sixteen, and we had some interesting times involved in the making of some interesting films! There was a sense that this production activity connected with a receptive home audience: *The General* was seen by over 50 percent of the Irish population, and *The Magdalene Sisters,* before its release on VHS or DVD, was watched by a quarter of the population. In May 2003, John Crowley's new film *Intermission* had made more than €2 million on a forty-print release. It is also true that no recent Irish film has been successful internationally, and distribution and marketing is a key aspect of this problem.[2]

Now

While we were doing all this, the wider context was becoming more difficult: it was even clear at the time I was leaving Channel Four in 1993 that a significant climate change was already happening in television. At my good-bye party I made some facetious remark about "ships leaving a sinking rat," and it has proved to be the case. You don't have to see too much of that station's output, or indeed current public service television throughout the world, to see that it has descended into what Saul Bellow called a "moronic inferno."

Meanwhile the international exchange rate in cinema has continued to deteriorate. It currently looks like this: The United States makes 96 percent of the films shown in Ireland. The United States makes 71 percent of the films shown in Europe as a whole. European film is only 4 percent of the U.S. market. Indeed, European film only constitutes 22.5 percent of its own home market in Europe overall.

The economy of production is in a very precarious state; the difficulty of achieving distribution pre-sales and the collapse of production and distribution operations like "Film on Four" at Channel Four are indices of this.

I went to college in the 1970s—once a structuralist, always a structuralist—so I wondered what might be the underlying causes of this worsening predicament. I had a minor epiphany when I was coming out of one of the cinemas in the Galway multiplex, having seen *Once upon a Time in the Mid-lands*, a nice enough, small enough film by Shane Meadows. I spied a young woman named Katie, about sixteen years old, who lives in our village—I knew her as she had babysat for us several times. I asked her what she thought of the movie: she didn't say anything really, just rolled her eyes to say "not much." Then I looked behind her and saw the cardboard cut-outs, marketing *Men in Black II,* and I just thought, "There is nothing we can possibly do that will get to where your taste is."

I think the fundamental process taking place may be that marketing has had its effect—it works to make itself a self-fulfilling prophecy and across time it has actually changed taste. Recently a European animation feature was shown to a test audience in California; the ratings on the test cards were 4–5 (on a 1–10 scale). The same film was rescreened to a different test audience with the Disney logo spliced at the front of the film; the test cards came back with average scores of 7–8. Branding can play a very effective role. Across the last few decades, mass marketing has predicated an increasingly limited version of cinema and has shifted audience taste toward it.[3]

I wondered why these changes are not noticed and argued about more. Maybe because it's a messy, complex situation and there are just a few small films that still succeed and, indeed, some big films that fail. Film festivals are a cornucopia, a celebration of cinematic diversity—but they are also short-term and illusory. The question still has to be, "What do most people watch most of the time?"

This is a dark picture I am painting, and I would much prefer a re-demptive ending. Maybe the tide comes up the beach and then it goes back. Maybe my expectations of a wider audience for cultural cinema (born of my involvement in early Channel Four, with its braver vision of how things could be) were always unfounded. Maybe I'm just passing fifty and losing the optimism of youth. Maybe we should remember Gramsci's line about "pessimism of the intellect and optimism of the will."

But I read Danny Morrison in the *Examiner* newspaper recently de-scribing the United States as "a plutocracy maintained by PR." If I were looking for just five words to explain the imperial structure, his phrase would be pretty succinct. We are part of an image system that has a hege-monic purpose: the reduction of the "inefficiency" of diversity. As Alpha Oumar Konare, the president of Mali, once said, "It's like standing in a burning library."

1. For a more detailed analysis, see Rod Stoneman, "Under the Shadow of Hollywood: The Industrial versus the Artisanal," *Irish Review* 24 (Autumn 1999): 96–103, and in *Kinema* (Spring 2000): 47–56. The article is available online at: http://www.kinema.uwaterloo.ca/stonm001.htm

2. See Stoneman, "All Generalisations Are False: Between *Monsoon Wedding* and *Behind Enemy Lines*," *Film Ireland* (November/December 2002): 16–18, and in *Kinema* (Fall 2002): 23–28. The article is available online at: http://www.kinema.uwaterloo.ca/stonm022.htm

3. For additional reflections on film and our current cultural predicament, as well as an account of the reconstitution of the Irish Film Board during its first ten years, see Stoneman, "The Sins of Commission II," *Screen* (Summer 2005): 247–64.

Dublin is in many respects a globalized city and understanding that fact
is essential to our understanding of contemporary Irish society.
—Hilary Tovey, in *Ireland Unbound: A Turn of the Century Chronicle*

Re-Imagining the Built Environment

Place, Community, and Neighborhood in the City of Dublin

MARY P. CORCORAN

In the late 1990s, Ireland entered an unprecedented period of economic
growth characterized by high levels of inward investment, falling unemployment rates, and rising income levels. These trends have been mirrored in the
record-breaking level of spending on homes, cars, holidays, clothes, drink,
food, and other consumables. The changes wrought over the last decade or
so have manifested themselves in a series of transitions, which are forcing a
re-imagining of the norms and values that underpin Irish society. Among
the identifiable transitions are: the move from a rural society to a high-
technology, urbanized, postindustrial economy; the replacement of a culture
structured around locality and localism with one more open to global influences; the decline of religious practice and its replacement by a creed of
conspicuous consumption; and the trend away from monocultural social
structures toward greater diversity and multiculturalism. These complex sociocultural transformations are dynamic and multidimensional. While some
of the changes occurring are dramatic (the accelerated rate of secularization),
others are slower and more piecemeal (reform of governance structures).

Furthermore, not all the changes have moved Irish society in a more progressive direction.

The fruits of Ireland's recent spectacular economic growth, for example, have been unevenly distributed.[1] Socioeconomic inequalities in Ireland have not attenuated but have deepened since the late 1990s. The global reorganization of capital that has contributed to the country's economic boom has had concomitant social costs. While there has been growth in the pharmaceutical, technology, and service sectors of the economy, the relatively secure and unionized "blue-collar" work that epitomized traditional manufacturing industries is in decline. The overheated property market has placed even modest houses in the central city beyond the reach of many. As a consequence, city populations are becoming more segregated along social and spatial lines.

Such divisions are brought into sharp relief in the city of Dublin, which is more spatially and socially segregated than other comparable European cities.[2] Resulting tensions and contradictions are very much a part of life in Celtic Tiger Ireland. They may be illustrated with reference to the built environment, which provides a useful benchmark for interpreting the social and spatial transformations that are occurring. Those tensions raise challenging questions about how we are re-imagining our cities, neighborhoods, and communities during this period of rapid social change.

The Urbanization of Ireland

Despite the establishment of a network of towns in the eighteenth century, the proportion of the Irish population that is urban-based historically remained relatively low in comparison with other European countries.[3] Nevertheless, the most recent census data available indicate that in 2002, just under 60 percent of the population was located in urban areas, that is, in settlements of 1,500 people or more. In the 1990s, Dublin consolidated its dominant position within the Irish urban system. The population of Dublin City is just below 500,000, while the Dublin region has a population in excess of 1.1 million.[4]

Dublin City has a thriving central business district that coexists with pockets of neighborhood dereliction which have recently become the targets of a range of integrated area development plans. Like many British and North American cities, Dublin suffered from poor planning in the 1960s and the 1970s. Much of the fabric of the city center was bulldozed out of existence, to create the semblance, at least, of a "corporate city in-the-making." Considerable profits were derived by key individuals from property development in the city center and land speculation on the outskirts. The City Council vigorously pursued a policy of relocating inner-city residents to new social housing schemes in the far-flung suburbs. The social fabric of the urban core and its capacity to form sustainable communities were systematically undermined. The erosion of inner-city communities through job loss and the disappearance of homes was paralleled by the growth of new ex-urbanized communities on the fringes of Dublin City, where population growth continues to increase at a dramatic rate.

More recently, a trend of "back-to-the-city" living has been manifested in the city of Dublin. This has largely been driven by developers, who have responded to a generous package of tax incentives made available under the Urban Renewal Scheme. The Urban Renewal Scheme was first launched in 1985 and was amended and extended throughout the 1990s. Thus, high-density apartment buildings have proliferated in designated areas of the inner city. Indeed, one of the fastest-growing demographic categories in Ireland, as in other Western countries, is the single-person household. Apartments have been one of the most successful growth sectors in the Irish property market over the last twenty years. Young urban professionals living in apartment buildings in inner-city neighborhoods readily avail themselves of a diverse range of retail outlets, restaurants, bars, and ancillary services now available in the city. In a short period, then, Dublin has been transformed from a provincial outpost to a fashionable European capital.

While the reclaiming and reshaping of inner-city neighborhoods proceed apace, the landscape of the countryside is also changing. New modes of urban living are taking shape in the suburban estates that encircle Dublin and other major Irish cities, increasing the concentration of commuters in peripheral towns. The suburb has emerged as the dominant urban form in Ireland over the last fifty years. Indeed, it can be argued that Ireland is becoming increasingly ex-urbanized, as many of these new forms of suburban living appear to be both posturban and postrural. They are postrural in the sense that vast housing estates, shopping malls, and leisure complexes are colonizing more and more of the countryside, threatening the sustainability of the rural landscape. They are posturban in the sense that the relocation of work, consumption, and leisure facilities to the edge of the city and, indeed, into small towns, reorients suburbanites away from the metropolitan core.

All of these transformations have occurred against the background of a virtual policy vacuum. Ireland, at least until recently, has envisioned itself in primarily rural terms. Memory, tradition, even the shaping of our modern history have been closely bound up with the land, and a visceral preoccupation with property rights, farm inheritance, and the "superiority" of the countryside. The urban explosion of recent decades has occurred in a haphazard, ill-considered, and ad hoc way. The continued, inexorable growth of Dublin, the disruption caused by major infrastructural projects, the revelations emanating from the Tribunal of Inquiry into planning matters in Dublin have combined to undermine public confidence in our structures of governance. Attempts to develop urban policies that are environmentally aware, take cognizance of the principle of sustainability, and seek to promote the idea of the "livable city"[5] are at a nascent stage.

From the Local to the Global and Back Again

In 2003, the Dun Laoghaire Harbour Company launched its plan to redevelop the Carlisle Pier, in Dun Laoghaire, Co. Dublin.[6] The pier, which was built in the 1850s, was a port of embarkation for emigrants for almost 150 years. Now it is to be redeveloped as a flagship harbor project, incorporating buildings of "international architectural significance" designed for recreational and commercial use. Four architectural practices were short-listed for the project, including Daniel Libeskind, the architect who is overseeing the redevelopment of the Twin Towers site in New York. The contract was eventually awarded to an Irish-based consortium, Urban Capital. Local opponents are concerned about the possibility of the privatization of the harbor and the loss to the public of access to an important local amenity. This story brings into sharp relief the kinds of tensions and contradictions that underlie the dramatic socioeconomic transformation of Dublin City in recent years. Twenty years ago, no one could have imagined a Dublin municipality taking its brief for a harbor redevelopment project onto the international stage. It says something for the newly emerged vision, self-confidence, and chutzpah of our city fathers that they now seek the highest possible architectural and aesthetic standards for a city once renowned for its drab provincialism.

But this latest harbor redevelopment project also raises a number of pertinent questions about the nature of the built environment that we might reflect upon: What kind of development and redevelopment is appropriate for a city such as Dublin? What set of values underpins current attempts at urban regeneration? Is it possible to reconcile the demands for commercial sustainability and the desire to respect the vernacular of place? Is there a way of

MARY P. CORCORAN ᏩᎧ

planning for urban futures that can achieve consensus among communities, planners, and developers? And finally, how is the changing built environment affecting our sense of identity, our sense of belonging, and our sense of place?

A number of key factors contribute to the development of a sense of place: First, environmental backdrops, both natural and constructed, come to be written into our place consciousness. Nature "both influences and takes on different reality depending on how, as a continuous matter, it lashes up with the other aspects of the local milieu."[7] Second, the existence of associational life at the level of locality is crucial to place attachment. Community voluntary associations are significant not only as integrating mechanisms that cover a range of fields of activity but because "they harbor memory traces through which something like a social structure can transpose itself from one time or institutional realm to the next."[8] Third, the capacity to develop a sense of place is predicated upon an "embeddedness" or "rootedness" within a particular culture that holds up familiar ideals and standards of "good" places to which we respond. In this way, certain landscapes and built forms become important cultural signifiers and a mechanism through which we develop self-identity. Place, then, is both a space of material reality and a focus of sentimental attachment.

A Tale of Two Communities

To shed particular light on the concept of place and its meaning in the concrete practices of everyday Irish life, I present two urban case studies. The first case study focuses on the proposed Spencer Dock development in Dublin's docklands and the response it elicited from the local community. The second involves a consideration of how community and neighborhood are currently being re-imagined in Fatima Mansions, one of the most notorious social housing projects in the city of Dublin. Together they illuminate how Dublin's sociospatial transformation is played out at the level of the neighborhood, how it impacts communities, and how those communities mobilize to advance their own vision of a "livable" city.

Following the perceived success of the International Financial Services Centre and the Temple Bar renewal schemes in Dublin, a new docklands regeneration scheme was put in place by the government. Under the guidance of a government-appointed supervisory body, the Dublin Docklands Development Authority (DDDA) aims to "provide homes for 25,000 people, create 40,000 new jobs and provide a menu of mammoth commercial schemes—a whole new thriving town in the heart of Dublin."[9] In 1998, the first proposal submitted for the development of fifty-one acres of the brownfield site emerged from a property consortium led by Treasury Holdings. An American-based architect designed a twenty-six-building complex for the site, including a national conference center, apartment blocks, office buildings, hotels, parkland, and the refurbishment and change of use of several listed buildings and structures. Partial planning permission was granted by Dublin City Council, in the first instance, but this decision was appealed by a range of parties, including the local residents, the DDDA, and the development consortium. As a result of the unprecedented scale of the scheme and the interest it had generated, an oral hearing was conducted by An Bord Pleanála in the spring of 2000. In July 2000, An Bord Pleanála rejected the bulk of the scheme, granting planning permission for the National Conference Center only.[10]

The hearing on the Spencer Dock development project provides some insight into how the idea of the city, its future, and its past can become the focus of contested claims. Conflicts between commercial interests (the Spencer Dock Development Company) and community values (docklands residents' associations) were largely grounded in arguments over the significance of place. On the one hand, the proponents of the scheme argued that the development would represent the most comprehensive urban project in the history of the state. It would be a landmark development that was, in the words of one architect, "timely and reasonable." Another architectural critic defended the development on economic grounds, suggesting that since Dublin was already part of the global information economy, it could capitalize on growth in that area by providing commercial buildings such as those proposed in the Spencer Dock scheme. He described the high-rise office towers featured in the development as "perfect machines for working in" and argued that the scheme was daring and adventurous, creating a new quarter that would constitute "an aesthetic as well as an economic breakthrough for a city too long held back by its own past."[11]

On the other hand, the residents (and a variety of other interested parties and groups) opposed the development on the basis of its architectural inappropriateness, excessive scale, environmental impact, disregard for the past, and social implications for the community. Oral testimonies by docklanders give us an insight into the importance of place in the everyday, taken-for-granted life of the city's historic neighborhoods. The residents' representatives employed a territorial, place-based identity as a basis for their political mobilization. The communities chose to represent themselves symbolically as a cluster of urban villages, linked through a powerful sense of attachment to the locality. They argued that their neighborhood retains a powerful sense of place, grounded in a shared historical past, working-class culture, and a web of familial ties. As one resident put it: "My husband's family have lived in this house since 1847 and worked on the railways. We feel cheated . . . It is ironic to see CIE [the Rail Transportation Authority] now part of a consortium attempting to get rid of former railway workers' housing."[12]

The proposed development was viewed as a threat to the neighborhood, so defined. Furthermore, in affirming the sense of a place-bound identity in the urban villages of the docklands, residents quite self-consciously rejected the "making over" of their place. One group of residents argued that, "Contrary to what people think, North Wapping Street, Major Street and Abercorn Road are not part of some Jim Sheridan film set. They are homes where people were born, parents died, brothers and sisters emigrated to America and Australia, and some have come back in their retirement."[13]

Here the residents distinguish between their lived experience of the character and tradition of their place, and its cultural representation in global space. The docklanders mobilized around the sense of place attachment—identifying the docklands as a geographically distinct place with a particular relationship to the city and the skyline. In addition, they made representations to the oral hearing about the significance of their neighborhood as a repository of Dublin's literary and historical heritage. Another resident asserted in his submission: "James Joyce and his brother Stan mitched from school and made their way to the Wharf swimming slip in East Wall. Sean O'Casey was a resident for years, as was Luke Kelly. The Sheridan brothers lived on Abercorn Road."[14]

Opposition to the proposed development crystallized around the clash between the global and the local, with the Treasury Holdings plan viewed as a kind of battering ram of globalization, which ultimately threatened to obliterate the "local" in Dublin. Local docklands opposition to the proposed development may therefore be interpreted as a questioning of the city's new globalized status, neatly summed up in the phrase "the Manhattanization of Dublin." Among docklanders and their supporters there appears to be a growing awareness that unfettered development that does not take account of the vernacular of the city can only lead to a Dublin which is much the same as anywhere else, and therefore, a nowhere place. When industrial buildings are destroyed or renewed as up-market apartment complexes, and when streets of row housing become gentrified, the locally rooted neighborhood milieu loses something of its character, popular memory, and tradition. The place runs the risk of becoming a dis-embedded milieu, its shared history and collective memory diluted by excessive development. As we have seen, local residents are not always powerless in the face of these changes and do articulate discourses of resistance.

The concerns expressed over the course of the oral hearing clearly indicated a desire for Dublin to retain its character and not succumb to placelessness through the importation of mammoth American-inspired architecture. There was a clear sense that, if Dublin was to look for models of development, it was not to America but to Europe that it should orient itself. Yet no party to the hearings could articulate a template or even outline the contours of an appropriate planning model for Dublin.

A few miles across the city, southwest of the river Liffey, lies a social housing project, Fatima Mansions. Here the community has also been actively mobilizing in order to exert some control over the shaping of their future. The re-imagining project in which they are currently engaged must be seen against the backdrop of decades of official neglect, which by the end of the 1990s had propelled the estate into a state of "structural crisis." Here too, as in the docklands, there is evidence of people drawing on a repository of memory and tradition to mobilize around the challenges of the present.

Fatima Mansions was built between 1949 and 1951 by Dublin City Council. The development originally consisted of fifteen blocks of four-story flat units, with an average of twenty-seven units per block. The complex is configured inwardly, which has had the effect of cutting Fatima Mansions off, both physically and symbolically, from the surrounding neighborhood of Rialto. While there is no doubt that the flats were a vast improvement on the tenements that had preceded them, they were essentially a "bricks-and-mortar" solution to the problems faced by the Dublin working class. Little thought was given to the provision of recreational facilities or to the highly salient issues of housing density and housing allocation policy.[15]

In the 1970s, a confluence of factors propelled the estate into a spiral of decline. The closure and, in some cases, relocation of local industry adversely affected job opportunities in the area. The impact of unemployment was compounded when stable tenants were offered incentives by the City Council to purchase local authority houses elsewhere. Such policy initiatives— which promoted home ownership—rewarded tenants who left Fatima Mansions. This gradually produced a residual effect, as less reliable tenants

MARY P. CORCORAN ᏹᎧ

frequently replaced those who had moved on, undermining the social fabric which had been the basis of a strong community. One resident explained the process thus:

> Flats were built in order to maintain social distinctions. Fatima were luxurious flats when they were built because they were third or fourth up the pecking order in the Corporation's housing. But you always had somewhere that was bottom of the heap. Keogh Square was where you went if you didn't pay your rent or you were evicted or whatever. In the fullness of time, Keogh Square got knocked down because it wasn't fit for human habitation. Once they got knocked down, the flats built in the 1940s and 1950s became bottom of the pile.[16]

Dublin City Council's services to the estate declined during the 1970s, with the removal, for example, of the uniformed officials who had informally "policed" the estate. It became more difficult for both the remaining tenants and Dublin City Council to exercise moral authority on the estate. A spiral of decline was set in motion, familiar to analysts of so-called "sink estates" in Britain, or inner-city housing projects in some U.S. center cities. The estate became vulnerable to problems of social disorder—vandalism, joy-riding, and later, drugs. Fatima Mansions earned the reputation of being an undesirable place to live.

By the late 1990s, daily life in Fatima had become a feat of endurance. The most common motif employed by residents to characterize their daily lives was that of imprisonment:

> "I feel as if I am in Mountjoy."
> "It's like a life sentence here now; I have seen too much of it."
> "We are like pigs in a pen here."
> "Our children are like caged animals."
> "We are like fish in a fishbowl."
> "In Fatima you become a person you don't recognize."
> "People shouldn't have to live like this."[17]

The origin of this sense of "doing time" can be traced directly to the problems that pervaded the estate. Trapped in an environment over which they had little or no control, they expressed feelings of hopelessness and despair. Their lives were dominated by two factors in particular: first, a breakdown of social order on the estate, which facilitated a drug economy and culture that continues to the present day; second, the inadequate upkeep and maintenance of the public areas of the estate. Both factors are of course interrelated; the degraded environment, with dimly lit stairwells and boarded-up flats, provided a safe haven for those seeking to buy and sell drugs without fear of apprehension. Residents had internalized the belief that they were perceived as "second-class" citizens by the statutory authorities, and that the quality of service provided to them reflected their overall status in society.

Alongside the simmering despair at the level of degradation into which the estate had fallen by the end of the 1990s, there was also a strong sense of an enduring social fabric and cohesive social networks. A high proportion of people in Fatima Mansions have lived there for more than twenty years, and in some families, tenancy has passed down through a second and third generation. Social ties with neighbors and extended families are extremely strong. Significant numbers believe there is a good community spirit in Fatima, and a majority expressed an interest in getting involved in lobbying to bring about change on the estate. Even though Fatima Mansions was generally deemed ungovernable, there were always blocks within the estate where neighbors, acting in solidarity, had managed to maintain social order. As one resident attested: "There wouldn't be a problem outside my door. They [troublemakers] wouldn't be allowed in the block. All the flats are occupied except one. There is a lot of nosy neighbors and nothing passes them. You'd be down at the shop and somebody would say, somebody is looking for you. Everybody does it and it's good, because everybody knows what is going on."[18]

Although people speak about the horrors of daily life and child rearing in Fatima, they nevertheless display remarkable resilience and a sense of humor in the face of these difficulties. There is a very real discrepancy between the total social breakdown which residents have had to live with on a daily basis—the physical degradation of the environment, the difficulty in securing adequate maintenance, the constant presence of drug dealers and users, the stigma attached to living in the complex—and their frequent reference to the great neighbors they have or have had, and the supportiveness of extended family networks. Clearly, the existence of associational life in the form of interactions, personal relations, and institutional practices at the level of locality act as an important bulwark against total social breakdown. This resource has helped not only to sustain the community but to enable the community to begin to re-imagine itself.

The "structural crisis" on the estate was evidenced by high rates of poverty and unemployment, low levels of educational attainment, and increased

MARY P. CORCORAN ᘒᓂ

criminality and drug-related activity. The problems on the estate can be identified as resulting from the spatial, social, and economic inequalities that characterize the city of Dublin. A structural crisis on this scale demands a structural solution. Thus, the local community came together with Dublin City Council in the late 1990s to set in motion a process of change. The local community development group, Fatima Groups United, became the driving force behind the estate's regeneration agenda and remains the key agent in the process of social change. This lobbying group acts as a catalyst for change by conceiving ideas and implementing initiatives that generally provoke or require a response from the statutory agencies. At the end of 2000, Fatima Groups United produced a manifesto that was the outcome of a creative-thinking exercise which involved the entire community of Fatima Mansions in articulating their visions and needs regarding the place where they live. *Eleven Acres: Ten Steps* comprised a brief from the community of Fatima Mansions to the planners, developers, and service providers tasked with the regeneration of the housing estate. It set out the community's vision for its future and invited Dublin City Council to enter into a dialogue on how the area ought to be regenerated. Crucially, the impetus for a plan for the regeneration came from the community, who placed themselves firmly in the driver's seat of the proposed regeneration.

In February 2001, Dublin City Council published its own plan for the regeneration, *Regeneration/Next Generation.* This plan commits to key principles of urban regeneration, including the creation of a socially balanced neighborhood made up of both social and private housing, with additional purpose-built community facilities. Research in Britain has demonstrated that compared with large deprived estates, socially balanced neighborhoods are likely to be less stigmatized by outsiders.[19] Central to the plan is the reimagining of the existing housing estate, its relationship to the adjacent neighborhood and to the wider city of Dublin. This plan seeks not just to create an integrated and sustainable community but to devise a new template for managing the process of urban regeneration. The new vision for Fatima Mansions is underpinned by the belief that the neighborhood is a key building block for the city and that it is at the level of neighborhood that democracy, participation, and integration must be achieved. Crucially, the plan maintains a dual commitment to both the physical and social needs of the area. The regeneration is guided by three aims: (1) to deliver new standards in quality of public housing and community facilities; (2) to undertake innovative actions aimed at breaking the cycle of poverty on the estate; and (3) to foster effective social integration and measures that promote and safeguard community participation in developing and sustaining the new Fatima, which will triple in size.

The physical regeneration plan is well underway, and the social regeneration agenda has been finalized. The regeneration board has established working groups which are addressing a range of issues including: antisocial behavior, health and well-being, education and training, arts and culture, and economic development. A strategic plan for the social, economic, and cultural regeneration of the estate will work in parallel with the physical regeneration plan. The community is determined to develop an international model of "best practice" for urban regeneration projects in deprived neighborhoods.

The experience of docklanders in opposing the original Spencer Dock development plan and of the residents of Fatima Mansions in generating their estate's renewal raises many salient issues about the process of urban regeneration in Dublin, and indeed in other cities coping with the effects of de-industrialization and marginalization. In particular, there are several key lessons that can be derived from those experiences:

· If the city is to be livable and sustainable, then attempts will have to be made to counteract tendencies toward social polarization in the city.

· Social polarization can be addressed by adapting a principle of equity that ensures that the benefits of urban renewal are more widely distributed across the urban population.

· Urban planners must retain sensitivity to the significance of a sense of place in the everyday life practices of city dwellers.

· Planning must proceed on the basis of a partnership approach that involves the local community as a co-equal stakeholder.

Re-Imagining the Built Environment of the City

Cities are in a constant state of formation, and nowhere is that more apparent than in Dublin at the turn of the twenty-first century. Building and rebuilding activities dissolve and re-create different areas as sites of activity and use. Whether it be the refurbishment of the Shelbourne Hotel or the development of a public plaza at Smithfield, the roadwork necessitated by

MARY P. CORCORAN ᗱᑎ

the building of Luas (a new public transport system) or the re-invention of O'Connell Street as the premier thoroughfare in the capital, Dubliners have become accustomed to living in a city that is somewhat chaotically in-the-making.

The building and rebuilding processes, however, raise important questions about the nature of the city itself. Of primary importance to a city's sense of place are the often intangible and always unique qualities associated with the city's character, the meaning and integrity imbued in the vernacular of streetscapes, building design, boundary vistas, and neighborhood configuration. A sense of place in Dublin has historically derived from a complex of factors including an architectural tradition, history and memory, literary narrative, and lively sociability. But in the wider context of the global economy, cities increasingly must compete for access to global capital, and to do so successfully, they must be prepared to re-invent themselves. Dublin has of late been attempting to reposition itself internationally as an attractive location for the global investor, on the one hand, and as a desirable object of the tourist gaze, on the other. This has necessitated a makeover, in terms of both the architecture and function of key urban landscapes. But the very openness of a city like Dublin to changes and to global influences also limits the city's capacity to sustain and cultivate its distinctiveness as a meaningful local place.

Attempts to delineate a clear vision of what kind of development is appropriate for the city center and its mosaic of urban neighborhoods, as well as for the green-field sites on the city's perimeter, are ongoing. Through social movements, community development associations, and environmental advocacy groups, the citizenry are being engaged in a variety of re-imagining projects that attempt to specify what the nature of place-specific and place-sensitive development might be. Clearly, evidence presented to the oral hearing on the Spencer Dock scheme points to the struggle to define and sustain the individuality of Dublin, amidst all those forces that threaten to render the city indistinct. And in Fatima Mansions, the community activists are driving forward an imaginative program of redevelopment that is requiring a good deal of "thinking outside the box." That community is confronting a history of ghettoization and marginalization and envisioning a new kind of urban living that will offer a template for other cities seeking to re-imagine their deprived neighborhoods. All interested parties, from communities to planners, developers, and politicians, must take up the challenge of identifying forms of development that are consensual across a broader spectrum of the citizenry and that are closer in design, scale, and aesthetic to the city's vernacular. In doing so, it may be possible to find a way that reaches out to the global, while simultaneously respecting the local.

NOTES

1. See for example, Denis O'Hearn, *Inside the Celtic Tiger: The Irish Economy and the Asian model* (London: Pluto, 1998); P. Kirby, L. Gibbons, and M. Cronin, eds., *Reinventing Ireland: Culture, Society, and the Global Economy* (London: Pluto, 2002); Colin Coulter and Steve Coleman, eds., *The End of Irish History? Critical Reflections on the Celtic Tiger* (Manchester: Manchester University Press, 2003).
2. See Daniel Berteaux, Thomas P. Boje, and Susan McIntosh, eds., *Between Integration and Exclusion: A Comparative Study in Local Dynamics of Precarity and Resistance to Exclusion in Urban Contexts,* Final Report. (Denmark: Roskilde University, 2002).
3. Kieran McKeown, "Urbanization in the Republic of Ireland: A Conflict Approach" in *Ireland: A Sociological Profile,* ed. Patrick Clancy, 326–43 (Dublin: Institute of Public Administration, 1986).
4. Central Statistics Office, *Preliminary Findings of the 2002 Census* (Dublin: CSO, 2002).
5. The Dublin City Development Board has produced a strategy development plan for the city of Dublin based on extensive research and consultation. See Dublin City Development Board, *Dublin: A City of Possibilities 2002–2012* (Dublin: DCB, 2002).
6. Olivia Kelly, "Dun Laoghaire Plans Unveiled," *Irish Times* (Dublin), 11 October 2003.
7. H. Molotch, W. Freudenburg, and K. E. Paulsen, "History Repeats Itself, But How? City Character, Urban Tradition, and the Accomplishment of Place," *American Sociological Review* 65 (2000): 794.
8. Ibid.
9. M. Keenan, "Dublin's Docklands Dizzy on Heights," *Sunday Tribune* (Dublin), 19 October 1997.
10. It is unclear whether or not the Conference Center will go ahead. Planning permission has been sought and obtained by Treasury Holdings for residential and commercial development in Spencer Dock. For more on the Conference Center, see Mervyn Horgan, "The Development of Dublin's Docklands," in *Culture of Cities,* ed. P. Moore and M. Risk, 138–45 (Toronto: Mosaic Press, 2001).
11. Judith Crosbie, "Dublin Held Back for Too Long by its History-Critic," *Irish Times* (Dublin), 7 March 2000.
12. "David v Goliath in Spencer Dock," *Sunday Business Post* (Dublin), 20 February 2000.

MARY P. CORCORAN ◯◌

13. Submission 16 to Spencer Dock Oral Hearing, 10 February–14 March 2000.

14. *An Bord Pleanála, Oral Hearing into the Development of Spencer Dock* (Dublin: An Bord Pleanála, 2000).

15. Pat Toibin, *Ways Ahead: A Case Study of Community Development in an Inner-City Area of Dublin* (Dublin: Barnardos, 1990).

16. Personal interview conducted by the author as part of research for the report *Making Fatima a Better Place to Live* (Dublin: Fatima Groups United, 1998).

17. Quotations from personal interviews and focus groups conducted by the author.

18. Quotation from personal interview conducted by the author.

19. B. Goodchild and I. Cole, "Social Balance and Mixed Neighborhoods in Britain since 1979: A Review of Discourse and Practice in Social Housing," *Environment and Planning D: Society and Space* 19 (2001): 103–21.

History, Memory, Diaspora

PAT COOKE

In an effort to explain his theory of relativity, Einstein asked us to understand, in defiance of common sense, that not only does the train move past the station, but the station moves past the train. There are, in other words, no fixed points of reference. All apparently stable phenomena are in motion in relation to each other; stability is a trick of perception. He went on to show how the light from distant stars is curved through space: what arrives is not quite the same as the thing that departed.

Likewise, history (time) and Diaspora (space) are bent and refracted through memory, creating unexpected and distorting effects, the products of cultural relativity.

One summer's day in 1997, I stood at the front door of Kilmainham Gaol with Joe Dolan, the director of the Irish American Heritage Museum at Albany, New York. I had just taken Joe on a tour of the Gaol, the place which, more than any other, crystallizes Ireland's struggle for political independence between the eighteenth and twentieth centuries. Leaders of all the key rebellions against British rule in Ireland had been imprisoned here, and some, like Robert Emmet and the leaders of the 1916 Rising, had spent their last nights before execution in its cells.

As Joe stood and watched that afternoon's stream of peak-season visitors pass through the front door, his face carried a look of increasing bewilderment, until eventually he asked the question that was bothering him: "Where are the Irish Americans?" In truth, he was observing a trail consisting overwhelmingly of French, Italian, Spanish, British, and Irish visitors, but no Americans.

I was not sure I could offer him a full explanation, but this much at least I knew: the trail of European visitors could be explained largely by the fact that they relied on independently researched guides (Berlitz, Fodor, Rough

Guides) in their own languages, whereas Americans tended to rely more heavily on promotional literature generated by Irish tourism agencies. But at that time (the year before the signing of the Belfast Agreement) and for most of the time that "the Troubles" had flared in the North, Irish tourism agencies had discreetly underplayed sites associated with Ireland's troubled modern history. In the early 1990s, for example, Dublin Tourism brought out a directory of the top-twenty visitor attractions in Dublin. Kilmainham was not among them. Instead, it appeared in a long list inside the back cover, headed "Items of Interest."

When I confronted a tourism executive about this anomaly, he explained that tourists came to Ireland to have an enjoyable holiday, not to wallow in the miseries of our history. Now at this stage it would be easy to blame all of this on the upbeat blandness, the cultural impoverishment of tourism's relentless commercialism. But it is precisely tourism's commercialism that makes the picture more complicated. Tourism people, after all, are marketing professionals who take considerable care to find out what their customers want and then try to give it to them. In this sense, the Irish tourism product is as much a reflection of Irish American *expectation* as of any willfully misleading intent on the part of those who fashion it. The elision of politics, misery, and suffering from the package of modern Irish history must surely result as much from how Irish Americans imagine an Irish holiday as from tourism industry guile.

During a lecture tour of the United States in 1999, I remember being struck forcibly by the widespread bitterness among Irish Americans toward Frank McCourt's *Angela's Ashes*. Whatever the literary merits of McCourt's memoir, it made little effort to gild an impoverished Irish childhood with those picturesque touches that palliate emigrant sensibilities. McCourt's tale appears to have disrupted a settled trope of immigrant Irish consciousness, whereby one could lay claim to spiritual origins in a culture as yet untainted by modernity, a culture valorized by honorable poverty and nonmaterialism, while rejoicing in the palpable boon of material prosperity which the act of emigration had delivered in the New World. Thus in tourism, as opposed to literature, people are given what they expect to find. A package holiday is a compendium of clichéd happy or reassuring moments. From the perspective of the heritage industry, which now pervades Ireland's efforts to meet and greet its visitors from abroad, the relationship between Ireland and Irish America has become as much a matter of customer relations as cultural relations. For this reason, any genuine effort to re-imagine Ireland in a way that permeates popular consciousness must reckon with the ideological power of the modern tourism industry.

But that is by no means the whole story. In our postmodern world, more and more people are equipped to fly beneath the radar of tourism and its surface effects. In doing so they discover the counterintuitive nature of culture as an antiproduct. This happened most significantly in the commemoration of the Great Famine over the years 1995–98. One of the most remarkable features of those commemorative efforts was the way in which Irish and Irish Americans came to share in the exploration of this deeply painful dimension of modern Irish history. The Emerald Isle's lush greensward was torn aside to reveal a landscape whose emptiness, as Fintan O'Toole put it, "is founded on catastrophe." Was this the moment in which a re-imagined Ireland became truly possible? In different but related ways, native and Diaspora Irish are products of a troubled history, and of a present that continues to be troubled by that history. History's capacity to disrupt complacencies must to a great extent lie at the heart of our re-imaginings.

Re-Inventing the Past

ROY FOSTER

Re-invent the past? Well, of course we do. It's what we do as historians, and often wearing other hats too. In Ireland everyone is a historian, using the past for the purposes of the present and the future. Kieran Keohane has aptly used the image of Joycean "metempsychosis," the shifting and recurrent pattern of the historical flow, with future and past interpenetrating. Yeats was preoccupied with such a view, which reminds me of a reflection by the great historian Lewis Namier, who pointed out that people don't remember the past and imagine the future; they imagine the past in terms of their own experience, and map the future upon analogies based upon the past, and so end up by imagining the past and remembering the future. Namier was a Pole by birth who became English (or thought he did), but when I read that, long ago, I thought of Ireland.

We do, of course, have our own variants. We're particularly keen in Ireland on scaling up microhistories into the history of the nation: the individual life carrying the weight of the national narrative. John Mitchel's *Jail Journal* is the great prototype. The whole notion of narrative is, of course, up for grabs; Irish intellectual exchange has been enlivened over the past while by literary critics attacking historians for their supposed innocence about theories of narrative and the philosophical presumptions behind them, which seems funny to those of us who were teaching Hayden White to our students twenty years ago. On an international front, the latest offensive of the narrative wars comes in the attack by Ashis Nandy and others on "history" itself as a discipline. They argue that it's ipso facto an elite narrative and can't replicate "experience," so we must "resist the oppression that comes as 'history,'" which Nandy, for one, sees as linear, progressive, and accumulative. It should be replaced with "experience" and a "defiant embrace of ahistoricity." This, we're told, is a therapeutic and creative necessity.

Nandy isn't referring to Ireland, but here too we're ahead of him. History as therapy is something we're old hands at. And in recent years it's right down into the marketplace, thanks to the heritage industry and the commemoration boom. Who owns history now? Not the professionals, which is as it should be. But as pop history takes over, it's worth sparing a thought for the poor old elite practitioners, who after all began, from the 1960s, a process of widening the parameters by buying into other disciplines and new approaches, stressing political relevance, and bringing historical research into the mass media—in Ireland as elsewhere. In the process, Pandora's Box may have opened wide, but, good or bad, the process was certainly significant.

All the more so because history in Ireland has always been of immediate political importance. The effect of, for instance, the Northern crisis on historical writing in Ireland is now itself the subject of historical research, and the concept of historical revisionism kept a lot of people happy for a long time. Bob Scally says that this moment has passed, and I couldn't agree more. But large subjects still lie to hand which need addressing. For subjects as vital as the rise of the Catholic middle class in the later nineteenth century, we still go to novelists like Kate O'Brien or Thomas Flanagan rather than to specific historical treatments. The same is true for the history of land in the twentieth century, or Ireland and the British Empire, though this (like the subject of Ireland and the First World War, or the history of Irish women) may be being opened up now. There are still areas which don't get written about enough, and whose centenaries don't attract much commemoration, and these absences and silences are, of course, significant in themselves. But we are moving away from linear history toward other kinds of "re-invention"—valuable historical work has recently been done on the evolution of, for instance, the Ulster Unionist stereotype, and the creation of St. Patrick's Day.

Simultaneously, though, the popular interest in history has been fueled by the rediscovery of the concept of collective memory and the way it's been inflicted on historical interpretation. The unified national history is collapsed into sectional memories, attached to certain "sites," sometimes speaking diverse meanings and setting up intimate and capricious relations between individuals and symbols: postmodern history. We know about this in Ireland too. It's often stated that the unique linkage we have to our past is mediated by group memory, which raises some awkward questions and involves some unexamined assumptions.

There's a danger—as in other cultures—of a dubious and propagandistic approach to supposed collective memory. In our case, I think particularly of the idea that we remember—or can be made to remember—the Famine, though preeminent scholars of the event and of folk culture, such as Cormac Ó Gráda and Niall Ó Ciosáin, have argued powerfully against this belief. The government has very deliberately used commemorative jamborees, not only of the Famine, whose celebration was pushed out of the way to make room for 1798.

The ensuing popularization and commercialization of historical events has some clear advantages for the historical profession among other beneficiaries, and I'm by no means opposed to all its manifestations. There were some marvelous exhibitions and genuinely illuminating conferences about both events. But the political impulses beneath, and the coded political messages, deserve some attention too. On a broader level, historians necessarily feel cautious about history repackaged as pageant. When a Famine Theme Park brochure promises, "It will be possible to experience first hand how 1,000 people struggled for survival at the height of the famine," is this a useful kind of reinvention, or invention? What lies behind is often a wish to simplify the apportioning of guilt, rather than reexperiencing pain. The notion of history as relived experience rapidly narrows down to vicarious victimhood, based on an assumption of steady-state oppression. It reached a point, in the mid-1900s, where we were told the entire nation had suffered since the 1840s from post-traumatic stress disorder.

Thus we run the danger of denying the shifting undercurrents of Irish history in favor of what a disillusioned Israeli historian has called, in another context, "the Olympics of suffering." What do the heritage presentations and commemorative action-replays really mean? To set sail in the replica *Jeannie Johnston* (after another million euros have been poured into her) or to fight the battle of Ballinamuck in full costume with plastic pikes, or to crouch for five minutes in a newly built mud cabin can provide fulfillment at various levels, but it's legitimate to ask how historically illuminating it is. You don't need to read Proust to know that, in the end, we can't reexperience the past. And much of the elaborate attempt to do so is a kind of self-glorifying effort to claim identity with those who suffered in the past, often for political purposes. By the end of the 1990s, well-fed politicians had become so high on this that they spoke as if they actually remembered a youth spent subsisting on nettles amid a landscape of ravaged skeletons. Cormac Ó Gráda has queried the oft-repeated claim that the Irish prominence in world famine aid comes from our memory of the 1840s. He thinks it's an invention of the 1980s and 1990s, and it's in fact the Irish missionary tradition which provides a far more direct influence. But that's much less fashionable to invoke these days.

We should consider the Irish appetite for virtual-reality historical replay—which the late, great humorist and social commentator Gerry Macnamara would have called silly-makey-uppy history—and note that it has flourished just as the country accelerates away from its past and into prosperity. I'd also like to point out that, in terms of concrete "heritage," there are large questions of abuse of environmental sites, buildings, and archaeological survivals, and that planning authorities in the localities can connive at this without fear of any effective cultural or administrative watchdog going for their throats—since the heritage organization, An Taisce, is effectively powerless, and a Fianna Fail government proudly axed the development board, An Foras Forbartha, as part of a much-touted economy drive, thus leaving them free to fill their pockets unhindered by planning guidelines (economy for whom?). It could also be pointed out that much of the government funds encouragingly earmarked a few years ago for postgraduate historical research have been suddenly slashed away. It's ironic that the actual, concrete ways in which we can experience historical continuity, through the existence and study of ancient landscape and artifacts, are being drastically compromised—while we simultaneously build theme parks and replicas. We seem ready on one level to ignore the destruction of real historical inheritance, and on another to reinvent an imagined "heritage."

A final point: I mentioned earlier the subjects we tend to leave out, and the areas where interesting analysis is beginning to be done. And above all it strikes me that recently we've paid surprisingly little attention overall to the pattern of communal confrontation in our past—the one sustained exploration of religious antagonism in Irish history has come from a journalist, not a historian. I previously mentioned the new-wave historical preoccupation which the generation of the 1960s began to prospect, in other countries as well as Ireland. Many of those historians went on to study the history of abstract themes like love, death, friendship, or fear. I think Irish historians might profitably study the history of hatred. It's an aspect of our own past which has no need, alas, to be reinvented.

The Triumph of Paisleyism

Re-Imagining the Future as the Past

SUSAN McKAY

Making Paisley Look Good

"Probably the worst thing I can say about the IRA," said U.S. Republican congressman Peter King, "is that they are making Ian Paisley look good. That takes a lot of work." This indictment, delivered in March 2005, came from a politician known for his support for Sinn Féin. Just two months earlier, King had called Paisley a dinosaur who had obstructed the Peace Process for years.

King's remarks were a measure of the dramatic changes which took place in the politics of Northern Ireland in the months which followed the breakdown of talks in December 2004. These were meant to see Paisley, leader of the Democratic Unionist Party, and Martin McGuinness, chief negotiator of Sinn Féin, installed as first and deputy first ministers in a power-sharing government at Stormont.

Those talks collapsed after Paisley's party refused to accept the IRA's offer to totally decommission its weapons, unless there was a photographic record of this process. Disregarding St. John's rebuke to doubting Thomas, patron saint of the literal-minded ("Blessed are they that have not seen, and yet have believed"), Paisley rejected a compromise under which a Protestant clergyman, selected by the DUP, would witness the decommissioning. Days before the deal was due to be concluded, Paisley declared in Ballymena, capital of his Bible Belt heartland of North Antrim, that "the IRA needs to be humiliated.

They need to wear their sackcloth and ashes, not in a backroom but openly." The IRA would not be humiliated, replied Sinn Féin leader Gerry Adams. The deal was off: "Dead and gone and buried in Ballymena."

Within days, an armed gang robbed the Northern Bank in Belfast, netting a massive sum of money. The chief constable of the Police Service of Northern Ireland (PSNI), Hugh Orde, blamed the IRA. The Taoiseach, Bertie Ahern, accused Adams and McGuinness of bad faith during the failed negotiations. The IRA and Sinn Féin were two sides of one coin—they must have known the robbery was planned, he said.

Days after that, Robert McCartney was beaten to death outside a Belfast pub. The PSNI's investigation led it to the Republican enclave of Short Strand, where police were met by rioters, and by Sinn Féin claiming harassment. McCartney's sisters went on to launch a powerful campaign for justice for their murdered brother. A local IRA leader appeared to have been deeply involved in the incident. It emerged that IRA men had forensically disposed of evidence and threatened witnesses, and that Sinn Féin candidates were in the bar that night. Some of the IRA men involved had spent the day commemorating the thirty-third anniversary of Bloody Sunday in Derry. This time, the murderers of an unarmed civilian weren't British paratroopers. The McCartney sisters said their efforts to get the killers brought to court had met with "a wall of silence."

Then gardai in the Republic swooped in on what appeared to be a major money-laundering operation. Bonfires of Northern Bank notes were interrupted in County Cork. Thousands of euros were seized which had been packed into a washing-powder box. Five IRA men were jailed after they were caught wearing fake Garda uniforms in a van belonging to a Sinn Féin supporter. Along with posters for a Sinn Féin member of Dáil Éireann, they had pickaxe handles and a lump hammer.

Congressman King's comment reflected the widespread public view, shared by the U.S., British, and Irish governments, that it wasn't Paisley who had humiliated the Republican movement. It had humiliated itself. Paisley was seen to be vindicated. The IRA had to go away, and be seen to go away, before any new negotiations were contemplated.

All of this played wonderfully well for Paisley. Genial interviews followed in the southern media. Of course he'd share power with Sinn Féin, he said. Once there were "no arms and no crime." He praised the Irish government for getting down to the basics in its condemnations of Sinn Féin and the IRA. "You couldn't ask for any better," he said—a rare compliment. The DUP particularly liked the anti–Sinn Féin fulminations of the minister for justice, Michael McDowell.

However, caution is required. I was not surprised when the deal was not done in December 2004 because, regardless of what was going on within the Republican movement, it seemed to me the DUP simply wasn't ready to do it. The "sackcloth and ashes" speech was clearly meant to scupper any chance of compromise. The photographs Paisley was concerned about, I suspect, were not of IRA guns. They were of the Reverend Ian "Never! Never! Never!" Paisley on the steps of Stormont with former IRA leader Martin McGuinness.

Paisley had unfinished business. The British General Election lay ahead in May 2005. His rout of David Trimble's Ulster Unionist Party needed to be completed before he could risk endorsing the Good Friday Agreement he'd vowed to wreck when it was signed in 1998. "Traditional Unionists have been revived and have partaken of a new zeal to defeat our ancient enemies and crush the vipers who poisoned our society," he'd said on the Twelfth of July, 2004. "That spirit must be further strengthened and every vestige of push-over Unionism erased from our midst. The Spirit of Trimbleism must be buried in a tomb from which there is no resurrection." Calling on the assembled Independent Orange Order to "renew our faith in the God of our fathers," he pledged that there would be "no compromise, no sell-out and no surrender."

From Captain Terence O'Neill in the 1960s to Trimble, Paisley has denounced the leaders of "official" Unionism as traitors, calling them "Lundy," after the governor of the city of Derry who favored a compromise with the Catholic forces of King James during the siege of 1688. "No surrender" was the cry of the working-class "apprentice boys" who saved Derry. Paisley has always claimed to represent the "nobodies" who had God on their side.

This has had a deeply inhibiting effect on Northern politics. After the Ulster Unionist Party's poor performance in the 2003 election, the party's Member of the European Parliament, Jim Nicholson, warned Trimble, "A political party should never get too far ahead of the people who are its supporters." Unionist leaders who have tried, however weakly, to reach accommodation with Nationalists have always been dragged back by the sectarian undertow of Paisleyism.

The Reverend Harold Good had no doubts about what he had witnessed in October 2005. "We are utterly certain . . . beyond any shadow of a doubt . . . that the arms of the IRA have now been decommissioned." Good, a former president of the Methodist Church, had, along with the Redemptorist

Father Alec Reed, accompanied General John de Chastelain to oversee the IRA putting its large armory beyond use.

The British, Irish, and U.S. governments cheered. But not Paisley. The DUP leader rummaged in his vast arsenal of destructive words and flung an armful out. It was the "falsehood of the century," he declared. There had been deceit, duplicity, dishonesty, and shameful betrayal. In any case, "There are other IRAs prepared to carry on the butchery . . . At the end of the day, we are no further forward."

Coasters

"You coasted too long." The final line of John Hewitt's 1970s poem about the start of the Troubles is a fitting comment on the outcome of the 2003 elections, which saw Paisley voted the leader of Unionism, and the leader of the biggest party in Northern Ireland.

This is the man who, according to the 1969 report of the Cameron commission into the earliest events of the Troubles, "must bear a heavy share of direct responsibility for the disorders." The man who calls ecumenism a cancer and has equated all Catholics with the IRA. The man whose followers think he is "God's man," a prophet sent to save them in their hour of need.

In May 2003, the British prime minister, Tony Blair, said anyone who believed a political deal could be struck with the DUP was talking "pie in the sky." He said it to try to save Trimble's skin—again. It didn't work. Things had gone too far.

Hewitt's poem is a satire on middle-class Unionists of the 1960s, doing well in business, pleased by their own "broadmindedness"—they had "a friend or two of the other sort"—convinced that "relations were improving," though the political institutions hadn't changed since the 1930s when the Protestant state was set up for the Protestant people. The poem goes on:

> When that noisy preacher started
> He seemed old-fashioned, a survival.
> Later you remarked on his vehemence,
> A bit on the rough side.
> But you said, admit it, in the club, "You know, there's
>   something in what he says."

Paisley's rise is due as much to the coasters as it is to the hardliners and fundamentalists at the core of his party. The UUP, members of which used to be simply known as "the Unionists," is in steep decline. The DUP says this is as a result of David Trimble's support for the Good Friday Agreement. In my view, it was Trimble's failure to support the Agreement which was disastrous. Having signed up to it, he never championed it.

He ignored the role of General de Chastelain's decommissioning body and made IRA arms the central issue at all times. This gave Sinn Féin a powerful bargaining tool—the IRA—and damaged the confidence of Unionists who wished to believe the war was over. The anti-agreement Jeffrey Donaldson and his allies were allowed to undermine the UUP from within, and the beleaguered Trimble tried to paper over the cracks, claiming the differences were "purely tactical."

Thousands of Unionists came out to vote for the Agreement in 1998 and haven't voted since. They thought that was their duty done, failing to grasp that politics is a process and a painful one. Their commitment to the Agreement was not fully tested, however, because Trimble did not demand it of them. When the Unionist parties collapsed the assembly in 2002 over claims of IRA spying, many Unionists didn't seem to notice or mind. But the DUP has learned much from Sinn Féin. It has a sharp press office, and it can mobilize an army of young party activists. The DUP got its voters out in 2003—the UUP did not.

When Donaldson finally defected to the DUP in 2003, his former ally in the UUP, David Burnside, MP, was asked would he be going too. "No," he said. "I'm no Paisleyite." "Paisleyite" is a derogatory term, meaning a bigot, a member of the rabble, a mindless follower of the Big Man. Business-class Ulster Unionists like Burnside would have a certain snobbish distaste for the DUP, though he did also want the parties to unite, on his terms.

However, the DUP is determinedly broadening its base. After the Agreement was signed in 1998, some of the Young Unionist movement defected. They included "baby barrister" Peter Weir, who stood successfully in the 2003 elections. He described his helpers on polling day: "I had a doctor at one polling station, an architect at another and a solicitor at another, along with people from housing estates." He admitted cheerfully that many of those who vote DUP would not admit it. "They want to seem more respectable."

The truth is, though, the DUP has become respectable. Paisley can still play to unabashed bigots—who shout, "No surrender" at every opportunity—but his North Belfast MP Nigel Dodds has a degree from Cambridge University. Like the Orange Order, the party aims to unite all classes under one banner, without, however, unduly disturbing the social order. In 2005, the Orange Order cut the link which bound it formally to the UUP. It had long since moved closer to Paisley's party, not least because of Paisley's consistency in championing it during the appalling events known as Drumcree in the mid- to late 1990s. Like the Order, the DUP is essentially a defensive organization.

In 2005, after a summer that saw Loyalists in Paisley's North Antrim constituency and elsewhere burning and intimidating Catholic families out of their homes, the Parades Commission put a minor restriction on an Orange Parade through North Belfast. Cue a piece of high Paisley: "This could be the spark that kindles a fire there will be no putting out," he announced. The Loyalist paramilitaries stated that they would clear the way for the march to proceed along its own chosen route (through a Catholic area, of course). The Orange Order called people out onto the streets to support its right to march. The leader of the UUP, Reg Empey, sang timidly from Paisley's hymn sheet.

Days of mayhem followed, with riots, gunfire, aggressive roadblocks, Catholic areas terrorized, and the extraordinary sight of Orangemen lunging with ceremonial swords at PSNI officers. In the aftermath, Paisley said he had been proved right. "There's matters in the Protestant community must now be faced up to," he said. The DUP leader claimed poverty and discrimination had pushed his people over the edge.

The Dynamite of Heaven

Paisley set up his first mission in the Belfast docks area in 1949. This was a crusade to defend Ulster Protestantism from "popery" and to expose its betrayal by traitorous ecumenists whose allies were Unionist "appeasers" of "the enemies of Ulster." In 1955, he preached that it was better "to face the stern facts now than to realize too late our peril when hopelessly wrecked on the reefs of disaster."

Billy Mitchell, born in poverty in 1940, was typical of the young men who were listening to Paisley in the 1950s and 1960s. Mitchell said, looking back, that life was good then. There was plenty of work, and it was the era of rock-and-roll. But he was into another kind of music, too, and it was as a member of a traditional Protestant flute band that he started to go to the rallies at which Paisley preached. "We got carried away with the rhetoric," said Mitchell. "We were told we needed to prepare for a doomsday situation. As time went on, the rhetoric got stronger, about the need to fight and the need to arm . . . Of course the preachers and the politicians say they were speaking in spiritual terms . . . but for us it was reality. We took them literally. It got out of control."

Mitchell joined the Loyalist paramilitary Ulster Volunteer Force (UVF) and proceeded into a career of violence, including murder. There were almost four thousand murders during the Troubles. Loyalists, who saw themselves as the "gloves-off" wing of the British security forces, were responsible for 30 percent of them. "We didn't have a coherent ideology," said Mitchell. "Our political analysis was that Ulster was being sold out. Our philosophy was, not an inch. We knew what we were against, but we didn't know what we were for."

In 1966, Paisley was jailed for three months for taking part in an illegal demonstration outside the General Assembly of the Presbyterian Church. In his prison diaries he wrote a prayer for power, based on a commentary on the phrase, "for it is the power of God" (Romans 1:16). "Gospel preaching is charged with the dynamite of heaven," he wrote. "Dynamite to be displayed in all its mighty potency must have the fuse and the fire. When the fuse of true prayer is set alight with the fire of the Holy Ghost and thus the gospel dynamite is exploded, what tremendous results occur."

In an essay called "Paisley's Progress," the Belfast-born poet Tom Paulin, noting that three years later, in 1969, the UVF helped bring about the downfall of Prime Minister O'Neill with a series of bomb attacks, wrote: "Puritan metaphor is a form of irony which has a habit of becoming literal." Another poet, W. R. Rodgers, wrote of Paisley that his "wordplay" inevitably became "gunplay."

Jack McKee began "thirty-five years of faithful service" to Paisley in the 1960s. He is from Larne in County Antrim, a tough port town with a large Loyalist population that gave rise to the expression, "Keep your head low like a Larne Catholic." His career as a loyal lieutenant charts his master's. He was in the Ulster Protestant Volunteers, set up by Paisley in 1966 to emulate Sir Edward Carson's UVF of 1912. It became the base from which Paisley would form the DUP in 1971. Billy Mitchell was one of the UPV's main organizers.

McKee used to sell the *Protestant Telegraph*, a paper founded by Paisley in 1966 and edited by him. One article compared Ulster to Rhodesia—both had a problem with "primitive natives." A letter referred to Catholics as "two legged rats" breeding in slums. McKee was by Paisley's side at Burntollet Bridge near Derry in 1969, when Loyalists ambushed a people's democracy march for civil rights.

"I was his election agent and presented him with a sword when he stood for Westminster in 1970," said McKee. Paisley became an MP in 1970 and has been one since. "I was in the Guildhall when he made his famous speech." In 1973, Paisley said, "Protestantism in Northern Ireland has been betrayed. We must now be prepared to use the mailed fist."

In the elections of that year, the DUP combined with other Unionists opposed to power-sharing to win twenty-seven seats to the twenty-one won by Unionists supporting it. After an executive was set up, Paisley and his followers, including a significant element of the UUP, dramatically increased the pressure. "I was in the Laharna Hotel in Larne with him for the first meeting to organize the Ulster Workers strike," said McKee. The 1974 "strike," the muscle for which was provided by loyalist paramilitaries, brought down the power-sharing executive set up under the Sunningdale agreement. Paisley paraded in front of ranks of masked men in Larne.

Journalists Andy Pollak and Ed Moloney, authors of the 1986 biography *Paisley,* wrote of Paisley's role as leader of the DUP back then: "His word is final and his freedom of action in policy formation, selection of election candidates and treatment of dissent is unique among Western political leaders. Only totalitarian regimes or military dictatorships have produced similar sorts of leaders."

They quoted an account of a 1979 meeting when Sammy Wilson, who had a reputation then as a radical in the party, spoke out against the British conservative party and praised the Labour government's economic policy in Northern Ireland. He warned that the Tories would adopt policies that would lead to unemployment and poverty. Then Paisley, who had arrived late, took the platform and said he trusted God would "deliver Ulster from the curse of socialism," which was against scriptural teachings. He prayed for the return of a conservative government.

W. R. Rodgers wrote of Paisley, "There, but for the grace of God, goes God." Paisley is the moderator of the breakaway Free Presbyterian church, which he founded. A DUP insider told Moloney and Pollak that Paisley had absolute authority simply because he was seen as God's man on earth. "In the Old Testament, God sent prophets at times of spiritual and political decline in Israel's history, and Ian Paisley is seen as one such man sent from the Kingdom to lead Ulster in her own troubles," he told them.

In 1981, Paisley organized a demonstration during which five hundred men marched up a County Antrim hill brandishing firearm certificates. "I was on the mountainside with my gun license," said McKee. "I led the largest group on Larne council for him." McKee was there, too, when Paisley told 100,000 demonstrators in 1985 that the Anglo-Irish Agreement of 1985 would be "resisted to the death" and claimed the British prime minister, Margaret Thatcher, would "wade knee deep in the blood of Loyalists for this document of treachery and deceit." He backed his leader's view of the Peace Process as "the worst crisis in Ulster's history since the setting up of the state" and "a partnership with the IRA men of blood."

Latterly, Jack McKee spoke out against Loyalist attacks on Larne Catholics. He was dropped as a candidate in 2003 and elected as an independent on Larne council. In 2004, he rejoined the DUP. "Back from the wilderness," he said. Billy Mitchell spent long years in jail for murder, emerging in the late 1990s to join the new Progressive Unionist Party, the PUP, which supported the Good Friday Agreement and was a thorn in the side of the DUP, which saw the Agreement as "a prelude to genocide." Paisley said 80 percent of Protestants in the Irish Republic had already been "eliminated." Northern ones would be next. Ian Paisley's son, Ian Junior, dismissed the PUP as "gangsters in suits."

It Takes a Long Time to Die

Paisley's view of history is apocalyptic. "Ulster's darkest hour" is always imminent. In 1997, he told a gathering of the Independent Orange Order that "the entire pan-nationalist front"—that is, the Catholic Church, Sinn Féin, the SDLP, and the Gaelic Athletic Association, which is to say, Northern Catholics—was "united behind the beast of fascism, the IRA." Preaching in 1998 near Portadown on the anniversary of the battle that led to the formation of the Orange Order, he declared that: "The same battle has to be fought today as was fought in the eighteenth century. The same enemy would still take our liberty. The same traitors are still among us who would betray us and sell us out to popery."

What was the root of Ulster's trouble, he demanded. "How did this province which was dreaded by its traditional enemies lose its strength? How was it robbed of its defiance? The blame lies in one place. The ecumenical movement." This was a time of "imminent disaster," he said. "But thank God, we can pray."

This was the year when Paisley warned that the authorities "had better" let the Orange Order march down the Garvaghy Road in Portadown, in opposition to the wishes of the Catholic residents of the area, before the day he called "the decider," the Twelfth of July, the highlight of the Orange year, anniversary of the Battle of the Boyne in 1690. "They'd be far better letting them down before the 12th of July because anybody here with any imagination knows what is going to happen on the 12th of July," he said.

In the early hours of that day, UVF men wearing Orange sashes manned roadblocks in Ballymoney, County Antrim, and a huge petrol bomb was thrown into the home of the Catholic Quinn family. Three little boys, Richard, Mark, and Jason, were burned to death.

In his fine poem "Ecclesiastes," Derek Mahon has written about the lure of Puritan Ulster:

> . . . Yes you could
> wear black, drink water, nourish a fierce zeal
> with locusts and wild honey, and not
> feel called upon to understand and forgive
> but only to speak with bleak
> afflatus . . . stiff
> with rhetoric, promising nothing under the sun.

This is the lure of Paisleyism. As Progressive Unionist Party leader David Ervine said, "It is all about keeping people afraid and angry and agitated."

The DUP has thrived on cultivating a sense of persecution among its people. They are God's chosen, beaten down by tyrants but righteous and sure to be delivered into glory in the end. One of the party's new MLAs (Members of the Legislative Assembly) said after his election in 2003: "The DUP has a different feel to other parties. There has always been a sense of being under siege. That binds people together."

After he topped the poll, as usual, in his Bible Belt heartland of North Antrim in 2003, Paisley was asked by a reporter if he would talk to Sinn Féin. "No," he shouted. "Do I have to take you by the throat? This is MY party and no one in MY party will talk to Sinn Féin IRA." Anyone who did, he threatened, would be thrown out. The talk of the old dictator.

U.S. Senator George Mitchell, who chaired the talks that led to the Good Friday Agreement, wrote in his memoirs that agreement would never have been reached had the DUP taken part in the negotiations.

However, led in the assembly by deputy leader Peter Robinson, it presented a different approach in practice. Robinson and North Belfast MP Nigel Dodds took to their work as ministers with enthusiasm. The DUP MLAs sat on committees alongside Sinn Féin representatives. Paisley himself led an agricultural committee, which included a Sinn Féiner, on a field trip to a hard-line Loyalist fishing village. Loyalists turned out to protest.

When Sinn Féin councilors were first elected to Belfast City Council in the 1980s, the DUP refused to allow them to be heard. Paisley's daughter Rhonda, then a DUP councilor, used to blow a trumpet when Sinn Féin's Alex Maskey rose to speak. But all that changed, over time. Sinn Féin became the biggest group on the council, and Maskey went on to become Belfast's Lord Mayor in 2002. "The DUP worked with us in every way," he said. "We've been to Tralee together and we've been to Peking."

The broadcasting organizations helped the DUP with the fiction that it didn't engage with Republicans, providing separate studios for DUP representatives during debates involving Sinn Féin speakers. By 2002, a perceptible thaw had occurred. The DUP speaker would sit in the same studio but would ostentatiously refuse to directly address or reply to the Sinn Féiner. Talk of "wrecking" has given way to talk of "renegotiating" the Agreement.

Paisley was notably absent from debates on radio and television during the election campaign. He turned seventy-seven in 2003 and was rumored to be in poor health. Certainly, although still "the Big Man" in the eyes of his supporters, he had become stooped and thin, and the voice no longer boomed. Challenged himself about why his deputies, mostly Robinson and Dodds, took his place during leaders' debates, he said, "I was needed out in the sticks." Paisley would later denounce "Romanist" journalists for maliciously claiming he was ill. However, in 2005, his son Ian Paisley Jr. admitted that his father had been "at death's door."

In the aftermath of the 2003 elections, the outgoing U.S. envoy to the North, Richard Haass, paid a visit to Belfast. Paisley called him a meddler who had been disgracefully sympathetic to Republicans. Peter Robinson said they had enjoyed a cordial and useful meeting. There would appear to be tensions within the DUP, but for the most part it has settled for a sort of double act, with Paisley doing the biblical vaudeville while Robinson, Dodds, and now also Jeffrey Donaldson provide the secular cunning. The party acknowledges no contradictions. When PSNI Chief Constable Orde criticized the judiciary for giving lenient sentences to paramilitaries, one senior DUP figure said he was right. Another said he was wrong. A third said he hadn't gone far enough.

The balance has obviously shifted now that Paisley is getting old. Others have power within the party. Born-again, evangelical Christianity of one sort or another is still, however, practiced by most of the senior figures. When the DUP emerged triumphant in 2003, the party's East Londonderry

MP, Gregory Campbell, declared, "God is good." Robinson said the Good Friday Agreement had been "laid in a Saducee's grave, never to rise again" (Paisley had said the same of the Anglo-Irish Agreement in 1985). Robinson also called on the IRA to "repent."

There is much wishful thinking about the DUP, particularly in the UK and the Republic of Ireland, based on largely unexamined notions that modernism, moderation, and pragmatism will take over as its guiding principles once Paisley "goes." He is well aware of this: "They say I am dying," he has said. "It takes a long time to die."

The Cameras Are Against Us

Paisley's dire warnings and demands for Loyalist resistance to the "foe" began long before the IRA's campaign. Then, during the 1970s, 1980s, and into the early 1990s, his blood-and-thunder rhetoric matched the horrors of the times. The IRA murdered nearly two thousand people, including policemen, soldiers, and civilians. There were scenes of carnage in the aftermath of car bombs exploded without warning. There were firebombs. There were even human bombs.

However, since the IRA cease-fire of 1994, Republican violence has declined dramatically. In 2002, the PSNI briefed a private meeting of the Policing Board that the IRA was still in a state of readiness for war, but that the PSNI didn't believe it was contemplating such a course of action. The DUP's representatives on the board rushed to tell the media the first part of the briefing, neglecting the second. The DUP claims the Real IRA and the Continuity IRA are not the enemies of the Provisional IRA, but its proxies.

Back in the 1970s, the DUP lamented the abolition of the sectarian constabulary known as the "B specials." It campaigned in the 1990s to save the Royal Ulster Constabulary, and in the first decade of the twenty-first century against the PSNI's recruitment policy. This was designed to get Catholics into a force which was more than 90 percent Protestant. It campaigned long after the paramilitary cease-fires to save those elements of the Royal Irish Regiment (a direct descendant of the B specials) set up to deal with the IRA at the peak of the Troubles.

There is intense denial among Unionists about Unionist violence. In 2001, a teenage Protestant boy, Glen Branagh, blew himself up throwing a blast bomb toward Catholics. Loyalists said Branagh was a hero who caught the bomb after it was thrown by Republicans at Protestant women and children.

Evidence on CCTV failed to dislodge this fiction. A young Loyalist once told me the reason an incident looked ugly on TV was "because the TV cameras are against us."

Branagh was a member of the youth wing of the UDA, which turned out in force at his funeral. The Loyalist paramilitaries continued to feud and kill and deal drugs. The DUP showed no signs of adopting policies to deal with the redundant foot soldiers of the war against the "enemies of Ulster." Its refusal to "sit down with terrorists" seemed to apply only to the Republican variety. One of its candidates in the 2003 elections was a former Ulster Volunteer Force paramilitary who had been jailed for sectarian offences. The UVF had not decommissioned its guns. Pressed, the DUP simply said the candidate had left his violent past behind him. The Orange riots of late summer 2005 gave the Loyalist paramilitaries a significant boost. It seemed the Unionist family still needed them, after all.

There have been frightening manifestations of twenty-first-century Loyalist rage. North Belfast is a fractured community, a jigsaw of segregated areas divided by peace-line fences. In 2001, the Protestant residents of one such area, Glenbryn, mounted a protest against children attending the Catholic Holy Cross primary school on the edge of their estate. The protesters shouted obscenities and hurled bags of urine and blast bombs at four-year-old girls and their parents. Pressed to explain themselves, they said they were being persecuted. A few years previously, a similarly hysterical and violent protest was mounted against Catholic churchgoers in Ballymena. A Ballymena man who took part in that protest was jailed in 2005 for the attempted sectarian murder of a Catholic.

In 2003, Loyalists began to drive Catholics from their homes in a mixed area adjacent to Glenbryn. One young woman found her child's pet cat dead on the doorstep one morning. Someone had cut off its paws and its tail. Loyalists daubed "Kill all taigs" ("Taig" is a frequently used derogatory term for Catholics) on the wall across the road from her house. Loyalists claimed Republicans were trying to seize their areas. Influenced by British white supremacists, Loyalists have also engaged in intimidation of immigrant families. Again, they claimed they were being overrun. The insecurity runs deep.

The Worm Has Turned

However, in a New Year's Message for 2004, Deputy Leader Robinson struck a different note. "A new spirit exists within Unionism," he said. "Buoyed up with a confidence and boldness that has been absent for a generation, Unionists can get up off their knees and meet their adversaries with self belief and assurance. We have for years been demonized and wronged. Everything British, Unionist, Loyalist or Orange has been despised and we have been pressed to apologize for our existence. The worm has turned."

This vision of Loyalists as the risen people is problematic. When the DUP was set up in 1971, Paisley's then right-hand man, barrister Desmond Boal, said it would be right-wing on constitutional issues, left-wing on social issues. In reality, it is right-wing across the board. Ian Paisley Jr. reacted in 2005 to the news that Trimble's political advisor, Stephen King, had married his male partner in Canada by declaring homosexual relationships as "immoral, offensive and obnoxious."

In working-class Protestant areas which traditionally return DUP candidates and have high levels of paramilitary involvement, just 3 percent of children pass the 11-Plus Exam. This selects the children who will go to grammar schools and have the chance to have third-level education afterwards. Working-class Catholics have a higher chance of passing the exam, but the group most likely to pass is children from middle-class and wealthy families.

The exam is controversial and was abolished by Sinn Féin's Martin McGuinness at the end of his brief tenure as education minister in the Stormont executive, in 2002. The DUP vociferously supports it. It is hard to see how it will deliver the disadvantaged among its voters to the new life of self-assurance promised by Robinson.

Tom Paulin, reviewing a biography of Unionist leader Sir Edward Carson, wrote that Carson's maiden speech in the British House of Lords in 1921 was "a spectacular example of the contradictory, self pitying, childish and festering sense of grievance which is at the center of the Loyalist mentality." Paisley sees himself as Carson's successor.

The DUP has encouraged the conviction that the Agreement was good for Catholics, and therefore bad for Protestants. Catholics get all the jobs now, they've said, producing misinterpreted statistics to prove it. Catholics get the houses. Catholics are taking over the police. Catholics are to blame for all that is wrong. During the 2005 Unionist riots, enraged Orange supporters yelled at PSNI officers: "Are youse Fenians in disguise?"

Can Unionism survive peace? It still relies heavily on the siege mentality for its coherence. "Waiting for the Barbarians," by the Greek poet C. P. Cavafy, deals with the order which prevails during the wait. No need to debate or legislate—the barbarians are coming. But night falls, and the barbarians don't appear. Word comes that there may not even be barbarians any more. The poem ends, "Now what's going to happen to us without barbarians? / They were, those people, a kind of solution."

Unionism has so far failed to re-imagine Northern Ireland as a place in which power is shared and the need for equality provides the dynamic for social change. An element within Unionism still hankers after the good old days of the Protestant state. In March 2005, Paisley said the Republican movement was "rotten to the core." There was no chance of a deal with it. Sinn Féin should be left behind.

Sinn Féin is the largest Nationalist party in the North, and the SDLP would be destroyed if it agreed to go into government with Unionists while excluding it. Paisley is talking about majority rule, again.

Plenty of Unionists don't want dominance. They want "just to get on with things." They've "nothing against Catholics." They need to face up to what Paisley's triumph means. "You coasted too long." The British, Irish, and U.S. governments have weighed-in behind Unionist demands for an end to the IRA. Unionists, still too preoccupied with what they are against, and uncertain what they are for, must come to terms with what the end of the IRA's long war in Northern Ireland actually means. Not the past, before the IRA, but a chance for democracy, at last, in Northern Ireland.

The Peace Process

FINTAN O'TOOLE

The old quip—English, of course—was that every time the Irish Question was about to be solved, the Irish changed the question. The Irish Peace Process was based on the realization that, in fact, changing the question might not be a bad idea. Eventually, the British and Irish governments and most of the political parties in Northern Ireland came to see that changing the question might actually be the way to answer it. For all the difficulties and disappointments of the process since the signing of the Belfast Agreement in 1998, its great success is that hardly anyone asks the old Irish Question any more.

The old question was about territory: "To whom does Northern Ireland belong—Ireland or Britain?" The old answer was: "To whoever can seize or hold it by force." The new question is about people: "Can Irish people of all persuasions live in the twenty-first century without knowing that they belong, once and for all, to a well-defined nation?" The peace deal is based on the belief that the answer is "Yes." For if the old question was about what people were prepared to die for, the new one is about what they are prepared to live with. It is about replacing the absolutes of identity, sovereignty, nationhood—all those big, abstract words—with the humbler contingencies of living with contradictions, ambiguities, and complexities. It is about accepting in the words of the old schoolmaster Hugh, in Brian Friel's play *Translations,* that "confusion is not an ignoble condition."

In order to get the positive answer to this new question that was delivered by the people of both the Republic and Northern Ireland in the referendums of 1998, the British and Irish governments had to blunt the edges of some very sharp words. In a series of texts, accumulated over a decade and a half, they subtly reworked the familiar language of the conflict. They were, in a sense, doing something more familiar to poets and novelists than to politicians— massaging fixed meanings so that they become supple and fluid; complicating the definitions of words so that they become open and ambiguous. If this exercise ultimately proves persuasive enough for the citizens of both parts of Ireland, it will be an extraordinary postscript to the bloody history of Europe's twentieth-century fascination with nationhood.

This leap of faith came about because of the failure of the conflict's absolutes to cancel each other out. By the early 1980s, it was clear to any rational protagonist that the IRA's "armed struggle" to coerce Protestants into a United Ireland could neither succeed nor be defeated. The IRA suffered reverses from time to time, but it was not going to be beaten by military means. Neither, however, could it force the British to leave. Britain simply could not abandon the Protestant majority of the Northern Irish population. Anyone watching the events of 1982, when Margaret Thatcher went to war with Argentina over the relatively meaningless Falkland Islands, had to realize that the idea of the same government surrendering a part of the United Kingdom to an army that consisted at any one time of a few hundred active terrorists was pure fantasy.

Yet the IRA's was not the only fantasy. For about seventy-five years, the United Kingdom pretended that Northern Ireland was a normal part of its territory, just like Bolton or Berkshire. The Republic of Ireland pretended that it was just a missing piece of its own state. Yet, behind the pretense, it was not at all clear that either state really wanted to own the troublesome province. In 1994, each abandoned its pretense. The British announced that they had "no selfish strategic or economic interest in Northern Ireland," a statement whose radicalism can be judged by substituting the United States for Britain and Arkansas for Northern Ireland. At the same time, the Irish declared that they had no interest in imposing "a united Ireland in the absence of the freely given consent of the people of Northern Ireland."

Behind these dry verbal formulae, there is an extraordinarily radical concept. The Belfast Agreement makes two important imaginative leaps. One is that Northern Ireland has become, essentially, a place that belongs to no state. The search for peace turned a place nobody quite wanted into a place nobody claims. The other is that sovereignty itself now resides quite literally inside people's heads. The Agreement states that the old question—British or Irish—is to be decided by the way a majority of the population thinks and feels. The province is British unless and until Nationalists can persuade Unionists otherwise. Northern Ireland has become a new kind of political space. Its people are in an extraordinary position—free to be anything they can agree to become. They have, in one sense at least, escaped from nations.

It's not as simple as that, of course. Northern Ireland remains a small space shared by people who can't agree about what nation they belong to. The conflict has shown what a difficult word "nation" really is. Depending on who is talking, it can mean very different things. For Irish Nationalists, the Protestants of Northern Ireland are part of the Irish nation. In their own minds, the Protestants belong to the British nation. But the Belfast Agreement suggests that that is where nations really exist—in the mind. It will let people in Northern Ireland be whatever they think they are—British, Irish, or any combination of the two. If you want to be British, you can take comfort in the fact that the place will still be formally part of the United Kingdom. If you want to be Irish, you can wave the Irish flag, carry an Irish passport, and argue for a United Ireland without being seen as a traitor. And if, like a lot more people than are acknowledged in the crudities of conflict, you feel that your place is really on the ragged borders between those two national identities, the Agreement acknowledges the rights of those who are "Irish or British or both." Those two little words—or both—seem to me to be among the most radical, and the most delightful, in any international treaty ever signed.

If we recognize that radicalism, we can perhaps understand, if not condone, the tedious progress of political events since the signing of the Agreement in 1998. It was not a statement of the status quo, but a map of a landscape whose lineaments have yet to emerge from the fog of war. It placed a flag on a hill and asked a political system to march toward it without worrying too much about the swamps and bogs that have to be crossed in order to get there. Just because we seem to be slogging forever through the swamp, however, we should not lose sight of the hill that has already, in the imagination at least, been climbed.

Re-Imagining Ireland

Unionism

ARTHUR AUGHEY

Moods can create their own reality. So this paper is not an attempt to justify Unionist attitudes; it is an attempt to explain them. It approaches the subject elliptically or, as Americans would say, from left field. Consider this: Imagine the scene from the recent Hollywood movie *Miss Congeniality*. For those who haven't seen it, Sandra Bullock stars as an undercover FBI agent at a Miss America beauty pageant. At that familiar point in the proceedings when the contestants are asked, "What is the one most important thing our society needs?" each one in turn looks dreamily at the jury and replies: "That's easy. World Peace."

When it's Sandra Bullock's turn (in the guise of Miss New Jersey), she looks seriously at the jury and answers: "Harsher punishment for parole violators." In the audience there is a sharp intake of breath. She pauses, smiles sweetly, and to great cheers, continues: ". . . and World Peace."

The philosophical insight of *Miss Congeniality* is this: The grander the objective, the more fantastic it becomes. The more expansive the aim, the more likely it is to be a cliché, like World Peace. On the other hand, being imaginative is often a question of being practical. And being creative does not mean losing touch with experience. Imagination springs from practical experience and must have knowledge of *means*.

The joke in *Miss Congeniality* is this: The disconnection between the piety of World Peace and the policy of harsher penalties for parole violators is the condition of absurdity. We laugh because we recognize that the sublime and the ridiculous are one and the same. This is what happens when one has only a vision of *ends*.

An absurd scenario, dangerously simplistic, a cheap Hollywood joke, yes; but it is a scenario, it is a danger, and it is a joke not without its significance for understanding Northern Ireland politics after the Belfast Agreement and for capturing the mood of Unionism in particular.

A few preliminary words on what I am *not* suggesting:

I am not suggesting we recycle the old myth about prosaic Unionism and visionary Nationalism only to invert it—that the times now require Unionist virtues and should dispense with Nationalist vices. That would be absurd.

I am not suggesting we peddle the similar notion that Unionists are somehow distinctively hardheaded, for this was never the compliment it appears. What it really supposes is that crass Unionist utility will ultimately succumb to poetic Nationalist idealism. In other words, Unionists will see reason once the ledger of pain outweighs the ledger of pleasure. It was once the belief of the Irish state and it remains the belief of Sinn Féin. That would be dangerous.

Finally, I am not suggesting that Unionism suffers from a crisis of identity. That is so 1970s (as Sandra Bullock might say) that it has become a joke.

This paper makes two relevant points, one general and the other specific. The general point has to do with reflections on the theme of "re-imagining." I am *not* challenging the value of imagination itself, for, without it, culture and the arts would wither. I am questioning the value of *one sort* of imagination in politics but *not all* forms of imagination in politics. Imagination in politics can tend toward romanticism.

Romanticism in politics is always problematic. Armed romanticism in politics is always dangerous. We should be careful not to forget this. As Edna Longley has pointed out, the Irish "imaginary"—in its elision of Unionism—can promote a dangerous political romanticism. Imagination in politics, then, is always a very qualified virtue and for the following reason. Contrary to impression, politics in Northern Ireland has not, I think, suffered from a lack of imagination. It has suffered from *over*-imagination of the fantastic (and deadly) kind. This is what Fintan O'Toole also alluded to when he spoke of the "panics" which had influenced Nationalism and Unionism at the beginning of the twentieth century. Such *over*-imagination has bequeathed to us a style of politics that can be called the politics of "endism," a politics at once sublime and ridiculous. The end for Nationalists, imagined as their destiny, is Irish unity. The end for Unionists, imagined as their demise, is also Irish unity. And these ends are easily disconnected from means. This is the politics of refusal:

First refusal: No first step *unless* it is a step toward Irish Unity—the Nationalist position.

Second refusal: No first step *because* it is a step toward Irish Unity—the Unionist position.

The Belfast Agreement is yet another attempt to shift the focus away from ends—upon which there is no agreement—to means: Whatever end one seeks, the way to achieve it is by peaceful, democratic, inclusive, and constitutional methods. Means then become ends in themselves. Nuala O'Loan and Inez McCormack have spoken eloquently and passionately on this theme and argued strongly that "means as ends," if you like, should become the basis of a new style of politics. To get to this stage, I would argue, involves a *Lampedusan Paradox:*

The Unionist side of that paradox is this: "If you want things to stay the same, things will have to change." In other words, to secure Northern Ireland's status within the United Kingdom requires sufficient reform to secure

Nationalist consent for that status. This is a point to which David Ervine constantly returns.

The Nationalist side of that paradox is this: "If you want things to change, things will have to stay the same." In other words, to secure sufficient reform within Northern Ireland, Nationalists need to accept the principle of consent for constitutional change.

On both counts, as Ed Moloney suggests, Unionist and Nationalist political parties can see the logic of that paradox, even though they still have difficulty accommodating themselves to the reality.

Working and living with paradox is a demanding act of the practical imagination. Unionism has not been particularly good at this. But then again, neither has Nationalism.

My second and specific point is this: What characterizes the current mood of Unionism is the disconnection between the rhetoric of peace and Republican "parole violations." The result has been growing disillusionment with the Belfast Agreement. In the referendum of May 1998, Unionist opinion divided 55 percent "Yes" and 45 percent "No." A narrow base of support, but not an insignificant one to build on. Today the figures are 33 percent "Yes" and 67 percent "No." Why has this happened?

It is a result of practical absurdity rather than of principled hostility. Polls consistently show willingness among Unionists for an honorable historic compromise. However, the distinctive Unionist sense of absurdity is related to the gap between what is experienced—the unnecessary evil of Republican irresponsibility—and what is asserted: that the Agreement is the best possible of all possible worlds and everything in it is a necessary good.

Or to put that otherwise, Unionists sense that parole violations are officially sanctioned while the local variety of World Peace remains to be delivered. And, as the final scene of *Miss Congeniality* affirms (tearfully), we "really do want World Peace." Indeed, we do. But it will not come by imagining it alone. It will only come by delivering it.

The Peace Process

ED MOLONEY

For nearly six years, longer if you go back to the first IRA cease-fire of 1994, the two governments were content to turn a Nelson's eye to examples of continuing but low-level IRA activity on the grounds that the Adams leadership needed to bring its hard men along with them. The hardliners in the IRA had to be satisfied that the version of the Peace Process that was sold internally to them, inside the IRA, was a credible one, which was that if the Process failed, then war would and could resume.

To make this a credible claim, the IRA had to continue to recruit, to train, to arm, to raise funds, and to gather intelligence on potential targets. The two governments were content to allow this to happen and to more or less ignore it, largely on the grounds that this strengthened the Adams leadership, but they also were aware of another reality about the Process—which was that with each day the cease-fire lasted, the more difficult it would be for the IRA to go back to violence.

But recently, as we have seen, there seemed to be a change of mood both in London and Dublin, and it will be interesting to see if it is translated into policy. I think this was brought about by three factors. First, this working out of the ambiguity, or dissembling, inherent in the process, may have eased the difficulties faced by Gerry Adams, Martin McGuinness, and their allies on the Army Council and in the leadership of Sinn Féin, but it was clearly destabilizing David Trimble's leadership of the Ulster Unionist Party, and with it the integrity of pro-Agreement Unionism. The Good Friday Agreement itself, the centerpiece of the process, was under threat from an election which probably would have seen enemies of the Process triumph within the Unionist camp.

Second, I rather suspect the two governments had become simply fed up turning blind eyes, especially when the IRA's activities became more and more outrageous and closer to home. It was one thing for the IRA to shoot alleged drug dealers dead or even the odd dissident inside their own communities, but it was an entirely different matter when it began mounting expeditions to the jungles of Central America—upsetting Washington in the process—or pilfering the contents of the British government's filing cabinets in Belfast.

Third, I believe the governments also calculated that the IRA's military decline had reached its inevitable conclusion, as the architects of its strategy must have known it always would, the point where a return to any sort of sustained and credible warfare was simply impossible, the moment at which the negotiating leverage available to the Adams leadership by the threat of renewed violence finally evaporated into thin air. And I think they also calculated that such was the investment in the Good Friday Agreement made by the Provos and the actual and potential electoral gains derived from it, that the IRA's political leadership would move heaven and earth to sustain the parliament and executive in Belfast.

And so they demanded that the IRA finally make good on the version of the Peace Process that was sold to the governments many, many years ago—an entirely different version from that sold by the IRA leadership internally—which was that the Process was all about the full and complete transition from paramilitarism to constitutionalism. The compliant, even submissive response from the IRA and Gerry Adams, the latter effectively admitting his senior status in the IRA in the process—something he had always resisted fiercely—suggests that London and Dublin read the situation pretty well and that the governments expect the Provos to do the rest that is being demanded of them, not least because they have no choice. That is how it looks at this point, although it is important to remember one crucial aspect of the way that this Peace Process has worked. Invariably things take longer to happen than they should or could, but inevitably at some point they do happen.

It is fitting and appropriate that the two governments have taken the lead in this way, for the political settlement that is inherent in the Good Friday Agreement is one that fundamentally satisfies the interests of both of them. The working out of the GFA (Good Friday Agreement), the working out of the Peace Process, promises to deliver something that both governments for years had relegated to the land of fantasy and pipe dreams. The settlement promises to produce a situation which combines the *minimum* degree of constitutional change with the *maximum* potential for stabilizing the Northern Ireland state, for completing the task of reform begun more than a generation ago by the leaders of the civil rights movement, not the revolution that the founders of the Provisional IRA plotted and planned for. And that is an outcome that the British and Irish governments had long prayed for but never hoped to realize—until, that is, the Adams leadership provided it, more or less on a plate.

This conclusion will come as something of a disappointment to those who have believed and preached for years that the Peace Process provides some sort of magical and even unstoppable route to Irish unity and independence.

But the prediction does not stand up to scrutiny or forensic examination. It does not do so because it fails to take into account the changes that, if it survives, the Process will impose upon the two ideologies at the heart of the conflict, Unionism and Republicanism.

To understand that, it is necessary to return to the fundamentals of those two competing views of the world and ask the following simple questions: "Why do members and supporters of the Provisional IRA behave in the way they do, and why do Unionists behave as they do, and how, if at all, will the Peace Process change their behavior?"

The answer to those questions is fairly straightforward. People joined the Provos, in my experience, not because of some yearning to reunite with the Southern state, but because of a deeply held belief that: (*a*) they could not live a safe and secure life in Northern Ireland, free from the threat of violence either from the state forces or from their supporters; and (*b*) because such is the nature of Unionism that they could never be certain of getting a square deal, a fair swig of the jug, so long as the Unionists were in charge of the show. They were, for the best part of a quarter of a century, committed to the destruction of Northern Ireland, not because they preferred to live in what many of them dismissively and sarcastically described as "the Free State," but because they literally hated the place. And Unionists behave as they do, through discrimination, bigotry, and anti-Catholic violence, because they believe that unless they keep their heel on the croppies' necks, they will be swallowed up and destroyed in a Catholic, Irish Republic. One set of fears and hatreds sustained another.

The Peace Process, the Good Friday Agreement, has the potential to change those definitions in a very fundamental way. In return for a significant say in how they are governed—and, as important, how they are policed and protected inside the state—and in return for a sense of ownership of Northern Ireland, the Catholics, through their most militant manifestation, the Provos, have agreed to put the issue of Irish independence and reunification on the back burner. They have done this by accepting, implicitly and explicitly, the principle of consent, the notion that Irish unity will not happen unless a significant number of Unionists, even a majority of them, wish it to be so. And the Unionists, admittedly with differing degrees of enthusiasm or even understanding of what is happening, have agreed that in return for constitutional security, in return for staying British, they will make Northern Ireland, to quote David Trimble, "a warmer place for Catholics." None of this is to say that this will be a speedy or easy transition, and there will be, and have been, bumps along the way. Many Unionists inhabit mental straitjackets and cannot see, never mind comprehend, what is going on all about them, but slowly, I believe, some of them are beginning to realize the change that has occurred and is occurring. The evidence is there in the pragmatic eagerness of some in the DUP to work the GFA, in the recent expulsion of Johnny Adair's supporters from North Belfast, and in the gradual decline in Loyalist violence.

It doesn't require a genius to work out what the implications would be for the definitions of Republicanism and Unionism should the GFA survive and thrive. If both are starved of the nourishment that sustains them, they will die off and be replaced or changed utterly. If Catholics can get a square deal within Northern Ireland and can identify with the policing system, then their hostility to the state will dissolve. If Unionists can be convinced that their constitutional and religious status will be guaranteed, then, notwithstanding the stupid and bigoted in their community, their hostility to their Catholic neighbors will inexorably melt away.

It doesn't require a genius either to work out that the most likely political outcome of that will be the demise of two extremes—one, physical force Republicanism; the other, irredentist Unionism—and their replacement by entities whose emphasis will likely be on the cultural rather than political differences that separate them. Northern Ireland will be a very different place than it was when Brookeborough ruled the roost or when the IRA Army Council bombed Belfast and Derry to smithereens. It will not be a Protestant state for a Protestant people, nor will it be the engine of the socialist Republic promised by the present IRA leadership way back in the 1970s.

The competing ideologies in the North will, if the process succeeds, have made their compromise and will have achieved a sort of security, perhaps the security of the eunuch, but security and stability nonetheless. It was this prospect, this particular re-imagining of Ireland, that prompted one Irish civil servant at the very dawn of the Peace Process, way back in 1986, to describe it as a "pearl beyond price." It is the reason why London and Dublin behaved as they did recently, and it explains why neither of them will, at this stage, let the process die.

Making Peace in Northern Ireland

NUALA O'LOAN

The governance and accountability of policing is a significant and complex issue in the Peace Process. Put simplistically, for Protestants the RUC (Royal Ulster Constabulary) was "their" police. Protestants still talk to me, as Police Ombudsman for Northern Ireland, about "our police"—55 percent of my complainants are Protestants. They often say they feel guilty about complaining about "our police," that the RUC were fighting a battle against terrorism—in which 302 officers died and almost 10,000 suffered injuries. They feel that whatever the police may have done, it is as if it is wrong to complain. Yet they do. They now demand a service of their police.

For Catholics, the story is very different. The RUC was 93 percent Protestant. Catholics had a history of alienation from the police. The reasons are well known. As a young law lecturer in the late 1970s, I remember clearly students coming to me to complain about being beaten up in the back of police and army Land Rovers.

One of the first complaints I received was from the family of a man called Sam Devenny, an ordinary family man, who was standing outside his little terrace house in William Street, Derry, in 1969. There was rioting nearby. A number of young men, trying to escape the police, ran up the road and into his house. Mr. Devenny followed them in, desperately trying to shut his door. The police arrived. Mr. Devenny and his friend were battered with police truncheons. Five of his little children were in the tiny front room. Several of them were beaten as they tried to protect their father. Mr. Devenny and his children were taken to hospital. The following day he suffered a heart attack; three months later a second heart attack, and he died.

There was a police investigation. There was no proper acknowledgment, though, of the terrible wrong done to an ordinary little Catholic family. We established exactly what had happened and articulated the injustice suffered by this family whose home and life had been shattered, whose father had died. Despite all they suffered, they are the most Christian, compassionate people. I have an enormous respect for them.

I remember also Pat Finucane, murdered by Loyalist paramilitaries, some of them informants, as he sat with his family eating dinner. John Stevens has stated that his murder could have been prevented, and solved. The police did neither. Stevens has also said that over the years, when the police received intelligence of threats, they did not, in many cases, warn Catholics, but they did warn Protestants.

Many people, bereaved by both Loyalists and Republicans, lives wrecked by the sudden death or serious injury of their loved ones, believe that the police either failed to prevent murders or did not investigate them properly. It is sad to have to tell these stories. They must be told—they are part of our history and part of the reason why we need a peace process. There are those who do not sleep at night because the men who murdered their loved ones came at night, who live with pictures in their heads of what they saw; children whose lives have been terribly fractured by what they have seen.

It is important to say that there are many honorable and courageous police officers in the PSNI (Police Service of Northern Ireland). As the Troubles progressed, the divisions deepened, and Catholic police officers became "legitimate targets" for PIRA (Provisional IRA). Anyone associated with the security forces faced the possibility of sudden, violent death. Many died. There were very few Catholic police officers—joining the police meant leaving family, friends, social life—a terrible price to pay for serving your community as police officers.

The police were fighting a battle against Republican terrorists. Many felt they did not have the same view about Loyalist terrorists who were very active, especially from the early 1980s. This led to a lack of confidence in the police, fear of the police, rumors and assertions about the police. It was a cruel and ugly time.

During the Troubles, the police became either reluctant or unable to police Catholic areas. Paramilitaries took control. They were ruthless. Informants were murdered. Punishment shootings, beatings, and exiling were frequent. The Loyalist community became somewhat separated from "their police," whom they no longer perceived as protecting them from the "other side." Loyalist and Republican paramilitaries ruled by fear, using methods of torture and intimidation for which they criticized the security forces. This still happens.

One woman came to me about her son, who had been murdered, she said, by a paramilitary police informant. She said the police had not investigated the murder because of this. She came in great fear, terrified of those who had murdered her son, too scared to tell me who she thought the murderer was, unable to say his name. I asked her to nod if I mentioned the name of the person she thought was her son's murderer. She nodded but did not speak, and I began to test names, until eventually I named a man and she nodded. Living with that terror and that anguish for so many years is hard to imagine.

Policing is essential to any society. It requires the consent of those policed. That consent was not present throughout Northern Ireland. Now we have the Report of the Patten Commission on Policing, the establishment of my office, the signing of the Good Friday Agreement. We are on the road to peace.

My contribution is to investigate totally independently all allegations and complaints against the police—from incivility to allegations of murder and collusion with paramilitaries. It is an enormous responsibility. I have a range of powers—a right to arrest officers, to access police materials, police premises, to take vehicles, uniforms, batons, firearms, etc. for forensic examination. I have a right of access to all police documentation including secret material. I must ensure the proper handling of the material we hold.

I investigate every death which may have been caused by the conduct of the police and every police use of firearms. The chief constable, the secretary of state, and the Policing Board can refer matters to me. I can investigate without any complaint or referral from anyone. The office is evidence driven. We use all criminal investigative techniques—DNA, fingerprinting, forensic medical reports, forensic analysis generally, computerized reconstruction of incidents, video analysis, etc. We must always respect and treat our complainants, our witnesses, and police officers with equal respect. Officers are innocent unless the evidence shows otherwise.

We will always articulate the evidence no matter what it shows. My Report on the Omagh bomb explosion, in which twenty-nine people and two unborn children died and hundreds were injured, established that a warning of an attack on Omagh on 15 August 1998 had been received by the police. They denied it. The warning was not properly dealt with. We will never know whether the explosion might have been prevented. The investigation itself was very flawed. It was a difficult time. I was told that I would not be able to report, that "they would get me in the long grass." I was reminded of John Stalker, who came to Northern Ireland to investigate "Shoot to Kill." He was not able to finish his investigation.

But it is a time of new beginnings. Change has come to the PSNI. We have made many more recommendations for change. By law, I must provide the service in the way I think best calculated to secure the confidence of the people and of the police in the Service. Independent surveys show that 84 percent of our community believe the office is independent; 78 percent believe we are impartial; 84 percent believe police officers will be treated fairly; 85 percent believe we treat people fairly; 78 percent of people believe we will help the police do a better job. We are determined to try to make the Service accessible to everyone. We go routinely and regularly into all sections and parts of our divided community. We have always been treated with respect.

So what is my vision? I look to the day when it is possible to protect life and prevent crime without fear of being bombed or shot, when people everywhere in Northern Ireland have confidence in the police, when paramilitaries do not control our streets, when there are no more kangaroo courts, no more savage and arbitrary punishments by paramilitaries.

Earlier I mentioned problems relating to informants. As a people we must come to understand that to be an informant is to provide to the police intelligence and information, which enables them to protect life and deter crime. It is the civic duty of any individual who can assist the police. It is not a thing to be despised, but a key to becoming a society that accepts and supports its police service.

Northern Ireland has established significant transparency around policing. We must continue to work for all the people. We must not flinch from difficult findings. We must tell society when false accusations are made. To do this we need the support of all the people and of the police officers whom we serve.

Peace and Northern Ireland

JOE LEE

In searching for a possible analogy between Virginia and Northern Ireland, my attention was arrested by an observation made in 1867 by the outstanding English journalist of his age, the editor of the *Economist*, Walter Bagehot:

> Ireland contains two peoples—one Irish, or if they like the word better, Fenian, and another which, though calling itself by many names is, in character, in creed, and in social circumstances, substantially Scotch. Not only is there no unity between these races, but there is no possibility of any. The hatred of a Venetian for an Austrian is feeble compared with the hatred of a Tipperary peasant for a Northerner; the pride of a Virginian to a Negro is gentleness compared with the pride of a Protestant of "Ulster" to any "native" whatsoever. The two peoples differ radically in race, creed and civilization, in their fundamental theories of land, in the tendencies of their dreams, in

their notions of social organization—in everything, in short, which has ever divided mankind.

The Venetian analogy is far from perfect, as Bagehot himself later recognized when observing that, "The real analogy of their position is not Poland or Venetia, but Bohemia, where four millions of Czechs, controlled by an immutable geographical position, vainly try to destroy the power of the million and a quarter of Germans quartered among them."

The Virginian situation bears a closer, though still far from perfect, resemblance. At the time of Bagehot's observation, Virginia had just been on the losing side in a "War between the States," partly provoked by the issue of ethnic relations. It would take well over a century, if even then, for the full implications to play themselves out.

But this makes a point that cannot be stressed too emphatically. It is the matter of time scale. The time scale for issues of identity politics, particularly where they revolve, as they usually do, around the alleged superiority and inferiority of conflicting identities, is very different from the time scale for purely pocket or even power politics untroubled by issues of identity. Disappointing though it naturally be for those who assumed a new day would dawn on the morrow of the Good Friday Agreement, that it languishes at this moment in institutional abeyance, it has only been in place for five years. The latest Troubles themselves have been going for little more than thirty years. But the issue was already old when Bagehot wrote, stretching back in popular memory to the Plantation of Ulster in the early seventeenth century by English and Scottish conquerors. If this perspective be kept in mind—that the Agreement is an attempt to resolve an essentially ethnic relationship, whose roots are nearly four hundred years old, what seems to me striking is not how little but how much change has occurred over so short a period. Only creatures of purely plastic identities can be expected to reconstruct their self-images, in effect to adopt new personalities, in so short a time. Least of all can they do so when identity issues involve real power issues, summed up in that basic question of all identity politics—who rules whom?

The pressure on personality in ethnic politics, in whatever idiom the sense of race may be expressed, when fundamental change is embraced, is analogous to tearing out a hitherto central component of their personality. The analogy is not perfect, but there are some parallels to a physical amputation. That amputation will be contemplated only if the patient can be persuaded that it is essential to guard against an even more horrible fate. As so many on all sides in the North are still loath to believe this, the Agreement had to be a masterpiece of drafting ambiguity for the participants to be satisfied that the new situation involved an improvement for them over the existing one. That is one reason why the smug dismissal by many in England, and indeed of some in the Irish Republic, of a plague on both their houses, is so fundamentally uncomprehending. It is based on the assumption that they themselves would not behave in the same way in the same circumstances.

I suggest that unless those of us living outside Northern Ireland can put our hands on our hearts and avow we would behave differently if born into those circumstances, we should be very slow to condemn—not least as England, to some extent abetted by the Republic, has contributed so much to creating the conditions conducive to conflict. Most such condemnations reveal far more of the capacity for self-delusion of the denouncer than of the denounced.

When one places the Northern Ireland situation in its proper comparative perspective, it seems to me that behavior has been normal rather than abnormal. It has long been fashionable to assert that Ireland in general, and Northern Ireland in particular, are obsessed by history, in contrast to allegedly more mature peoples who do not allow themselves to be imprisoned in the coils of the past and focus their energies on the two really serious things in life, money and sex. But the observation is unhistorical because it is based on a false analogy.

That analogy in the Irish case is essentially with England, given the habitual provincialism of what passes for comparative perspective in Irish affairs, not least the provincialism of those Irish who fancy themselves somehow cosmopolitan simply because they internalize the perspectives of the bulk of the London media, often themselves highly insular. The assumption of the "imitation mind" is that if one's own experience deviates from that of one's erstwhile masters, then one is deviant not only from them, but deviant from the normalcy of human nature—it being a standard technique of all dominators and dominatrices to persuade the dominated to adopt their values as "normal" and dismiss any deviation as not only a deviation from themselves, but from all humankind.

The truth of the matter is that all collectivities with a national sense appeal to history as an affirmation of their identity when they feel themselves under pressure. That is why the English analogy is false not only for Northern Ireland, or Ireland in general, but for most of humankind. It has been England's great good fortune not to find its sense of identity under pressure through-out most of its history.

On the happily rare occasions when it has felt the threat of conquest and occupation, it too has responded in the normal manner—with an appeal to history, most dramatically of all in Churchill's great speeches of 1940, striving to rouse resistance to the threat to English identity by invoking the greatness of the English past as a spiritual weapon at a time when material resources appeared sadly inadequate to resist the threat of invasion.

American identity likewise has happily only rarely come under enough pressure to oblige it to invoke history as a weapon. But it is no coincidence that the one part of America which has known military defeat and occupa-tion is the part of America in which a sense of history seems most devel-oped—as the great Yale historian, himself a southerner, C. Vann Woodward, observed in *The Burden of Southern History.*

So when people in Northern Ireland are accused of behaving abnormally by those who have no remotely comparable experience of such circum-stances, my response would be that they are behaving quite normally, maybe even with greater restraint than normally, for the circumstances in which they find themselves. That does not of course solve the problem. But at least it redefines the diagnosis, and therefore the most likely enduring prescription.

The issue is one of power, not of history—who rules whom? Of course, power in divided societies reflects the outcome of historical conflicts. But the appeal to history has nothing to do with a search for historical truth, and everything to do with the use of history as a weapon in the power struggles of the present. Re-imagining in these circumstances is no problem for the fic-tion writer. For the historian, however, it does pose a fundamental problem. The whole raison d'être of the historian is to discover the truth about the past—otherwise historical writing simply becomes another form of fiction, which of course is what its critics, from the uncomprehending to the oppor-tunistic, claim it to be anyway, which carries for the critics the comforting corollary that they can write any rubbish they like about the past and call it history. But let us at least recognize that the claim that the present is the pris-oner of the past is itself a highly present-centered contention which largely succeeds in concealing the fact that rather than the present being the pris-oner, it is the past which is in danger of regular reinvention in the image of the preferred future.

Re-Imagining Irish Revisionism

KERBY A. MILLER

Re-imagining Ireland is nothing new. Irish bards and English conquerors, Catholic and Protestant clergymen, Nationalists and Unionists, British observers and spokespersons for the Irish Diaspora: for centuries these and others have contested the "facts" and interpretations of Ireland's troubled history, interrogating "what it means" and has meant to be "Irish" at home or abroad.

Contemporary Irish historians, like their predecessors, have played a major supportive role in the "re-imagining" process. From the 1930s and especially since the 1960s, their dominant paradigm has been "revisionism."[1] Revisionist interpretations have permeated Irish scholarship as well as Irish education, media, and, despite some resistance, political culture and popular consciousness. Purportedly blessed with unbiased, "value-free" perspectives and armed with new "scientific" methodologies, revisionists have claimed to write "objective" history. Their efforts have been prodigious and in some respects praiseworthy: they have uncovered new evidence, illuminated experiences of hitherto neglected groups, and "imagined" novel and challenging ways of understanding Ireland's past.

The revisionists' main objective, however, has been to deconstruct, destabilize, and expel from the realms of "responsible" discourse (public as well as academic) what they condemn as the "dangerous myths" of Irish Nationalist history: the "traditional" accounts and interpretations of Conquest and

Resistance that allegedly fostered the Easter Rebellion of 1916, the Irish Revolutionary and Civil Wars of 1919–23, the sociocultural and political inadequacies of independent Ireland, and, most critically, the recent "Troubles" in Northern Ireland. Indeed, their anti–Irish Nationalist sentiments are often so obvious that one wag has suggested that revisionists, if miraculously granted the opportunity to prevent just *one* occurrence in the Irish past, would choose the Easter Rising rather than the Conquest, the Famine, or Partition. Compromised by that agenda, much revisionist scholarship seems scarcely more "objective" than the much-maligned "old-fashioned" Nationalist history that it has largely supplanted. Perhaps more damning is that, after decades of dominance, and despite its practitioners' undeniable sophistication, much revisionist history—once innovative and stimulating—has become tediously predictable.

No history, popular or professional, Nationalist or revisionist, is "value-free" but rather is conditioned, consciously or unconsciously, by the historians' political culture: by the socioeconomic, cultural, political, and academic hierarchies—the prevailing systems of rewards and punishments—in which they function. As Fintan O'Toole suggests provocatively, one of the independent Irish state's greatest failures was that, out of parsimony or philistinism, from the 1920s it failed to co-opt most of Ireland's young intellectuals into the state's "founding" Nationalist and Catholic mythologies, thus alienating them and obliging them to seek nourishment from other sources that were contemptuous of those mythologies and/or of the new state itself.[2] Yet complicating O'Toole's analysis is that after 1921, the Irish state's leaders and apologists were themselves necessarily ambivalent toward at least some Nationalist mythologies, as in the wake of Partition and Civil War the logic and emotive power of thirty-two-county Republicanism threatened "from within" the new state's stability and legitimacy.

The 1960s, however, marked the Irish establishment's critical if long-disguised break with traditional Nationalism. The state's abandonment of autarchic, Sinn Féin economic policies—"capitalism in one country"—for total immersion in an international "free market" controlled by Anglo American financial and corporate capitalism, and the explosion of Northern Ireland's smoldering conflict between Irish and British/Unionist Nationalisms, persuaded most Irish academics to embrace new socioeconomic and historical mythologies better suited to the needs of the globalized, post-Nationalist future which, Dublin's politicians and pundits now promised, would bring Ireland the economic prosperity, social stability, and political closure which the old beliefs had failed to deliver.

Revisionist interpretations of Irish history generally reflect this convergence of neoliberal economic and of (allegedly) post-Nationalist political perspectives.[3] Indeed, historical revisionism is somewhat akin to that neoliberal panacea, privatization. In Ireland both revisionism and privatization find their greatest enthusiasts in periodicals like the *Irish Independent* and among Progressive Democrats and other ideological denizens of "Dublin 4." Both strip "property" (material or cultural) from national, public ownership or common understanding and entrust it to privileged, "cosmopolitan" elites. Both purport to be objective, inevitable processes that liberate individuals from the stultifying effects of "mistaken" past policies and understandings. Both appropriate liberal or humanistic terms and values— concerning individual "freedom," "dignity," and "agency," for instance—to condemn the alleged dangers of "paternalism," "dependency culture," or "victimization history." Yet both subvert such terms to validate new forms of economic and cultural domination—and *old* forms as well: for just as privatization's apostles ignore its consequent inequities of wealth and power, revisionists (despite their post-Nationalist pose) rarely critique British Nationalism or Ulster Unionism with the vigor and asperity they apply to Irish Nationalism. Finally, despite their advocates' disdain for Nationalist or Leftist "ideologues," both impose degrees of legal, structural, or philosophical conformity designed to preclude policy reversal or intellectual challenge.

Thus, just as the ascendancy of neoliberalism has constricted public debate on contemporary socioeconomic and political questions, so the hegemony of revisionism has restricted research or marginalized alternative perspectives on many critical issues in Irish history. Yet revisionism itself needs to be deconstructed and its basic assumptions denied their mystifying authority—not only to restore a healthy equilibrium to Irish historical scholarship but perhaps also to help Ireland's inhabitants "re-imagine" a more coherent vision of themselves, their past, present, and possible future. In the remainder of this essay, therefore, and drawing largely on my own research, I propose to interrogate revisionist interpretations of three historical issues of contemporary importance: Ulster Protestant identities; the causes and consequences of Irish migration; and Irish relationships, past and present, with empire and imperialism.

Ulster's Protestants: Complex Identities

In Ireland, historically and currently, questions of ethnoreligious or "national" identities invariably have political connotations. Unfortunately, the prevailing revisionist model of Irish ethnic identities and relationships—the "two-traditions" paradigm—is deficient. The term suggests the paramount and permanent existence of only two Irish groups whose adherents have totally distinct historical experiences, antagonistic political cultures, and conflicting material interests. One group is characterized as Gaelic, Catholic, Nationalist, and "Irish"; the other as English/Scottish, Protestant, Unionist, and "British."

The two-traditions paradigm does not promote full understanding of the Irish *past*. By merely substituting a two-traditions model for the old unitary Nationalist one, revisionists have failed to grasp the complexity they normally celebrate. Ironically, in the guise of "pluralism" the two-traditions paradigm simply reifies what Frank Wright calls the Ulster Protestants' "settler ideology" as well as the "natives'" Manichean analogue.[4] Consequently, the binary model ignores or deemphasizes similarities, common interests, and instances of cooperation between Protestants and Catholics, and it ahistorically homogenizes both traditions, slighting the diversity, complexity, and sociocultural and (among Protestants) denominational conflicts within each group. And although the two-traditions paradigm purportedly illuminates *cultural* distinctions, its concept of culture is limited: culture is conceived as an independent variable, divorced from socioeconomic and other contexts; and culture and cultural conflicts are "naturalized" as virtually primordial and eternal.

In fact, ethnic cultures and identities are impermanent, situational, contingent on ever-changing historical and environmental factors. Among them, demographic factors are crucial but are often ignored, although between the early 1700s and early 1900s dramatic population changes surely conditioned the development of Irish Protestant identities. For example, between 1732 and 1911, the proportion of Ireland's Protestants who lived *inside* the future Irish Republic fell from nearly 51 to less than 29 percent, primarily because in the 1700s, long before the rise of Daniel O'Connell's Irish Catholic Nationalism, southern Ireland's Protestant communities began to decline precipitously, largely due to high emigration rates that exceeded those among Ulster's Protestants. As a result, by 1911 the six counties of the future Northern Ireland contained almost three-fourths of the island's Protestants. Equally important, between 1831 and 1911, the Protestant proportion of those six counties' inhabitants rose from 57 to 67 percent, and yet between the early 1700s and the early 1900s, the *Presbyterians'* share of that region's Protestants fell from at least three-fifths to less than half. The sociocultural and political

KERBY A. MILLER Ꮼ

implications of these and other demographic changes were surely momen-
tous—for the rise and fall of eighteenth-century Irish Protestant Nationalism, for instance, or for the subsequent consolidation and concentration of
Ulster Unionism.

The two-traditions paradigm is equally unhelpful for understanding *contemporary* Northern Ireland—for contextualizing its ethnoreligious divisions or imagining their future transcendence. Instead, the two-traditions
model is a prescription for eternal sociocultural and political partition in
Northern Ireland and between it and the rest of the island. Likewise, the
paradigm's most recent elaboration, by those promoting a pan-Protestant
"Ulster Scots" identity, arguably only historicizes and exacerbates ethnoreligious polarization by implicitly denying all associations with "Ireland" and
the "Irish." Moreover, in its common usage the term erases from historical
consciousness the large and important body of northern Anglicans, primarily of English descent, who are subsumed in an "Ulster Scots" hegemony
which in turn logically implies Presbyterian primacy in the North's sociocultural and political history. Yet, as we have seen, during the last three hundred
years Ulster's Protestant population has steadily become *less* Presbyterian,
from over 60 percent in the early 1700s to less than 40 percent by 1971. Crucially, it was the Ulster Presbyterians whose disputatious political culture—
once the bane of Anglican bishops, landlords, and officials—was subsumed
in the zealous monarchism and Tory conservatism that traditionally characterized Ulster's Anglicans, as well as in the latter's most distinctive institution,
the Loyal Orange Order.

For the past half century, revisionist historians have "re-imagined" the
Irish Nationalist tradition—subjecting it to intense analysis, exposing its
contextual nature, its ambiguities, contingencies, and inadequacies. However, the re-imagining process must be impartial if relationships in Northern
Ireland, and between northern Protestants and the inhabitants of the rest of
the island, are to achieve peaceful and constructive resolution. If the interrogation and deconstruction of Irish Nationalist "mythologies" are healthy,
valuable exercises, then it would be fair and salutary to interrogate and deconstruct those of Ulster Unionism as well. Revisionists claim to anticipate
the emergence of a post-Nationalist Irish society. We should also imagine and
discuss the possibilities of a "post-Unionist" Ireland.

In the 1790s, the United Irishmen asked if Irish Protestants and Catholics
were forever condemned "to walk like beasts of prey over fields which [their]
ancestors stained with blood?"[5] Ironically, one "field" that members of the

two traditions might explore mutually and profitably is the Great Famine of 1845–52, perhaps in the process discovering that historically they have more in common than hitherto imagined. Of course, the Famine's traditional interpretations appear to corroborate a Manichean view of Irish history. In Nationalist mythology, the Famine confirms the malevolent nature of the Union with Britain and the rapacious character of the Protestant landlord class, whereas in Unionist mythology there was no Famine in "Protestant Ulster" because God spared his Chosen People to reward their fidelity to the Union and their sociocultural and moral superiority to Ireland's "feckless" and "disloyal" Catholics.

And yet, between 1831 and 1861, Ulster's Presbyterian and Catholic populations declined by nearly identical rates—by 18 and by 19 percent, respectively. It was the Famine-era experience of Ulster's *Anglicans* that was exceptional, for their numbers fell merely 13 percent in the same period. Patronage from an overwhelmingly Anglican landlord class and magistracy, membership in Ireland's legally privileged church, and fellowship in the Loyal Orange Order (then still predominantly Anglican): all these may have sheltered poor communicants of the Church of Ireland from the pressures that starved or exiled poor Presbyterians and Catholics.

Local studies discover even more remarkable patterns. Between 1841 and 1851, for instance, the population of ten contiguous, overwhelmingly Protestant and heavily Presbyterian parishes in mid- and east County Antrim declined overall by more than one-seventh, and losses in several parishes were comparable to those in west Munster and Connacht: minus 21 percent in Glenwhirry parish, minus 24 percent in Raloo, and an appalling minus 36 percent in Kilwaughter.

When Kilwaughter's Presbyterian cottiers and other poor Ulster Protestants died of hunger or famine fever, suffered eviction, or migrated to the disease-ridden slums of Belfast or of cities overseas, their fates were determined not by members of the "other tradition"—by their "ancient Catholic foes"—but instead by Protestant landlords, officials, merchant-creditors, and employers: in short, by Ulster's upper and middle classes, whose members mythologized the Famine as devoid of Protestant suffering and, a few decades later, mobilized the North's poor Protestants to defend a Union and a socioreligious hierarchy that had signally failed to protect many of their ancestors from destruction and dispossession.

In early 1848, John Mitchel, a Protestant Irish Nationalist from Newry, County Down, published his "Letters to the Protestant Farmers, Labourers, and Artisans" of Ulster, urging them to join Ireland's Catholics in revolution against a government and a landlord class which, he argued, were responsible for the "Great Hunger."[6] However, Ulster Protestants' political culture, as it had evolved since 1798, allowed for neither a Nationalist nor a class-based interpretation of the Famine experience, as between 1798 and the 1840s a combination of socioeconomic, religious, and political factors (not least the massive emigration of disaffected Presbyterians) had largely eradicated among northern Protestants the ecumenical Nationalism of the United Irishmen—creating instead a pervasive loyalty to the Union and its upper- and middle-class Protestant champions.

Consequently, Ulster Protestant victims of hunger, evictions, and parsimonious relief could not express their pain, grievances, and resentments within the context of a hegemonic religious and political culture that denied their very existence. Likewise, the confines of their "tradition" generally forbade the Famine's Protestant survivors to join or even applaud later Nationalist movements, such as the Fenians or the Land League, that challenged the landlord class or wrung from the British government enormous concessions—such as the abolition of tithes, reduced rents, protection from eviction—that benefited ordinary Protestants (as well as Catholics) and were gained despite fierce opposition from affluent Unionists and from the Orange Order.

The means by which a dominant class achieves cultural and political hegemony over its adherents can be coercive or subtle, ranging from physical punishment (as in 1798) to exclusion from religious fellowship, to everyday signals that "loyal" or "respectable" behavior is a prerequisite for favorable leases, decent wages, steady employment, easy credit, or rapid promotion. Did the disproportionately heavy Ulster Presbyterian emigration of the early and mid-nineteenth century reflect the operation of such pressures, thus promoting the consolidation of Unionism and conservatism—both traditionally Anglican and landlord projects? Did Presbyterian departures and Famine-induced insecurities help ensure, among their remaining coreligionists, the authority of Rev. Henry Cooke and others who led their people into a Unionist alliance with Anglican proprietors, evangelicalism, and the Orange Order—fealty to which increasingly became the poor Presbyterian's most reliable protection against eviction or unemployment? And was the construction of Unionist hegemony encouraged or even mandated by elite Protestant needs to control, or to ignore the very existence of, poor Protestants—and to ignore the intracommunal conflicts which their existence implied—by ratcheting up a sectarian and supremacist rhetoric that sharply and simplistically divided Ireland's and Ulster's inhabitants into merely two traditions—Protestant and Catholic, Unionist and Nationalist, loyal and disloyal, "worthy" and "unworthy"?

Hopefully, the two-traditions paradigm offers no more infallible guide to Ireland's future than it does to Ulster's past. Perhaps a critical perspective may discover or "re-imagine" other, conflicting "traditions"—one or more of which may provide better guideposts to a brighter future than the perpetual polarization and partition to which the revisionist model would consign us.[7]

Irish Migration: Home and Away

At its peak in 1845, the Irish population was about 8.5 million. Remarkably, between 1600 and 2000 roughly the same number of Ireland's inhabitants emigrated. During the seventeenth century, about 100,000 Catholics—often banished by English conquerors—went to Europe or the West Indies. In the 1700s, between 300,000 and 500,000 people—predominantly "Scots Irish" Presbyterians from Ulster—settled in the New World. During the nineteenth century, at least six million Irishmen and -women, most of them Catholics, left the island—nearly two million during the Great Famine—primarily for the United States but also for Britain, Canada, Australasia, and lesser destinations. Finally, during the past century perhaps two million Irish, largely Catholics, went abroad, mostly to England.

Yet if Ireland has been an "emigrant nursery,"[8] to a lesser degree it also has been a migrants' destination: for the Celts in prehistoric times, for Vikings and Normans in the Middle Ages, and for 250,000 to 400,000 Protestant settlers, principally English and Scots, between the 1500s and the early 1700s. Even in the nineteenth and twentieth centuries, small numbers of British entrepreneurs and laborers crossed the Irish Sea, and in recent years perhaps 100,000 "new immigrants" and refugees, primarily from eastern Europe, Africa, and Asia, have come to Ireland.

Thus, Ireland's people have for centuries been familiar with what is now called globalization, as geography and history placed their island at the Atlantic crossroads of the emergent Anglo American economic and political empires. During the nineteenth and early twentieth centuries, most Irishmen and -women enjoyed only a tenuous, temporary grip on "home." Even before they emigrated, many became more familiar with "away"—with the Bostons

KERBY A. MILLER ରୀ

and the Liverpools whence their relatives sent letters, money, and passage tickets—than with other parts of Ireland itself.

Indeed, Fintan O'Toole has suggested that, in recent decades, vastly accelerated changes—rapid travel, instant electronic communications, the globalization (read Anglo-Americanization) of corporate commerce and popular culture—have virtually erased conventional distinctions between "home" and "away." As a result, today's Irish migrants—especially the well-educated, ambitious, and upwardly mobile—often feel more comfortable in Manhattan, Brussels, or Sydney than in an Ireland which they, unlike their predecessors, can visit easily.[9]

To be sure, many recent emigrants remain poor and unskilled, and few experience migration in purely positive, painless ways. O'Toole's argument, however, highlights the fact that the "story" of Irish emigration has always been contested. The interpretations of its causes, character, and consequences have long been subjects of controversy for the Irish in Ireland, the non-Irish members of the "host societies" overseas, and the emigrants and their descendants in the far-flung Irish Diaspora. Contending "meanings" and disputed "lessons" of Irish emigration have emerged from dialogue and debate both among and within these groups. Invariably the results of these contentions—the voices and interpretations that became dominant—reflected the interests and outlooks of those classes that enjoyed the greatest social and cultural authority. Put simply, the "meaning" of Irish migration was and is a profoundly political question, inextricably related to power relationships in Ireland and in the Diaspora.

For example, Ireland's own "possessing classes"[10] have always "explained" Irish emigration in ways that buttressed their sociocultural and political hegemony—often in conflict with variant interpretations advanced by representatives of subordinate groups. This was true even in the 1720s, when Ulster Presbyterian clergymen described their people's migration in starkly religious and political terms—as flight to a New World "Canaan" from "Egyptian bondage" to rack-renting landlords and persecuting Anglicans. By contrast, Irish magistrates and ministers of the legally established Church dismissed Scots Irish grievances as "imaginary" and insisted their departures were due merely to economic ambitions or "strange humours."

Likewise, during the nineteenth century British officials usually contended that Irish emigration was natural and beneficial—the inevitable result of free-market forces—whereas Irish and Irish American Nationalists argued that emigration was at root involuntary "exile" caused by poverty and famine, which in turn were the results of British misgovernment and landlord oppression. Much evidence, historical and contemporary, served to corroborate the Nationalist interpretation, as in the minds of Irish Catholic countrypeople the conquests, confiscations, and persecutions of the past merged seamlessly with *An Gorta Mór* and the wholesale evictions that occurred during that and other crises. Of course, the Nationalists' interpretation of emigration-as-exile caused by political malevolence served to mobilize the Irish at home and abroad against British rule and landlordism. Yet it also *de*mobilized the impoverished masses in Ireland and overseas, for it obscured the socioeconomic and cultural conflicts between them and the Irish and Diasporan middle classes, whose economic, religious, and political enterprises benefited immeasurably from the departure (or, overseas, from the arrival) of Ireland's dispossessed.

For instance, the wealth of Ireland's "strong farmers" and graziers often derived from the fields and flocks of their evicted and emigrated neighbors, while the former's security against reprisals was ensured by the mass departures of disgruntled peasants. Likewise, the Catholic Church's influence at home was strengthened both by the disappearance of lower-class, nonpracticing Catholics and by remittances from the faithful overseas, while the Church's expansion abroad was based largely on the Diaspora's increasing size and wealth. Finally, emigration ensured that in Ireland bourgeois Nationalists were rarely threatened by class conflict, whereas the great numbers of Irish overseas enabled both Diasporan Nationalists and ordinary ethnic "machine" politicians to build and fund successful organizations.

In the early twentieth century, the semi-official Irish Catholic interpretation of emigration-as-exile, caused solely by British/landlord tyranny, remained pervasive—despite occasional objections from socialists such as James Connolly, and although logically it soon became untenable, since after 1921 it was the Catholic bourgeoisie, empowered by Irish independence, that proved unwilling or unable to stem mass migration. From the late 1950s, however, Irish politicians and economists formulated new strategies to attract massive foreign investment and create an export-based, high-tech economy fully integrated into a U.S.-controlled, transnational capitalism. Ideally, they promised, the consequent prosperity would halt and even reverse the tide of emigration. But when departures soared again in the economically troubled late 1970s, 1980s, and early to mid-1990s, Dublin's political establishment hastened to excuse and even encourage the new exodus, both to reduce welfare costs and to protect their new economic order from social and political upheaval. In turn, the establishment's neoliberal and revisionist intellectuals produced new interpretations of Irish emigration.

In the new dispensation, historic and contemporary Irish migrations no longer were viewed in negative, communal, or nationalistic terms. Nor were they interpreted as resulting from systemic inequalities within Catholic Irish society or from the regional imbalances and social inadequacies of the globalization process. No longer was the Irish emigrant a homesick "victim" of British misgovernment or a vengeful "exile" whose "atavistic" Nationalism might destabilize Anglo-Irish relations or lend support to Northern Irish Republicans. Rather, in an ironic echo of nineteenth-century British voices, Irish emigration became the natural result of politically uncontrollable yet ultimately benign "market forces" operating on "a small island." The Irish emigrant was now portrayed as either a fortunate escapee from a repressively "traditional" Catholic Ireland, still blighted by *its own* perverse failure to fully embrace capitalist modernity, or, more commonly, as a confident, ambitious, adaptable individual who—after a few years of certain success abroad, honing entrepreneurial skills in Los Angeles, London, or another "world city"— would return to help indoctrinate Irish society and culture in the techniques and outlooks of global capitalism. "Home" and "away" thus became indistinguishable and irrelevant—with the lure of opportunity dimmed only slightly by occasional jet lag.

Thus, with emigration as with the two traditions, revisionists merely substituted one monolithic explanation ("opportunity") for another ("exile"). Like its antecedents, today's interpretation of emigration serves the interests of Ireland's economic, political, and intellectual elites, most representatives of which deify the market, advocate untrammeled capital and labor mobility, and regard traditional Irish Nationalism as at best embarrassing and leftist criticism as abhorrent and "divisive." For them, the neoliberal interpretation promotes "social stability" by "explaining" all Irish emigration, past and present, as the product of voluntary, individualistic, rational, market-based decisions rather than as the result of flawed policies or social inequalities susceptible to political solutions.[11]

Both the old and the new hegemonic interpretations of emigration help explain why the Irish in Ireland have had an ambivalent relationship with the Irish of the Diaspora. The old notion of emigration as involuntary "exile"—as an occasion for communal grief expressed at American wakes as well as in political and religious rhetoric—contrasted starkly with the cold welcome the Irish usually gave to less-than-affluent returned emigrants. For the "returned Yanks," it was feared, might demand a share of the island's resources—and those were both meager and, thanks to mass departures by the dispossessed and disinherited, increasingly concentrated in the hands of the Irish bourgeoisie.

Similarly, the emigrant's current image as resourceful entrepreneur has enjoyed a mixed reception, at least among some of the Irish abroad. To be sure, many of the Diaspora's members and spokespersons—attuned to the triumphal siren songs of neoliberalism or eager to "prove" their emigrant ancestors' "respectability"—have embraced revisionist interpretations. This is perhaps especially true in Canada, Australasia, and the United Kingdom, where British laws, social patterns, and pressures—plus the reality or hope of state funding for Catholic schools, as well as the presence of large and politically influential communities of Irish *Protestants*—had from the beginning fostered an "accommodationist" model among their Irish Catholic Diasporas. Of course, many Irish overseas, particularly in the United States, find it difficult to jettison the heroic imagery of oppression, poverty, exile, and rebellion that has been integral to their communal identity. But such "traditionalism" merely confirms the Irish establishment in its suspicion of the Diaspora (in America, especially) and in its refusal (virtually unique in Europe) to grant voting rights to emigrants.

The "Celtic Tiger's" recent troubles—soaring housing costs, public sector cutbacks and privatizations, wholesale political corruption, environmental degradation, and other results of rapacious and uneven "development"— may yet again stimulate mass migration, as may also the Irish establishment's efforts to suppress Sinn Féin's increasing political support, itself largely a response to the inequities and inadequacies of Irish "progress." Whether these will generate challenges to the dominant, depoliticized interpretation of Irish emigration is problematic. Mary Robinson's "Light for the Diaspora" may still burn in the Irish presidential residence, but the recent closure of the Republic's *only* center for Irish migration studies (at NUI Cork) is a more accurate reflection of the Irish elite's real attitude toward those it formerly eulogized as "Mother Ireland's Banished Children."[12]

The Irish Empire

The notion of an "Irish Empire" overseas, recently advanced by historians, filmmakers, and journalists,[13] at least partly reflects the same political impulses driving revisionist interpretations of Irish migration and Nationalism.

KERBY A. MILLER

Apparently, the revision of Irish migration demands more than the latter's divestment of traditional, communal, and Nationalist connotations, or its "normalization" as modern, individualistic, and market-driven. It also requires its conceptual relocation in the matrix of British imperialism, specifically, and of Western (or "white") military, economic, and cultural conquest, colonization, and exploitation of native peoples in the Americas, Australasia, Asia, and Africa, generally.

Revisionist logic is simple: If the Irish Catholic experience abroad can be reinterpreted as one of enthusiastic participation in British and American imperial and colonial adventures, and in genocidal assaults on dark-skinned peoples (as well as in the Catholic Church's offensives against indigenous cultures), then the "exceptionalist" assumptions that underpin traditional Irish identity and Nationalism—and the latter's alleged affinities with Third World suffering and resistance—can be fatally discredited.[14]

Of course evidence exists to corroborate the revisionists' image of Irish migrants and their descendants as racist and imperialist. Although Daniel O'Connell provided an authentically "Irish" language of antislavery and antiracism, most of his countrymen overseas rejected his injunctions. Indeed, it is arguable that Irish Americans often played pivotal (if subaltern) roles in the construction of racial hierarchy in the United States, their efforts to gain acceptance and advantage by "becoming white" expressed through urban politics, trade union practices, policing, and race riots.[15] Likewise, it is true that during the nineteenth century, in India and elsewhere, Irish Catholics often comprised a disproportionate number of ordinary soldiers in the British Army overseas—as also in the U.S. Army on the western frontier and in the Spanish-American War. In short, many Irish responded as members of oppressed groups often do when they encounter others even lower in status or more vulnerable than themselves.

Yet the revisionists' basic assumptions are confused and faulty. To the degree that those assumptions are neoliberal, stressing individual volition or "choice" (as in the emigration-as-opportunity thesis), they fail to recognize that attitudes and behavior regarding race and imperialism, like those respecting ethnic or national identity, are socially constructed as well as situational and contingent.

Irish Catholic migrants overseas (and especially in the U.S. and British armies) encountered social structures, legal systems, and hegemonic cultures that were already hierarchical and often deeply discriminatory. Their own "alien" or "undesirable" characteristics—as Irish, Catholic, working-class, impoverished, and often Irish-speaking—posed major obstacles to employ-ment or even sufferance in what were often highly insecure, ruthlessly com-petitive, and even trenchantly hostile environments. Few migrants enjoyed wealth, power, or incentives sufficient to do aught but adapt to their host societies' basic "rules." In the process of accommodation, moreover, most migrants created and relied heavily on their own familial, social, and cultural-religious networks, which in themselves also promoted ethnically exclusive (and perforce "white") attitudes and behavior.

Enmeshed in such circumstances, it was not surprising that Irish mi-grants usually internalized and demonstrated loyalty to both their host society's and their own subsociety's reinforcing conventions, particularly when it seemed both "natural" and in their material and political interests to do so—*and* also when failure to do so threatened to incur economic depri-vation, social stigma, and even legal punishment. A wholesale Irish rejection of American slavery, for example, likely would have generated—and prob-ably institutionalized permanently—a nativist backlash far more powerful than the "Know-Nothing" movement. These are not "excuses" but merely sad and almost inescapable realities.

However, the Irish Empire thesis is at least equally flawed to the degree that, paradoxically, its underlying assumptions are also (as in the two-traditions model) homogenizing and essentialist. Indeed, the thesis implies a kind of "racial" essentialism: the "Irish" were "white" and therefore must always have formed a part (however subordinate) of the "master race" and its thrust to global empire. Yet it is revealing that revisionists often can sus-tain the Irish Empire thesis only by ignoring the two-traditions paradigm. Indeed, sometimes they willfully conflate the identities of Irish Catholics and Protestants abroad—obscuring key distinctions among those they lump indiscriminately together as "Irish"—in order to imply that the for-mer's allegedly hyper-"collaborationist" record overseas belies Nationalist analogies between the historical experiences of Ireland's Catholics and of the dark-skinned subjects of "real" colonial exploitation in the Anglo American empires.

However, the distinctions that revisionists thereby slight were real and im-portant. For example, it was Scots Irish Presbyterians, not Irish Catholics, who, if simply by chronological precedence and sheer numbers, perpetrated most of the "Irish" violence against Native Americans in the eighteenth and early nineteenth centuries. For the same circumstantial reasons, it was the Scots- and Anglo Irish in the United States who comprised the great majority of the "Irish" who practiced slavery and legalized white supremacy in their crucial, formative periods. Further, it was Anglo Irish Protestants, not Irish Catholics, whose status and connections enabled them to constitute the overwhelming majority of the "Irish" officers in the British Army overseas, the British East India Company, and the British colonial administrations and police forces. More recently, it was Ulster Protestants, not Irish Catholics, who availed of such connections to compose most of the "Irish" members of the South African police and prison services under the apartheid régime. Thus, to the degree that it *is* legitimate to speak of an "Irish Empire" abroad, it was an empire dominated, not by Irish Catholic Nationalists, but by Irish Protestants—and, in the British colonies, principally by wealthy and privileged Irish Protestants, that is, by the same kinds of people who dominated Ireland itself.[16]

The point of this argument is not to invert the political implications of the two-traditions paradigm. Irish Catholic migrants were not morally "superior" to, or more "innocent" than, Irish Protestants. It was primarily factors such as timing, class, and circumstance that implicated many of the latter more broadly or deeply than their Catholic countrymen in imperialist and racist systems abroad. It may be that Irish Protestants could transpose a "settler ideology" overseas—and colonial governors often re-"planted" them in frontier regions in part precisely because of that belief. However, Catholic Ireland's conquest and colonization—and the elaborate systems of rewards and punishments thereby imposed—also inevitably generated emulative and even collaborationist responses. Likewise, as noted above, poverty, ambition, and the need to please no doubt fostered adaptation to dominant systems and outlooks that promised acceptance, opportunity, even privilege to migrants longing to escape from customary deprivation and proscription.

Nevertheless, revisionist advocates of an Irish Empire ignore a remarkable amount of contradictory evidence. This evidence suggests that—because of a complex of sociocultural, political, and psychological factors, rooted in their own legacies of conquest and colonization—individuals of Irish Catholic birth or descent (along with Irish Protestants who shared similar perspectives) may indeed have been disproportionately prone—relative to other "British" migrants—to interact with native or subject peoples overseas on comparatively equal terms, to empathize with their plight, and even to support their struggles for liberation.

For example, nineteenth- and early twentieth-century Irish and Irish American Nationalist newspapers almost invariably applauded "native" uprisings against British colonialism, and the Irish American press (both Nationalist and Catholic) strongly criticized U.S. imperialism in Cuba and the Philippines. Many Irishmen of Gaelic or Old English origins—such as William Johnson in early eighteenth-century New York, R. R. Madden in mid-nineteenth-century Cuba and Western Australia, and "His Majesty [David] O'Keefe" in early twentieth-century Micronesia—were unusually successful in mediating sympathetically between native and imperial, traditional and capitalist, societies and cultures. Remarkably, the records of almost every major slave revolt in the Anglo American world—from the West Indian uprisings in the late 1600s, to the 1741 slave conspiracy in New York City, through Gabriel's Rebellion of 1800 in Virginia, to the plot discovered on the Civil War's eve in Natchez, Mississippi—were marked by real or purported Irish participation or instigation. Even Frederick Douglass, a bitter critic of Irish American racism, related how Irish laborers in Baltimore offered to help him escape from slavery.

In class and national conflicts, the evidence of disproportionate "Irish" (often including Protestant—especially Presbyterian—as well as Catholic) migrant participation in protest, radicalism, and rebellion is even greater and more varied. Transatlantic examples range from the "London hanged," the Nore and Spithead mutinies, the Democratic-Republican Societies, and the Whiskey Rebellion of the 1700s, through the Latin American revolutions and the activities of the Chartists, the Molly Maguires, and the Knights of Labor in the 1800s. In Australia, notorious Irish involvement in sociopolitical unrest extends from the convict rebellions of the early 1800s to the Eureka Stockade in 1854, from the legendary exploits of bushrangers like Ned Kelly to the dockland radicalism of the early 1900s. In New Zealand, even the Maori uprisings were reputed to have support from disgruntled Irish Catholic immigrants, as were the Canadian rebellions of 1837 and later of Louis Riel (himself of Irish descent).

Much Irish involvement in such activities is incontrovertible, but much must be qualified by words like "alleged," "rumored," or "reputed." Yet this is one instance in which *reputation* is as important as reality. Reports of "Irish" insubordination, unrest, conspiracy, and rebellion generally originated among governing officials and conservatives—lay and clerical, the latter Catholic as well as Protestant, many of whom were often Irish themselves. These men felt they had ample reasons to fear what they perceived as a perennial "Irish" danger to hierarchy or empire. Prominent figures such as Boston's John Adams, for example, saw inevitable threats to "law and order" from the "motley rabble of . . . Irish teagues" whom he blamed (alongside "saucy boys, negroes and molottoes, . . . and outlandish jack tars") for the "mobs" that in 1770 precipitated the Boston Massacre.[17]

Indeed, in the late 1700s such allegations were legion. Influenced by American, French, and Irish radicalism, many Protestant as well as Catholic Irish, at home and in the New World, embraced a broadly and politically "Irish" identity that embodied for them (and for their adversaries) dreams (or nightmares) of political revolution, social upheaval, and personal liberation. Unfortunately, however, in 1798 the United Irish Rising failed, and the "Age of Revolution" soon became one of political and religious reaction and repression. In Ireland, most Protestants fled to the shelters of Unionism, of evangelicalism, and/or of America, while most Catholics gravitated to "faith and fatherland" movements that were narrowly sectarian and bourgeois-controlled. In the United States, conservatives posed a modernized "Scotch Irish" ethnicity as an exclusively Protestant, socially "respectable," and politically "safe" alternative to the formerly ecumenical and ultrademocratic connotations of "Irishness."[18]

Contrary to the revisionists, therefore, it was not the much-maligned Irish Nationalists of the nineteenth and early twentieth centuries who first constructed the image of Ireland's Catholics (and their former Protestant allies) as inveterate rebels against political and social authority. Rather, it was earlier Protestant (and Catholic) conservatives and counter-revolutionaries for whom "essential" (or "wild") "Irishness" seemed the inveterate enemy of the hierarchical systems, deferential habits, and genteel norms that maintained the prevailing unequal distributions of rights, property, and power. Perhaps the Irish Empire thesis appeals to modern conservatives, who wish today's Irish to acknowledge and fulfill their allegedly imperialist legacy. But much evidence suggests that a once-extensive "Irish *Anti*-Empire"—"When 'Irish' Meant 'Freedom'"—might provide more fruitful themes for historical inquiry as well as for popular inspiration.

In conclusion, the revisionists' failure to "re-imagine" adequately the history of Ireland's people—Catholic and Protestant, at home and abroad—is rooted in their failure to fulfill their own injunctions to boldly explore and fearlessly expose the complexities of the past. Too often, their project to deconstruct Nationalist/Catholic essentialism has merely juxtaposed or substituted other essentialisms alongside or in its place. Thus, the two-traditions paradigm simply reifies the hoary native/settler dichotomy, hedging the old

Nationalist monolith with another equally distorting in its alleged homogeneity and permanence. Ironically, the revisionists' interpretation of emigration implicitly explodes both traditions, replacing them with a neoliberal model of *homo economicus* to counter the old Nationalist belief in emigration-as-exile. Finally, with the Irish Empire we see the return of monolithic essentialism, in which the former "victim" or "rebel" is refigured as "oppressor" and, by extension, as "hypocrite."

By contrast, my research suggests that both traditions were malleable, interwoven, and crosscut by class, politics, and (among Protestants) denomination in ways that demographic evidence and Irish emigrants' letters only begin to reveal. Similarly, the varied Irish responses to mass migration can only be understood through analyses of class and politics, as well as culture, that pose alternatives to the Nationalist and the neoliberal interpretations alike. Last, only "re-imaginings" of even greater breadth and complexity—ranging across the histories of Ireland, its Diaspora, and the latter's host societies—can explain (without justifying) Irish complicity in imperialism and racism and still also appreciate the magnitude and importance of anti-imperialist and even antiracist themes that may yet make at least some Irish history relatively (perhaps even proudly) "exceptional."

NOTES

1. The critical literature concerning Irish historical revisionism is voluminous. Perhaps the most balanced survey is Ciaran Brady, ed., *Interpreting Irish History: The Debate on Historical Revisionism* (Dublin: Irish Academic Press, 1994), and one of the most important short critiques is Luke Gibbons, "Challenging the Canon: Revisionism and Cultural Citicism," in *The Field Day Anthology of Irish Writing*, ed. Seamus Deane, 3:561–68 (Derry: Field Day Publications, 1991). I would like to thank my colleague at the University of Missouri, Ted Koditschek, for his insightful comments on early drafts of this essay.

2. Fintan O'Toole, *The Ex-Isle of Erin* (Dublin: New Island Books, 1996), 95–96.

3. Revisionism is not ideologically homogeneous, however, despite its practitioners' shared aversion to the Irish Nationalism of Tone, Mitchel, Pearse, and Connolly. For instance, revisionism tolerates a handful of Marxist-Unionist (but not Marxist-Republican) practitioners. Also, revisionists include some devoutly Catholic "traditionalist" scholars, who dislike many aspects of *secular* Nationalism (its Enlightenment, Protestant, and sometimes Socialist inspirations and/or its revolutionary methods) that, in their view, compete with faith and Church for historical prominence and popular allegiance. Despite profound philosophical

differences, secular and clerical revisionists maintain an alliance of convenience, as illustrated by the former's lavish praise for Fr. Francis Shaw's influential article "The Canon of Irish History—A Challenge" (*Studies* 61, no. 242 [Summer 1972]: 113–53), which criticized the Irish Nationalism of Tone and others from an essentially theocratic perspective.

4. Frank Wright, *Two Lands on One Soil: Ulster Politics before Home Rule* (New York: St. Martin's Press, 1996), 20 and passim.

5. Cited in Nancy J. Curtin, *The United Irishmen: Popular Politics in Ulster and Dublin, 1791–1798* (Oxford: Clarendon Press, 1994), 21.

6. Mitchel's "Letters" first appeared in his newspaper, the *United Irishman* (Dublin), 28 April and 13 May 1848; reprinted in *An Ulsterman for Ireland* (Dublin: Candle Press, 1917).

7. The 1831–61 demographic data in this section are described and interpreted in greater detail in Kerby A. Miller, with Bruce D. Boling and Liam Kennedy, "The Famine's Scars: William Murphy's Ulster and American Odyssey," in *New Directions in Irish-American History,* ed. Kevin Kenny, 36–60 (Madison: University of Wisconsin Press, 2003); originally published in *Éire-Ireland* 36, nos. 1–2 (Spring/ Summer 2001): 98–123.

Additional research indicates that large discrepancies between Presbyterian and Anglican growth and out-migration rates also prevailed in the 1766–1831 period, particularly in Mid-Ulster—the birthplace of the Orange Order and a cockpit of religious and political conflict from the 1780s. See Kerby A. Miller, Arnold Schrier, Bruce D. Boling, and David N. Doyle, *Irish Immigrants in the Land of Canaan: Letters and Memoirs from Colonial and Revolutionary America, 1675–1815* (New York: Oxford University Press, 2003), appendix 2: "Irish Migration and Demography, 1659–1831" (with Liam Kennedy), 656–77.

Many of these arguments are elaborated in Kerby A. Miller, "Ulster Presbyterians and the 'Two Traditions' in Ireland and America," in *These Fissured Isles: Varieties of British and Irish Identities,* ed. Terry Brotherstone et al. (Glasgow: Hambleton Press, 2005), and "Forging the 'Protestant Way of Life': Class Conflict and the Origins of Unionist Hegemony in Early Nineteenth-Century Ulster," in *Transatlantic Perspectives on Ulster Presbyterianism: Religion, Politics and Identity,* ed. Mark G. Spencer and David A. Wilson (Dublin: Four Courts Press, 2005).

8. Jim Mac Laughlin, *Ireland: The Emigrant Nursery and the World Economy* (Cork: Cork University Press, 1994).

9. O'Toole, *Ex-Isle of Erin,* especially the introductory and final sections.

10. J. J. Lee, *Ireland, 1912–1985: Politics and Society* (Cambridge: Cambridge University Press, 1989), 376, 390, and passim.

11. Arguably, the same perspective may buttress the global-capitalist project of cheap-labor migration *into* Ireland, for both neoliberals and those genuinely sympathetic to the new immigrants' plight brand that project's critics as provincial and racist. Many of the latter merit such pejoratives, but neoliberal critics often ignore

the plight of those "left behind" by Irish "progress," who unfortunately sometimes seek easy, xenophobic answers for their own absolute or relative deprivation.

12. The results of my research on transatlantic Irish migration are set forth or summarized in various publications, especially in *Emigrants and Exiles: Ireland and the Irish Exodus to North America* (New York: Oxford University Press, 1985); in "Emigration As Exile: Cultural Hegemony in Post-Famine Ireland," in *A Century of European Migration, 1830–1930*, ed. Rudolph J. Vecoli and Suzanne M. Sinke, 339–63 (Urbana: University of Illinois Press, 1991); and, on eighteenth-century migration, in Miller et al., *Irish Immigrants*.

Regarding contemporary Irish migration, my interpretations are similar to those of Jim Mac Laughlin in *Ireland: The Emigrant Nursery and the World Economy*, and *Location and Dislocation in Contemporary Irish Society: Emigration and Irish Identities* (Notre Dame: University of Notre Dame Press, 1997).

13. In addition to the recent documentary film series *The Irish Empire* (1998), see, for example, Keith Jeffrey, ed., *An Irish Empire? Aspects of Ireland and the British Empire* (Manchester: Manchester University Press, 1996), and the chapters in "Part Three: The Empire," of Andy Bielenberg, ed., *The Irish Diaspora* (Harlow, Essex: Longman, 2000); it should be noted that the authors of the essays in these works vary in their interpretations of—and enthusiasm for—the Irish Empire concept.

14. To be fair, at least some who employ an Irish Empire concept have a different project, namely, to challenge the complacency and insularity of many Irish and Irish Americans by summoning them not to abandon Nationalist ideals or anti-imperialist sentiments but to extend their application beyond mere rhetoric and the confines of their own communities.

15. This is the argument made by leftist scholars of race in America, such as Noel Ignatiev in *How the Irish Became White* (New York: Routledge, 1995), and David Roediger in *The Wages of Whiteness: Race and the Making of the American Working Class* (London: Verso, 1991). Of course, these scholars are worlds apart, ideologically, from neoliberal revisionists who seek to discount the radical and internationalist aspects of Irish Nationalism. Nor do they view Irish American racial identity as essentialist but rather as historically constructed and therefore amenable to deconstruction (perhaps even destruction as well). However, I suspect that Ignatiev and Roediger, as New Leftist scholars, may overattribute "agency" to ordinary Irish immigrants and thus underestimate the constricting socioeconomic and other subaltern contexts in which Irish American "whiteness" developed.

16. Moreover, however harshly one judges Catholicism's record among American, Asian, and African natives—and to be fair its performance must be compared with those of the Protestant churches that sent "Irish" representatives overseas—the Catholic Church's vaunted "Spiritual Empire" was everywhere (including Ireland itself) predominantly "Roman," not "Irish." Indeed, one might contend that institutional (that is, official) Catholicism in Ireland has not been indigenously or distinctively "Irish" since the impositions of the Gregorian Reforms in

the Middle Ages or of Tridentine Catholicism or the "Devotional Revolution" in the early modern and modern periods, respectively.

17. Adams cited in Alfred F. Young, *The Shoemaker and the Tea Party: Memory and the American Revolution* (Boston: Beacon Press, 1999), 96–97. Revealingly, the "Irish" killed in the Massacre (Caldwell and Carr) were men who later would be called "Scotch Irish." Thus, for Adams and other Anglo American conservatives, it was not religion that marginalized and stigmatized such people as "Irish teagues" or "wild Irish"—epithets traditionally applied only to Irish Catholics—but rather their poverty, "subversive" social and political ideas, and "dangerous" or "rebellious" behavior.

18. These arguments are elaborated in Miller et al., *Irish Immigrants*, especially in the introduction, the chapters in part 7, and the epilogue.

The Two-Migrations Myth, the Scotch Irish, and Irish American Experience

PATRICK GRIFFIN

The Irish American experience makes little sense without including the Scotch Irish. At first blush, such an assertion may seem absurd. After all, we know that when we discuss the Irish American experience we mean the migration, settlement, and adaptation of millions of Catholics who left Ireland during the nineteenth and twentieth centuries to travel to American cities, that we are studying the people who would identify themselves and be identified by the moniker "Irish American."

Why would historians of Irish America explore a smaller movement, one that numbered somewhere between 100,000 and 200,000 over the course of the eighteenth century to colonial America? Why study a group of people who moved by and large to rural areas? Why examine a largely Protestant people who defined themselves against Catholics, who suggested they were anything but "Irish"? Indeed, we would be hard pressed to find two more distinctive experiences.[1]

But viewing these experiences as mutually exclusive has come at a great cost to each. In fact, by dividing the "Scotch Irish" from the "Irish American" experience we have lost sight of the big picture. Conventional perspectives—enshrined in popular American memory and in scholarly literature—that celebrate each of these traditions as distinctive have blurred the enduring lines that have tied Ireland to America for four centuries. For the Irish American experience only makes sense if we understand that Ireland was yoked to America from the first days of settlement, and that the scope and tenor of migration changed in response to the changing relationship between the two places.

The two-migrations myth emerged full-blown at the tail end of the nineteenth century after shoals of poor Irish began arriving into American cities.

Real and imagined descendants of the eighteenth-century movement from Ireland re-invented themselves as "Scotch Irish." Their ancestors, they asserted, were a brave, hardy, anti-authoritarian "race" of men and women who left a decrepit Old World during the formative years while the American nation "matured." These "Ulster" migrants were Protestant to a man and woman, individualistic, and attracted to the rigors of the frontier. They appeared as the storm troopers of civilization and epitomized the ideals that made America a distinctive place. These sentiments dovetailed nicely with the frontier and nationalist schools of scholarship. According to historians such as George Bancroft, and especially Frederick Jackson Turner, America was exceptional—the frontier especially so—and these people as described by their self-styled descendents were its exemplars. They were the first Americans.[2]

Catholics, of course, had no place in this drama. They did not arrive in America during the formative period. Moreover, the Irish Catholic experience of the nineteenth and early twentieth century was defined by city life and its corrupting influences. This violent and ignorant "race"—un-American by contemporary nativist standards—bore little resemblance to those men and women who came over after they gained a little seasoning in Ireland to prepare them for their true mission in America. The island and its Catholic inhabitants, they argued, had no influence on shaping, or tainting, migrating Protestants. It was a stopover that left no indelible mark on the character of the "Scotch Irish" race.

Like all myths, this tale mixes truth and half-truth to deal with uncomfortable contradictions. Catholics did come over during the eighteenth century; indeed, at least a quarter of those from Ireland who traveled to America from 1718 to 1775 were Catholic. And many lived on the frontier and cooperated with Protestants from Ireland. At this time, Protestants had no real sense of Scotch Irish identity. At times, especially during the last few decades of the eighteenth century, they called themselves "Irish," proudly so. The first challenges to this protean notion of group identity came with changes in Ireland. An intensification of sectarian violence and confessional allegiance as the eighteenth century came to a close strained any notion of Irish-ness. Close on the heels of this transatlantic reformulation of identity came the new migration. And understandably the descendants of the men and women who came over during an earlier period sought to reinvent themselves as anything but Irish.[3]

The tables, of course, have been turned. Truth be told, today the Scotch Irish appear marginalized. Most people still see the Scotch Irish as a distinct group, not really Irish, and view their movement as smaller in scale and not as significant, say, as the huge and influential movement of Catholics that dwarfed the earlier migration. The mythmakers—reformulating the past—had no way of knowing what the future would hold. They could not foresee the day when Catholics would be mainstreamed, nor could they imagine the influence of the alien group on American culture and society. And today, the Scotch Irish face an uphill battle competing with Irish America for a more privileged place in American memory.

This is a shame. The two-migrations myth has marginalized the great contributions to the American experience of eighteenth-century migrants. Moreover, it skews our views of subsequent migrations and the larger Irish American experience because it seems to suggest that the "Irish American" experience is of recent vintage and is a Catholic-only story. In fact, the narrative of Ireland's role in peopling America goes back to the early seventeenth century, involves both Protestants and Catholics, and reflects the enduring tensions and shifting notions of identity within Ireland, as well as Ireland's abiding ties to America.

To understand the Irish American experience means viewing migration from Ireland as a continuum. When we stand back and look at the Irish American experience over nearly four centuries, some fascinating patterns emerge. Ireland was part of America from the beginning, as were Irish men and women. From the early seventeenth to the late twentieth century, different groups were affected over time by and responded differently to the processes of Anglicization and commercialization that tied England and later Britain to America and Ireland. The Irish migration experience reflected the growing reach of British markets and British cultural norms in Ireland and the extent to which Britain and America formed coherent parts of a larger Atlantic system. These processes gripped different regions of Ireland and the lives of different groups at different times. Rather than thinking of two distinct migrations, we must conceive of one long thread of experience, of Protestants and Catholics moving through an Atlantic system—mediated by British culture and commerce—that tied Ireland to America culturally, politically, and economically.

The transatlantic story begins in the seventeenth century in the Caribbean and in the Chesapeake, the two most crucial Atlantic outposts of English society, when large numbers—certainly for the time period—left Ireland for the New World.[4] It continued in the eighteenth century as the direction of migration—and British trade and influence—shifted to the Middle Colonies. The next chapter was played out in the nineteenth century as American cities and an Irish hinterland became linked through British cultural mediation and international labor and capital markets. The flow of migration corresponded to changes in the Atlantic economy, Britain's role in reconciling (often in brutal and uncaring fashion) the transatlantic system and Irish society, and how and when different groups were enmeshed in this process. In the seventeenth century, those Catholics described by contemporaries as "vagabonds" and "rogues," military and political prisoners, sailors and the dispossessed—in other words, those directly affected by English expansion into Ireland—left for places like Montserrat. In the eighteenth century, by and large dissenters from Ulster would enter this Atlantic world by spinning and weaving a central commodity of empire, linen, before migrating. Finally, with the industrial age, these dynamics grew in scale and scope, reaching deeply into hitherto isolated corners of an increasingly English-speaking Atlantic. Ireland's Catholics were once again in the crosshairs of the Atlantic system.[5]

This approach, I hope and believe, will get us past two myths, the older and by now discredited one that the only migration that mattered was the eighteenth-century Protestant/rural migration, and its newer variant that only the Catholic/urban experience is worthy of study. For better or worse, both movements were part of a single migration that made Ireland's destiny American, and made America's destiny Irish.

NOTES

1. The literature on these two migrations and experiences is too large to be mentioned here, but for a view of the state of the field, see Kevin Kenny's *The American Irish: A History* (New York: Longman, 2000). The best study still remains Kerby Miller's *Emigrants and Exiles: Ireland and the Irish Exodus to North America* (New York: Oxford University Press, 1985).

2. For the Scotch Irish in America and their sense of identity, see Patrick Griffin, *The People with No Name: Ireland's Ulster Scots, America's Scots Irish, and the Creation of a British Atlantic World* (Princeton: Princeton University Press, 2001).

3. Griffin, *The People with No Name*, and Kenny, *The American Irish*, passim; David Doyle, *Ireland, Irishmen, and Revolutionary America* (Cork: Cork University Press, 1981).

4. See Donald Akenson, *If the Irish Ran the World: Montserrat, 1630–1730* (Montreal: McGill-Queen's University Press, 1997); and Graeme Kirkham, "Ulster Emigration to North America, 1680–1720," in *Ulster and North America: Transatlantic*

Perspectives on the Scotch-Irish, ed. H. T. Blethen and C. W. Wood (Tuscaloosa: University of Alabama Press, 1997).

5. For a promising look at this approach, see Kerby Miller, David Doyle, Arnold Schrier, and Bruce Boling, eds., *Irish Immigrants in the Land of Canaan: Letters and Memoirs from Colonial and Revolutionary America, 1675–1815* (New York: Oxford University Press, 2003).

Protestant Identity in a Borderland Context

HENRY GLASSIE

Mindful that identity is always situated and multiplex, that it is firm and fluid, stable and negotiable, ascribed and voluntary, a matter of both difference by contrast and sameness by affinity, I will restrict myself to a description of identity among Protestant people in a particular place at a particular time, telling a touch of what I learned during a decade of intense ethnographic work. The place is South Fermanagh—a borderland where Catholics form the majority and Protestants are, largely, adherents of the Church of Ireland. The time is the decade that began with 1972, the bloodiest year of the Troubles, a period of violence and deprivation.

The first fact of identity was stated proverbially: "A man must follow his father and be what he was born." There had been religious conversions in the past. Some Protestants had Irish Catholic as well as English and Scottish, Anglican, Methodist, and Presbyterian, forebears. But in the 1970s, people were born, fixed, into religious difference. They were Protestants, or they were Catholics.

Birth led to religious identity, but Protestant religious identity did not lead inevitably to Loyalist or Unionist political commitment. In public, among unknown others, they aligned loyally with their side, cheering as the Orange Lodges marched though Enniskillen on the Twelfth of July. But only a few were politically active, and at home, in private, they were vexed and ambivalent. Their personal identities, by gender, by age, by character, molded private opinions on the conflict that ranged from compassionate to bitter. Some wanted an autonomous Ulster, some wished to be part of the United Kingdom, some wanted a united Ireland. But one generalization is possible. Protestant people were not, in their minds, British. Though mainly English by ultimate origin, they were hostile to English ways. English manners were haughty and indecorous, they thought. English accents galled them. Scottish things were preferable, as symbolic alternatives, but, in context, kilts and pipes and Jacobite laments were, like the Union Jack and the Orange banner, signs of a distinct Irish tradition. Irish is what they called themselves.

They were Protestant and Irish in private, Orange and Loyal in public. But little of their waking, working lives passed in the private or public spheres. In communal space, where most of life transpired among well-known others, they were farming people, members of the "three-fifths," the working majority, composed of Protestants and Catholics alike. None of them were, in their own thinking, members of the elite that ran Ulster.

As workers in their community, they identified themselves, and were identified, as big farmers, middling farmers, small farmers, or landless laborers. Protestants fell into all classes. But, to them, identity by economic class mattered less than identity as a good farmer. A good farmer is industrious; he keeps a neat farm, hacking the hedges back and clearing the fields of rushes. It was bad to be lazy, but worse to be a "rusher" who tolerated unkempt fields in the frenzied quest for cash.

He was identified by the size and look of his farm, she by the cleanliness and generosity of her kitchen. All wished to be known as good workers. And as good neighbors. The neighbor is the one who stays when the exile abandons the land and seeks success over the sea. The neighbor is one who cooperates, swapping labor at agricultural tasks, helping in times of emergency, when a neighbor falls sick or a house burns down. The neighbor follows Our Lord's chief commandment, which they put like this: "Love your neighbor as yourself, and in this you shall live."

The neighbors were Protestants, and they were Catholics. And that fact set the dilemma of identity. Born Protestant or Catholic, you are drawn toward conflict. Born Christian, you are commanded to love. Life, then, was sprung with tension. No final release, short of death, seemed possible. All resolution was momentary, situational. People identified themselves, and acted upon their identities, differently, contradictorily, in private, communal, and public settings.

Structurally, Protestant and Catholic identities were identical. Catholics, too, were born into their religion. They were identified politically in public as Republicans or Fenians. And they were identified in the community as workers and neighbors. The result was that Protestants and Catholics acknowledged difference, adopted a wide range of political positions within an Irish frame, and then, day in and day out, they worked hard and worked together, using polite behavior and kind gestures to counter within the community the differences they felt in private and expressed in public.

In Gortdonaghy, the Cutlers live at the top of the hill, the Lunnys down the slope. When the turf were bad, Billy gave them a hedge for firing. When the potato crop failed, John James came up with a cart of spuds and put them in the shed at the back without a word. Tommy brings fruit, picked from his trees, when he comes to call, and Ellen gives him a seat by the fire and a mug of sweet, creamy tea. The Cutlers are Protestants. The Lunnys are Catholics. They are neighbors, and they use small gifts to bridge difference and affirm community.

In Derryhowlaght West, Bobbie Thornton is the big farmer. He marches with pride at the head of his Lodge on the Glorious Twelfth. In a time when he owned one of the few cars in the district, he would rise from his warm bed and speed through the night, getting the wife of one of his farmhands to the hospital so that another Catholic child could come healthily into the world.

It takes a while to understand. The observer in a hurry—the journalist with a deadline, the social scientist with a questionnaire—reduces people to the public and political dimensions of their identity. Such reduction is convenient for writing but false to the human reality. The ethnographer's slow understanding counters the journalist's account of spectacular violence or the historian's political narrative—both based on rare public expressions of identity.

In Northern Ireland, at the height of the Troubles, life for most people, for most of the time, was a matter of getting through another day, working diligently and living decently among others. And that is the basis upon which the heroic efforts at making peace will succeed.

Contributors

ARTHUR AUGHEY is a Professor of Politics at the University of Ulster at Jordanstown whose most recent work is *Northern Ireland Politics: Beyond the Belfast Agreement* (2005). His *Nationalism, Devolution, and the Challenge to the United Kingdom State* (2001) was nominated for the UK Political Studies Association WJM McKenzie Prize. He is a member of the Northern Ireland Advisory Committee of the British Council, sits on the management board of the Institute of Ulster-Scots Studies, and is a former member of the Northern Ireland Community Relations Council and the Northern Executive of the Irish Association. He was a member of the Working Group on the Bicentenary of the Irish Act of Union and a contributor to the first volume of *British Island Stories: Histories, Identity, and Nationhood* (2004).

ANGELA BOURKE is a Senior Lecturer in Irish at University College Dublin and has been a Visiting Professor at Harvard University, the University of Minnesota, and the University of Notre Dame. She is the author of *Caoineadh na dTrí Muire* (1983), a study of the Crucifixion in oral religious poetry, and the short-story collection *By Salt Water* (1996). Her *The Burning of Bridget Cleary: A True Story* (1999) was awarded the Irish Times Literature Prize and the James S. Donnelly, Sr., Prize (from the American Conference for Irish Studies, for the Best Book on Irish History or Social Studies). Her most recent book is *Maeve Brennan: Homesick at "The New Yorker"* (2004). Bourke is a coeditor of *The Field Day Anthology of Irish Writing*, vols. 4 & 5, *Irish Women's Writing and Traditions* (2002). She is a member of the Royal Irish Academy, the editorial boards of *Éire-Ireland* and the *Canadian Journal of Irish Studies*, and is a regular guest contributor to TV and radio programs in Ireland.

JEAN BUTLER, a native of New York, has been dancing professionally since her debut with the Chieftains in 1988. She is best known for her work in *Riverdance* and for her own show, *Dancing on Dangerous Ground*. The 1999 recipient of the Irish Post Award for her "outstanding contribution to Irish Dance," she was 2003–2005 Artist in Residence at the Irish World Music Centre at the University of Limerick. The Good Will Ambassador for the Irish-based charity "The Forgotten Children," she works to spread awareness of the plight of the Rwandan people.

NICHOLAS CAROLAN is Director of the Irish Traditional Music Archive in Dublin and a lecturer and writer on Irish traditional music. He researches and presents the long-running archival television series *Come West along the Road* on RTÉ, Irish national television, and *Siar an Bóthar* on TG4, the national Irish-language channel. He is the author of *A Harvest Saved: Francis O'Neill and Irish Music in Chicago* (1997) and editor of *A Collection of the Most Celebrated Irish Tunes* (2005 facsim. ed. [1724]).

MICHAEL COLLINS was the first Irish Traveller to become a member of Equity, the actors' trade union. For more than ten years, he played the part of Johnny Connors in *Glenroe*, a highly successful serial drama on Irish television. He has also acted in several films, including *Trojan Eddie* and *Man About Dog*, and has appeared with the Abbey Theatre. An advocate for Travellers' rights, he is a member of the executive of the Irish Travellers Movement and works with Pavee Point, also known as the Dublin Travellers Education and Development Group.

PAT COOKE is the Curator of Kilmainham Gaol on behalf of Ireland's State Heritage Service, at the Office of Public Works. A former Visiting Research Fellow at the Policy Institute, Trinity College Dublin, he is also Curator of Dublin's Pearse Museum. The author of *Kilmainham Gaol: Interpreting Irish Nationalism and Republicanism* (1997), he lectures on heritage issues at the postgraduate level at University College Dublin.

MARY P. CORCORAN is a Senior Lecturer in Sociology at the National University of Ireland, Maynooth. She is coeditor (with Mark O'Brien) of *Censorship and the Democratic State* (2005), and coeditor (with Michel Peillon) of *Place and Non-place: The Reconfiguration of Ireland* (2004) and *Ireland Unbound: A Turn of the Century Chronicle* (2002). Corcoran is author of *Irish Illegals: Transients between Two Societies* (1993). Her many essays include chapters in *Location and Dislocation in Irish Society* (1997) and *Encounters with Modern Ireland* (1998), as well as articles and reviews in the *Canadian Journal of Urban Research, European Societies, Eire-Ireland,* and the *International Journal of Migration*. A founding member of the National Institute for Regional and Spatial Analysis at NUI Maynooth, she is currently a Taoiseach's [prime minister's] nominee to the National Economic and Social Forum. She is a frequent commentator on radio and television.

THEO DORGAN is the author of such volumes of poetry as *The Ordinary House of Love* (1991), *Rosa Mundi* (1995), and *Sappho's Daughter* (1998), and of the prose memoir *Sailing for Home: A Voyage from Antigua to Kinsale* (2004). In 2004, his libretto *Jason and the Argonauts,* set to music by Howard Goodall, was premiered in London's Royal Albert Hall. His most recent publication is *Songs of Earth and Light,* translations from the Slovene of the poet Barbara Korun. A member of the Arts Council (An Chomhairle Ealaíon) of Ireland, he is the former Director of Poetry Ireland (Éigse Éireann), where he managed *Poetry Ireland Review*. He was presenter of *Poetry Now* on RTÉ Radio 1, and later presented RTÉ's television books program, *Imprint*. Dorgan is editor of *Irish Poetry since Kavanagh* (1996) and coeditor of *The Great Book of Ireland* (1991), *Revising the Rising* (1991), *Watching the River Flow* (2000), and *An Leabhar Mòr/The Great Book of Gaelic* (2002). He is a member of Aosdána, Ireland's national assembly of the arts.

RODDY DOYLE is the author of the Booker Prize–winning, international bestseller *Paddy Clarke Ha Ha Ha*. His works also include *The Commitments, The Snapper,* and *The Van* (known collectively as *The Barrytown Trilogy*); *A Star Called Henry;* and *The Woman Who Walked into Doors*. His most recent novel is *Oh, Play That Thing*. He has written screenplays, plays, and the four-part BBC television series *Family*. Doyle worked for fourteen years as an English and Geography teacher at Greendale Community School, in Kilbarrack, North Dublin. He achieved widespread recognition when his novel *The Commitments* (1987) was made into a motion picture in 1991. Since 1993 he has been dedicated to writing full-time.

ROY FOSTER is the Carroll Professor of Irish History at the University of Oxford. He is the author of *Modern Ireland: 1600–1972* (1988), *The Irish Story: Telling Tales and Making It Up in Ireland* (2001), the *Oxford Illustrated History of Ireland* (1989), and *Paddy and Mr. Punch: Connections in Irish and English History* (1993). He is also the author of *W. B. Yeats, A Life*, vol. 1, *The Apprentice Mage, 1865–1914* (1997), which won the James Tait Black Prize for biography, and vol. 2, *The Arch-Poet, 1915–1939* (2003), which completes the authorized biography of the poet, among others. He is a fellow of the British Academy and a well-known broadcaster and critic.

LUKE GIBBONS is the Keough Family Professor of Irish Studies at the University of Notre Dame, Indiana, and Dublin, and is Director of the Graduate Program in Irish Studies at Notre Dame. He is the author of *Edmund Burke and Ireland: Aesthetics, Politics, and the Colonial Sublime, 1750–1850* (2003). His other books include *Gaelic Gothic: Race, Colonialism, and Irish Culture* (2004), *The Quiet Man* (2002), *Transformations in Irish Culture* (1996), and (with Kevin Rockett and John Hill) *Cinema in Ireland* (1988). He was a contributing editor to *The Field Day Anthology of Irish Writing* (1991) and is a coeditor of *Reinventing Ireland: Culture, Society and the Global Economy* (2002) and *The Theatre of Irish Cinema* (2002).

HENRY GLASSIE is a Professor at Indiana University, with appointments in Folklore and Ethnomusicology, American Studies, Near Eastern Languages and Cultures, Central Eurasian Studies, India Studies, and as Codirector of Turkish Studies. He is former president of the American Folklore Society and of the Vernacular Architecture Forum, as well as a former member of the National Council on the Humanities. Books that he has authored include *Folk Housing in Middle Virginia* (1976), *All Silver and No Brass: An Irish Christmas Mumming* (1976), *Irish Folk History* (1982), *Passing the Time in Ballymenone* (1982), *Irish Folktales* (1985), *The Spirit of Folk Art* (1989),

Turkish Traditional Art Today (1993), *Art and Life in Bangladesh* (1997), *Material Culture* (1999), *The Potter's Art* (1999), *Vernacular Architecture* (2000), and *The Stars of Ballymenone* (forthcoming in 2006).

PATRICK GRIFFIN teaches history at Ohio University. He is the author of *The People with No Name: Ireland's Ulster Scots, America's Scots Irish, and the Creation of a British Atlantic World, 1689–1764* (2001), as well as *American Leviathan: Empire, Nation, and Revolutionary Frontier* (2006). He has received a number of fellowships including most recently one from the American Council of Learned Societies. He has been a visiting fellow at the Centre for the Study of Human Settlement and Historical Change at the National University of Ireland, Galway.

NOEL IGNATIEV is author of *How the Irish Became White* (1995); coeditor of *Race Traitor* (1996); winner of an American Book Award; and editor of *Lesson of the Hour: Wendell Phillips on Abolition and Strategy* (2001). He teaches in the Department of Critical Studies at Massachusetts College of Art and is a fellow of the W. E. B. Du Bois Institute for Afro-American Research at Harvard University.

PEADAR KIRBY is a Senior Lecturer in the School of Law and Government at Dublin City University, where he lectures in the Master's Degree program on International Relations and Globalization. He is codirector of the University's Centre for International Studies. He is the author of *Introduction to Latin America: Twenty-First Century Challenges* (2003) and *The Celtic Tiger in Distress: Growth with Inequality in Ireland* (2002) and is coeditor (with Luke Gibbons and Michael Cronin) of *Reimagining Ireland: Culture, Society, and the Global Economy* (2002). His latest book, *Vulnerability and Violence: The Impact of Globalization,* was published late in 2005.

LARRY KIRWAN, Irish musician, novelist, and playwright, is cofounder, lead singer, and guitarist for the band Black 47, known for tackling controversial issues and mixing Irish traditional music with rock, rap, reggae, and political, street-smart lyrics. Black 47 has recorded nine albums, including this year's *Elvis Murphy's Green Suede Shoes.* Kirwan has also recorded two solo albums, *Kilroy Was Here* and *Keltic Kids.* His books include *Mad Angels: The Plays of Larry Kirwan* (1994), *Livin' in America* (1995), *Liverpool Fantasy* (2003), and *Green Suede Shoes—An Irish-American Odyssey* (2005). He is currently working on *Transport,* a musical, with Thomas Keneally, and a new novel, *Rockin' the Bronx.*

JOE LEE, Director of Glucksman Ireland House, is Glucksman Professor of Irish Studies and Professor of History, New York University, and former Head of the Department of History, University College Cork. Author of the prize-winning *Ireland 1912–1985: Politics and Society* (1990) and *The Shifting Balance of Power: Exploring the Twentieth Century* (2000), he has served as an Independent member of the Irish Senate and as Chair of the Irish Fulbright Commission.

AODÁN MAC PÓILIN is the Director of the ULTACH Trust, a cross-community Irish-language funding body in Northern Ireland. He is a board member of the Columba Initiative, and a member of An Foras Teanga (the Cross-Border Language Body) and Comhairle na Gaelscolaíochta (the Council for Irish-Medium Education). He was on the editorial board of *An Leabhar Mòr na Gaeilge/The Great Book of Gaelic*. He has published on issues of cultural and linguistic politics, language planning, broadcasting, and education. Mac Póilin has been Irish-language editor of *Krino* and edited *Styles of Belonging: The Cultural Identities of Ulster* (1992), *Ruined Pages, New Selected Poems of Padraic Fiacc* (1994), and *The Irish Language in Northern Ireland* (1997).

MALCOLM MACLEAN is CEO and Creative Director of Proiseact nan Ealan/the Gaelic Arts Agency, the national development agency for Scotland's Gaelic arts and culture. The agency was established in 1987 and is also an arts production company (www.gaelic-arts.com). He is a board member of Iomairt CholmChille/the Columba Initiative, a funding agency that supports developing cultural links between Gaelic Ireland and Scotland. He is also curator and editor of the international touring exhibitions and books *As an Fhearann* (1986) and *An Leabhar Mòr/The Great Book of Gaelic* (2002 and following). Maclean helped create Peacock Printmakers (Aberdeen), An Lanntair Arts Centre (Stornoway), the Feisean nan Gaidheal—the Association of Scottish Gaelic Arts Youth Tuition Festivals, the Tosg theater company, the Ceolas music summer school (South Uist) and the Columba Initiative (Scotland/ Ireland). He was producer of the award-winning *Craobh nan Ubhal/The Apple Tree* touring theater production (1993) and the Oran nan Gaidheal concert series at the Edinburgh International Festival (1998). His film and television production credits include *Uamh an Oir* (CH4, 1995), the *Tacsi* TV series (STV/BBC, 1997–2001), and *Is Mise An Teanga* (BBC/RTÉ 2004).

TRISH MCADAM is a writer and director of feature and documentary films and Chair of the Screen Directors' Guild of Ireland. Her work includes the feature *Snakes and Ladders* (1996), the three-part television documentary series *Hoodwinked* (on the role of women in Irish society since 1920), and the documentary *Flirting with the Light* (on the making of an independently financed and distributed CD, *Glare*) with the production company Dreamchaser. She is currently working with Samson Films on a feature film based on the James Stephens novel *The Crock of Gold*.

FRANK MCCOURT was born in Brooklyn, the child of Irish immigrant parents. When he was four years old, the family moved to Limerick. He wrote about his childhood in the critically acclaimed and internationally popular *Angela's Ashes* (1996), which won the Pulitzer Prize, the National Book Critics Circle Award, the ABBY Award, the Los Angeles Times Book Prize, and was named among the best books of 1996 by numerous newspapers. He spent thirty years in the New York City public school system, including seventeen years at the Stuyvesant High School in

Manhattan. Those years formed the basis for his second book, the bestselling 'Tis, which was published in 2000 and received the New York Society Library Award and Italy's Riccardo Bacchelli Award. His most recent book, *Teacher Man*, a memoir about teaching, was published in November 2005. In 2002, he contributed an introduction to the book *Brotherhood*, a collection of photographs paying tribute to the losses suffered by the New York City Fire Department on September 11, 2001. He is collaborating with composer David Amram on a New York City–inspired Mass called *Missa Manhattan*.

DECLAN McGONAGLE is Chair in Art and Design at the University of Ulster, Belfast, and a board member of the City Arts Center, Dublin, which he formerly headed (2001–4) as Director of the Center's Civil Arts Inquiry. McGonagle was the first Director of the Irish Museum of Modern Art (1991–2001), the founding Director of the Orchard Gallery in Derry, and is former Director of Exhibitions at the Institute for Contemporary Art, London. He was short-listed for the Tate Gallery's Turner Prize in 1987 and served on the Turner Jury in 1993. He has also served on the juries for the John Moores and Jerwood Prizes. He acted as Ireland's Commissioner at the 1993 Venice Biennale and the 1994 Sao Paulo Biennale. He is currently Chairman of the Board of the Liverpool Biennial. A contributing editor of *ArtForum*, he has curated numerous international exhibitions and projects in Ireland and Britain and writes and lectures regularly on contemporary art and museum issues, as well as on the relationship between art and society.

SUSAN McKAY is the author of *Without Fear: A History of the Dublin Rape Crisis Centre* (2005), *Northern Protestants: An Unsettled People* (2000), and *Sophia's Story* (1998). She writes for the *Irish Times* and the *Irish News* and was formerly Northern Editor of Ireland's *Sunday Tribune*. She has made several television documentaries and is a regular radio and television commentator on arts and politics on Radio Telefís Éireann (RTÉ) and the BBC. Her awards include Irish Feature Writer of the Year (2002), the Amnesty International Award for Human Rights Journalism (2001), and the Irish Print Journalist of the Year (2000). McKay's work is featured in anthologies including the *Field Day Anthology of Irish Writing* (2002). She is a former community worker and founder of the Belfast Rape Crisis Center.

MARTIN McLOONE is Professor of Media Studies (Film, Television, and Photography) attached to the Centre for Media Research at the University of Ulster, Coleraine, and was formerly the University's Head of School of Media and Performing Arts. He is the author of *Irish Film: The Emergence of a Contemporary Cinema* (2000) and has contributed to and edited *Television and Irish Society* (1984), *Culture, Identity, and Broadcasting in Ireland* (1991), *Border Crossing: Film in Ireland, Britain, and Europe* (1994), *Broadcasting in a Divided Community: Seventy Years of the BBC in Northern Ireland* (1996), and *Big Picture, Small Screen: The Relations between Film and Television* (1996).

PETER MCVERRY, SJ, is a Jesuit priest, born in Northern Ireland, who has worked mainly with homeless young people in Dublin. McVerry runs three hostels and a residential drug detox center, serves as Director of the Arrupe Society for Homeless Young People, and has worked in the inner city and in Ballymun, a high-rise estate in the suburbs of Dublin.

KERBY A. MILLER is Middlebush Professor of History at the University of Missouri, Columbia. He is the author of *Emigrants and Exiles: Ireland and the Irish Exodus to North America* (1985), the primary author of *Irish Immigrants in the Land of Canaan: Letters and Memoirs from Colonial and Revolutionary America, 1675–1815* (2003), and coeditor of *Irish Popular Culture, 1650–1850* (1998). He is also primary author of two books for general readers, *Journey of Hope: The Story of Irish Immigration to America* (2001), and *Out of Ireland: The Story of Irish Immigration to America* (1997). He has won numerous scholarly and teaching prizes.

ED MOLONEY is a journalist and author who has written for the *Washington Post,* the *Economist,* and the *Guardian.* Elected Irish Journalist of the Year in 1999, he has spent two decades writing about the IRA, first as Northern Ireland Editor of the *Irish Times* and then as Northern Editor of the *Sunday Tribune.* While researching his book *A Secret History of the IRA* (2002), Moloney gained unprecedented access to the IRA.

MICK MOLONEY is Global Distinguished Professor of Music and Irish Studies at New York University and author of *Far from the Shamrock Shore: The Story of Irish American History through Song* (2002), a book and CD. An academic folklorist, he has recorded and produced over forty albums of traditional music and is cofounder of the Green Fields of America, an ensemble of Irish and Irish American musicians, singers, and dancers. A promoter of Irish musical interchange with America, he served as music/humanities consultant for the PBS documentary *Out of Ireland* and as a public radio and television host. In 1999, he was named a National Heritage Fellow, the highest official honor a traditional artist can receive in the United States.

LIZ O'DONNELL, TD, a Senior Deputy in the Irish National Parliament, represents Dublin South and is Chief Whip of the Progressive Democrats. Originally a lawyer, she has been a member of the Irish parliament since 1992. She is a former Minister of State to the Government and a Minister of State at the Department of Foreign Affairs, representing the Irish Government at the multiparty talks which culminated in the Good Friday Agreement of 1998. She presided over an unprecedented expansion of Ireland's Overseas Aid Program to the poorest countries and remains vocal on issues of international justice and development.

NUALA O'LOAN, Police Ombudsman for Northern Ireland since November 2000, is a solicitor with a long-standing interest in matters of law, the police, and consumer rights. Mrs. O'Loan was a former Senior Lecturer holding the Jean Monnet Chair in

European Law at the University of Ulster. She was a former Chairman of the Northern Ireland Consumer Committee for Electricity and formerly held membership on the Police Authority, the Northern Health and Social Services Board, and the General Consumer Council for Northern Ireland. She was also a legal expert member of the European Commission's Consumer's Consultative Council and a Special Commissioner at the Commission for Racial Equality.

FINTAN O'TOOLE has been a columnist and critic with the *Irish Times* since 1988, was elected Irish Journalist of the Year in 1993, and was drama critic of the *New York Daily News* from 1997 until 2001. His *White Savage: William Johnson and the Invention of America* (2005) is the first book in a trilogy about the Irish experience in America (the second will deal with the story of Billy the Kid, and the third with the relationship between the Irish and African Americans in nineteenth-century America). His other books include *The Ex-Isle of Erin: Images of a Global Ireland* (1996), *Traitor's Kiss: The Life of Richard Brinsley Sheridan* (1997), *The Lie of the Land: Irish Identities* (1998), *The Irish Times Book of the Century* (1999), and *Shakespeare Is Hard, but So Is Life: A Radical Guide to Shakespearian Tragedy* (2002).

HELEN SHAW is Managing Director of Athena Media, a media innovation company based at the Digital Hub, in Dublin, and the author of the *Irish Media Directory and Guide.* She was previously Head of RTÉ Radio (Irish national public broadcasting), was the first woman appointed to RTÉ's board, and launched Lyric FM, the Irish national music and arts channel, for RTÉ in 1999. In 2002–3, she was a Visiting Fellow at Harvard University's Weatherhead Center for International Affairs, where she conducted advanced research on media globalization, and she is now participating in a pan-European digital radio research project called DRACE. She spent much of her early career as a journalist with the *Irish Times,* RTÉ, and the BBC. In 1997, she received a Gold Sony for her BBC Radio work.

LENWOOD SLOAN is an African American arts activist and historian who has a career as a director, choreographer, dancer, and actor. His great-great-grandfather was an Irish activist who lived and worked among free blacks and those enslaved in the American South. Sloan was formerly a director of Performing Arts programs at the NEA. Perhaps the only African male ever to enter the World Championship of Irish Step Dance, he is the producer and director of *Vo-Du MacBeth* and director of cultural and heritage tourism programs for the State of Pennsylvania.

ROD STONEMAN is the Director of the Huston School of Film and Digital Media at the National University of Ireland, Galway. He was Chief Executive of Bord Scannán na hÉireann/the Irish Film Board until September 2003 and previously worked as a Deputy Commissioning Editor for the Independent Film and Video Department at Channel 4 Television, London. He has made a number of documentaries for television—including *Ireland: The Silent Voices* and *Italy: the Image Business*—and has written on film in various journals, including *Screen, Sight and Sound, Kinema,* and *Film Ireland.*

Colm Tóibín is the award-winning author of *The Master* (short-listed for the 2004 Booker Prize) and other fiction, including *The South* (1990), *The Heather Blazing* (1992), *The Story of the Night* (1996), and *The Blackwater Lightship* (short-listed for the 1999 Booker Prize). Among his nonfiction books are *Bad Blood: A Walk along the Irish Border* (1987), *Homage to Barcelona* (1992), and *The Sign of the Cross: Travels in Catholic Europe* (1994). His debut play, *Beauty in a Broken Place*, opened at the Abbey Theatre in Dublin in 2004. He has been awarded the E. M. Forster Prize from the American Academy of Arts and Letters, the Irish Times Prize, and the Ferro/Grumley Prize for the Best Gay Novel of 1997.

Andrew Higgins Wyndham is Director of Media Programs at the Virginia Foundation for the Humanities (VFH). He conceived and organized the international VFH conference and festival "Irish Film: A Mirror Up to Culture" (1996) and organized and directed the 2003 "Re-Imagining Ireland" conference and festival, winner of the 2004 Helen and Martin Schwartz Prize awarded by the Federation of State Humanities Councils. He also executive-produced and directed the nationally broadcast *Re-Imagining Ireland* documentary. Wyndham has coordinated the VFH fellowship program and now directs the Southern Humanities Media Fund. He is Executive Producer of *With Good Reason*, a weekly radio interview program broadcast throughout Virginia, and created and directs VFH Radio's statewide Humanities Features Bureau and other new radio initiatives.

Index

Dublin (*continued*)
Irish-speaking communities planned for, 100–101; Manhattanization of, 175; population of, 170; representation in film, 152–55; rural Ireland contrasted with, 148; sense of place in, 181; spatial and social segregation in, 170; Spencer Dock development, 173–76, 181; and urbanization of Ireland, 170–72

Dublin Docklands Development Authority, 173–74

Duleek, 129

Dun Laoghaire, 172

Dunne, Colin, 140, 143

Easter Uprising (1916), 4, 43–44, 184, 224

economic boom: Catholicism affected by, 14; Celtic Tiger, 16–25; EU enlargement to the east and, 24; as externally driven, 12; ills attributed to, 17; international significance of, 7–8; Ireland as fastest-growing economy in world, 21; Peace Process and, 13–14; reappraisal of identity resulting from, 147; recent troubles in, 234; socioeconomic transitions resulting from, 169–70; uneven distribution of fruits of, 13, 170

education: 11-Plus Exam, 204; English-language-only, 84; free secondary, 91; Irish language in, 87, 89, 90–91, 96; for poor children, 19; for Travellers, 75

Egan, Seamus, 42

11-Plus Exam, 204

emigration: contested interpretations of, 230–34, 240; by Protestants, 226; scale and duration of, 5. *See also* Irish Diaspora

Emmett, Dan, 128

Emmett, Robert, 184

Empey, Reg, 196

England: Irish immigration to, 230, 234; Irish music in, 123; London, 36, 126; Northern Irish nationalism compared with that of, 221–22; South Fermanagh Protestants and, 248–49

English language: education restricted to, 84; in Gaeltacht, 83; Irish Americans learning, 42, 96–97; Irish speakers using, 82, 102; Irish speakers wanting their children taught, 89; learning as buying into British way of life, 55; as second official language of Republic, 90; "speaking English, thinking Irish," 122

Enniscorthy, 36

Enya, 94

Eorpa (television series), 103

Ervine, David, 200, 211

ethnicity: ethnic options for Irish Americans, 61–66; and race, 59–61; in two-traditions paradigm, 226–30. *See also* race

European Media Program, 164

European Union (EU), 13, 21, 23, 24, 53

Evans, Marc, 157, 158

Famine, the: commemorations of, 62, 186, 188; emigration caused by, 230; Nationalist versus Unionist interpretations of, 228–29; propagandistic approach to, 188; and world famine aid, 189

Fanning, Bryan, 56

Fatima Mansions, 173, 176–80, 181

feminism, in development of Ireland, 13

Ferrier, Kathleen, 36, 37

Fethard-on-Sea, 151

Field Day Theatre Company, 118

film, 145–68; of John Ford, 60–61, 63, 79, 147, 149; Hollywood, 147, 163–65, 166–67; industrial model of production of, 164, 165; in Irish language, 95; as mediator of change, 161–62; Peace Process as depicted in, 148, 156–61; rural Ireland as depicted in, 148–52; Scorsese's *Gangs of New York*, 58, 79–81; as slow to develop in Ireland, 147; traditional cinematic image of Ireland, 148–49; traditional cinematic representations of the Irish, 161–62; urban Ireland as depicted in, 152–56

Filmbase, 165

Finucane, Pat, 216–17

Fíor-Ghaeltacht, 89–90

"First Programme for Economic Expansion" (1958), 8

FitzGerald, Garret, 38–39

"Five Points" (Black 47), 80

Flaherty, Robert, 121

Flanagan, Thomas, 187

Flatley, Michael, 42

Fleadh Cheoil na hÉireann, 133

Flick (film), 155

Flight of the Doves, The (film), 63

Foinse (magazine), 95

Foras Forbartha, An, 189

Foras na Gaeilge, 97n2

Ford, John, 60–61, 63, 79, 147, 149

Ford, Patrick, 57

Forgetting Ireland (Connelly), 95

Fort Apache (film), 61

Foster, Roy, 55

Fragmens sur les Institutions Républicaines IV (Cullen), 121–22

free-market economics, 12–13, 23, 233

Free Presbyterian Church, 198

Friel, Brian, 122

Fuentes, Carlos, 24

full employment, 21, 22

Gaelic Act (Scotland), 103–4

Gaelic American (newspaper), 127

Gaelic League, 85–86, 94, 131, 132

Gaelscoileanna, 96

Gaeltacht, 82–98

Gaeltacht Commission, 88–90, 94

Gaeltarra Éireann, 90–91, 92

Gàidhealtachd, 82, 103, 104, 105, 109

Galway to Clifden railway line, 85, 86

Gangs of New York (film), 58, 79–81

Gardiner, Kevin, 16

Garner, Steve, 57

Garrison, William Lloyd, 81

gender, artists exploring issues of, 120–21. *See also* women

General, The (film), 152, 166

Gill, Liz, 154–55

globalization: Hollywood and, 163; identity in global context, 26–35, 112–13; Irish emigration and, 230, 231; of Republic, 7–8, 9–12, 113; revisionism and, 224; urban development affected by, 181

Goldfish Memory (film), 154–55

Goldhagen, Daniel, 53

Goldsmith, Oliver, 65

Good, Harold, 193–94

Good Friday (Belfast) Agreement (1998): as achieved by changing the question, 206–8; ambiguity of, 221; Democratic Unionist Party on, 199, 200, 204; and "helicopters-on-the-lawn" syndrome, 2; intellectual achievement of, 6–7; international significance of, 7; Irish Diaspora and, 14; Irish-Scottish conversion encouraged by, 106; as languishing, 220; model of negotiation provided by, 119; promise of, 213–15; as shifting focus from ends to means, 210; Unionist support for, 195, 211. *See also* Peace Process

Gortdonaghy, 250

Graceville (film), 95

Graham, Len, 28

Green Fields of America, 141

Greetings (McCarthy), 113

Guerin, Veronica, 153

Haass, Richard, 201

Hamill, Robert, 6

Hamilton, Hugo, 49

harp, Irish, 32, 126

Hartigan, John, 64–65

Haughey, Charles, 11, 17, 62

Heaney, Joe, 37

Heffernan, Liam, 78

Henry, Paul, 88

Herder, Johann Gottfried von, 53

heritage industry, 187, 188–89

Hewitt, John, 194

Higgins, Michael D., 147, 148

Hindley, Reg, 92–93

history: Northern Ireland as obsessed with, 221–22; reinventing, 186–90; revisionism, 187, 223–43

Hollywood, 147, 163–65, 166–67

homelessness, 18–19

home ownership, 20

Horse (film), 150

Horslips, 124

housing, cost of, 18, 234

Howell, Ron, 80

Hoyle, Fred, 9–12

Hyde, Douglas, 85, 131

IDA (Industrial Development Authority), 10

identity: African American Irish, 47–48; arts in reconstruction of, 112–22; in borderland context, 248–50; built environment affecting, 173; economic boom and Peace Process leading to reappraisal of, 147; English response to threat to, 221–22; finding in global context, 26–35, 112–13; for Irish Americans, 40–42; and lifestyle, 63; music and, 37–38, 124–25; symbols of Irish American, 133–34; time scale in politics of, 220; of Ulster Protestants, 225–30. *See also* Irishness

Ignatiev, Noel, 14, 242n15

immigration: as challenge, 14; for cheap labor, 241n11; increase in, 12, 21; intolerance toward immigrants, 58; long history of, 230

imperialism, Irish immigrants opposing, 238

Incident (Doherty), 116

Industrial School system, 3

inequality, increase in, 13, 170

Inglis, Tom, 92

Intel, 11

Intermission (film), 154, 166

Internet, the, 84, 95–96

Into the West (film), 149

Iomairt Cholm Cille (Columba Initiative), 108

IRA (Irish Republican Army): cease-fire of 1994, 202, 212; continuing low-level activity of, 211, 212–13; in Cullen's *Fragmens sur les Institutions Républicaines IV*, 121–22; decline in violence by, 202; Good Friday Agreement's implications for, 7, 214–15; making Paisley look good, 191–94; offer to decommission its weapons, 191, 193–94; police as targets of, 217; referred to as terrorists after September 11, 2001, 59; representation in film, 156, 157; as unable to succeed or be defeated, 207

Ireland: and "Celtic" identity, 125; disproportionate attention paid to, 2–5; Irish-Scottish conversion, 102–9; pastoral myth of, 113; racism in, 49–68; traditional cinematic image of, 148–52, 161–62; two peoples of, 219–20. *See also* Irish Diaspora; Northern Ireland; Republic of Ireland

Irish Americans: African Americans as, 46–48; Americanism questioned, 59–61; colonialism and imperialism opposed by, 237–38; dance among, 42, 140; difference between Irish and, 39–43; emigration as interpreted by, 234; English learned by, 96–97; ethnic options for, 61–66; forgetting to remember, 43–46; *Graceville*, 95; in minstrel shows, 128; music of, 42, 44, 45, 123–24, 126, 127, 133–34; in New York Draft Riots of 1863, 58, 79–81; racism among, 54, 57–58, 235, 236–37, 238; radicalism among, 238–39, 243n17; Scots Irish, 230, 236–37, 239, 244–48; South Boston Irish, 80; symbols of Irish identity of, 133–34; tourism by, 184–86

Irish civil war of 1923, 3

Irish dance, 123–44; commercialization of, 142; costumes, 140–41, 142; current state of, 143; free-form arena needed for,

235, 236–37, 238; and Irish Jews, 56; media and, 51, 66n3; and national character, 52–53; in New York Draft Riots of 1863, 58, 79–81

radicalism, 238–39

radio, 84, 91, 92, 93, 103

Raftery, Blind, 133

Raidió na Gaeltachta, 84, 91, 92

railways, 85, 86, 88

rebellion, 238–39

"recovery of roots" phenomenon, 63

Redpath, Jean, 39

Reed, Alec, 194

Reed, Carol, 147

religion, secularization of, 22, 152, 169. *See also* Catholicism; Protestantism

Renan, Ernest, 55

Republic of Ireland: American-style social structure of, 13, 17; conservative values of, 8–9; economic reform of late 1950s, 8, 9–10; emigration from, 232–33; free-market economics and development in, 12–13; as globalized, 7–8, 9–12, 113; Irish Film Board, 147–48, 166; new constitutional position in, 119; and Northern Ireland, 207; outrageous comparisons with Africa and Eastern Europe, 3–4; urbanization of, 170–72. *See also* Dublin; West of Ireland

Republicanism: extreme of, 215; Good Friday Agreement's implications for, 214–15; Irish language associated with, 104; Irish Republican Brotherhood, 43–44; representation in film, 156–57. *See also* IRA (Irish Republican Army)

Resurrection Man (film), 157, 158

revisionism, historical, 223–43; as anti-Nationalist, 223–24; contested interpretations of emigration, 230–34, 240; heterogeneity of, 240n3; Irish Empire thesis, 234–39, 240; moment for has passed, 187; privatization compared with, 225; two-traditions paradigm, 226–30, 239–40

Riverdance, 63, 124, 132, 133, 140, 141–42, 143

Robinson, Mary, 62, 109, 234

Robinson, Peter, 200, 201, 202, 203–4

Rodgers, Jimmie, 69

Rodgers, W. R., 197, 198

Roediger, David, 14, 54, 242n15

romanticism, in politics, 210

romantic nationalism, 52–53, 124

Rorty, Richard, 59

Rosmuc, 86, 87

Royal Ulster Constabulary (RUC), 202, 216

Ryan, Frederick, 57

Sabhal Mòr Ostaig, 103

Sands, Bobby, 44, 45

Sayers, Peig, 12, 94

Scally, Bob, 187

Scél Lem Dúib (*Brief Account*) (anonymous), 110

Schumacher, Joel, 153

Scorsese, Martin, 58, 79–81

Scotland: Anglo-Saxonism in Lowland, 52; and "Celtic" identity, 125; Gaelic-speaking areas of, 82, 103–4, 107; Ireland's status compared with that of, 37, 38, 39; Irish Gaels in settlement of, 105; Irish-Scottish conversion, 102–9; music of, 106, 126; *Sruth na Maoile* radio program in, 92

Scots (Scotch) Irish, 230, 236–37, 239, 244–48

Séadna (Ó Laoghaire), 87

Seawright, Paul, 117

secularization, 22, 152, 169

Seeley, Sir John, 53

sense of place, 173, 181

Separate Car Act (1890), 47

September 11, 2001, attacks, 59

"settler ideology," 226, 237

Sheridan, Jim, 149, 175

Sigerson, George, 57

"signature" culture, 113–14, 118

Sinn Féin: economic policies of, 224; Paisley and, 200–201, 205. *See also* IRA (Irish Republican Army)

slave revolts, 238